NEXT WEEK — the story of a dramatic escape from the island of Crete.

Printed and Published in Great Britain by D. C. THOMSON & Co., Ltd., 12 Fetter Lane, Fleet Street, London, E.C.4.

LEAKEY'S LUCK

A TANK COMMANDER WITH NINE LIVES

REA LEAKEY WITH GEORGE FORTY

SUTTON PUBLISHING

First published in the United Kingdom in 1999 by
Sutton Publishing Limited · Phoenix Mill
Thrupp · Stroud · Gloucestershire · GL5 2BU

British Library Cataloguing in Publication Data
A catalogue record for this book is available from the British Library

ISBN 0 7509 1731 5

Endpapers: *Victor* magazine © D.C. Thomson & Co. Ltd.
Frontispiece: Rea Leakey in his summer dress-uniform as GOC Malta and
Libya. Note the CB around his neck, the DSO and MC (with Bar) on the
right-hand end (as worn) of the row on his chest, before the WWII campaign
medals, then followed by the UN Medal (for service in Korea) and last of all
the Czech MC (foreign decorations are always worn last). (*A.R. Leakey*)

Jacket illustrations: Front: Major-General Rea Leakey (*Maj-Gen Rea Leakey's
private collection*); Tank Cruiser Mk I (A9) (*Tank Museum*). *Back, top*: 7
RTR with Matilda Mk II heavy infantry tanks (the 'Queen of the Desert')
(*Tank Museum*); *bottom*: Rea Leakey gives orders over the radio to his tank
commanders (*Maj-Gen Rea Leakey's private collection*).

 ^{TM} ALAN SUTTON^{TM} and SUTTON^{TM} are the
trade marks of Sutton Publishing Limited

Typeset in 10/12 pt Plantin Light.
Typesetting and origination by
Sutton Publishing Limited.
Printed in Great Britain by
Biddles, Guildford, Surrey.

CONTENTS

Plates and Illustrations

Plates

Between pages 86–87

Illustrations

Foreword

by Field Marshal Lord Carver GCB, CBE, DSO, MC

'Fear Naught' is the motto of the Royal Tank Regiment of which General Leakey is such a distinguished member. Nobody could have lived up to it more fully than he, whether in his many daring exploits on the battlefield or in his equally frequent acts of insubordination towards higher authority. It is remarkable that he got away with both almost scot-free, and he acknowledges that he owed much to 'Leakey's Luck'.

Rea Leakey has always been thirsting for action and spoiling for a fight. The reader of these lively memoirs will relish his vivid descriptions of the many adventures he met with on his way up the military ladder from Subaltern in Egypt before the Second World War to Major General, responsible for British troops in Malta and Libya when they were about to leave both places in 1967.

Introduction

As Lord Carver has indicated in his Foreword, Rea Leakey was one of that remarkable band of men who made up the Royal Tank Corps between the wars. Intelligent, capable, bursting with enthusiasm, they typified all that was best in the prewar British Army, yet constantly had to fight against the prejudice and crass stupidity of many Senior Officers in the War Office and elsewhere, who still saw the horse as the primary means of providing shock action on the battlefield. My favourite example of this, which I have to say I have quoted many times before, was the statement made by the then Secretary of State for War (Duff Cooper), when he introduced the Army Estimates for 1936, in which he apologized to the Cavalry for having to start mechanizing eight of their regiments, saying, 'It is like asking a great musical performer to throw away his violin and devote himself in future to the gramophone.' Many brave men who then had to fight in obsolete, under-armoured and under-gunned light tanks would have to give their lives to make up for such ostrich-like idiocy which delayed mechanization.

Some of the wartime adventures of Maj Gen Arundel Rea Leakey, CB, DSO, MC and Bar, Czech MC, have in fact appeared in print on a number of occasions before this book. For example, his devastating raid on Martuba aerodrome during Wavell's campaign when he destroyed all the Italian aircraft and his subsequent actions in Tobruk, both of which earned him Military Crosses, were briefly recounted in David Masters' wartime best seller of 1943, *With Pennants Flying*, subtitled: *The Immortal deeds of the Royal Armoured Corps*. Later, one of his exploits with the Australians in Tobruk in August 1941 was featured in picture script format on the front and back covers of the *Victor* magazine, in July 1969, while I used yet another of his battles in my book, *Tank Action*, to illustrate the bravery of British tank crews, fighting in their paper-thin A9s against much superior German PzKpfw IIIs and IVs. This, however, is the first time all his wartime service has been fully documented. His autobiography actually includes the postwar years as well, but space has prevented us going any farther than the end of 1945, except in brief summary.

My first meeting with General Rea was as a member of Intake 1 at the Royal Military Academy, Sandhurst, when it reopened after the war between 1946 and 1947. He was my Company Commander in Dettingen Company, Old College, and one of the main reasons why, in July 1948, I was commissioned into the 1st Royal Tank Regiment. Our paths naturally continued to cross and when I attended the Staff College, Camberley, in 1959, I discovered to my great good fortune that he was my College

Commander and, at the end of the course, he was instrumental in getting me my first staff appointment as GSO 2 at the Army Air Corps Centre at Middle Wallop. Sadly, neither of us knew that I was colour-blind, so the only thing I eventually flew – after some fairly hair-raising lessons in a Chipmunk – was a desk!

It has been both an honour and a great delight for me to be permitted to edit Gen Rea's memoirs. I did a similar job some years ago with Sgt Jake Wardrop's diary in my book, *Tanks Across the Desert*. Jake was a tank driver, then a Sgt Tank Commander in 5 RTR, which Gen Rea later commanded. Jake was another of the wonderful breed of tank soldier who went so bravely into battle in 1939, their *esprit de corps* and fighting ability more than making up for the gross imperfections in their equipment. Sadly, he was one of those who did not survive to share with us the postwar years. As I did with his memoirs, I have tried again to explain a little of the background to the period covered by each of Rea's chapters, without being too obtrusive. I trust the reader will find my remarks of interest and valuable – but of course if they are superfluous then please ignore them!

After thirty-two years of active soldiering with the RTR, in which I served with the 1st, 2nd, 4th, 7th and 42nd RTR, followed by thirteen years of 'part-time' soldiering running the Tank Museum (where I finished up with almost more tanks than the entire British Army!), and now after a further five years editing the Regimental Journal, *Tank*, I believe I know my Regiment fairly well, certainly well enough to be able to say with conviction that every potential RTR officer should read, mark, learn, and inwardly digest Gen Rea's remarkable memoirs and then try to emulate his fighting spirit in their careers – and at the same time of course endeavour to have just as much fun and excitement as he clearly did: FEAR NAUGHT!

George Forty
Bryantspuddle, Dorset
1998

Chronology

Date	Event/Unit/Formation	Rank/Appointment	Location
30 Dec 1915	Born		Nairobi
1935	Entered RMC	GC	Sandhurst
Jan 1936	Commissioned into RTC	2nd Lieutenant	
1936–7	4 RTC	2Lt	Catterick
1938–41	1 RTC/1 RTR	2Lt to A/Major	Egypt & Western Desert
1941	Awarded Military Cross – *London Gazette* 8/7/41		
1941	Awarded Bar to MC – *London Gazette* 4/11/41		
1941	Staff College	Lt	Haifa
1941	451 Sqn RAAF	A/Maj	Western Desert
1942–3	252 Indian Armd Bde	A/Maj (BM)	Persia
1943	3 RTR	A/Maj (Sqn Comd)	Tunisia
1943–4	44 RTR	A/Maj (Regt 2IC)	Italy, UK & Normandy
1944	7 RTR	A/Lt Col (CO)	Normandy & Holland
1944	Awarded Czech MC – *London Gazette* 24/5/45		
1945–7	5 RTR	A/Lt Col (CO)	North West Europe
1945	Awarded DSO – *London Gazette* 11/10/45		
1947–8	RMA Sandhurst	A/Maj (Coy Comd)	Sandhurst
1949–50	HQ East African Command	Major (MS)	Kenya
1950	Married Muriel Irene le Poer Trench		
1950	Son Nigel born		
1951–2	Staff College	A/Lt Col (DS)	Camberley
1952	Son David born		
1953–4	5 RTR	Major (Regt 2IC)	Korea
1954–6	1st Armd Car Regt, Arab Legion	Lt Col (CO)	Jordan
1957	3 Inf Div	Lt Col (GSO1)	Colchester
1958–60	Staff College	Col (DS)	Camberley
1961–3	7th Armd Bde	Brigadier (Comd)	Germany
1964–6	War Office/MOD(AD)	Maj Gen (DGFV)	London
1967	Appointed Companion of the Bath (CB)		
1967–8	Br Tps Malta & Libya	Maj Gen (GOC)	Malta
8 May 1968	Retired from the Army		
1968–80	Wolfson Foundation	Director & Secretary	London
1980–2	St Swithun's School	Fund Raiser	Winchester

CHAPTER ONE

Born in Kenya

Editor In this opening chapter, Rea Leakey gives a vivid impression of growing up in the wilds of East Africa, his father literally having to carve out a home for his family from the virgin bush with his bare hands. Leakey senior must have been one of the Allied troops who fought against the redoubtable Col (later Gen) Paul von Lettow-Vorbeck, a determined and resourceful German guerrilla leader who had hoped to influence the war in Europe by pinning down a disproportionately large number of Allied troops in the area which had been German East Africa (Deutsch-Ostafrika), which became included in what is now Kenya. He finally surrendered twelve days after the Armistice and returned to Germany a hero. Kenya was established as a British Protectorate in 1920 (British East Africa) with the British East Africa Company holding commercial control. This remained the situation until just after the Second World War.

Like the children of so many colonial families, Rea was forced by his circumstances to come back to England to complete his education and, as he explains, this led to him becoming a 'GC' (Gentleman Cadet) at the Royal Military College – 'the little hell over the hill' as it was called by the then Master of Wellington College, which was situated a few miles away! Over 50 per cent of the GCs were the sons of Army officers (hence normally penniless), the remainder being sons of members of the ICS (Indian Civil Service) or more rarely of the liberal professions. Few – under 5 per cent – had not been to one of the recognised public schools. Fees were considerable, although there were scholarships to be won which were awarded from the funds of disbanded Irish regiments. The RMC had the typical outlook of most of the British Army between the wars as one historian later explained: 'Sandhurst remained throughout the years between the wars an isolated military encampment in a chiefly anti-military Britain (with a traditional class background), there was no sign of the radical changes which were shortly to transform the character of war. . . . The entire emphasis, indeed, of military recollection after the First World War dwelt on those battles where the tactics had been perhaps fumbling or even non-existent but where the casualties had been heaviest – not on those conflicts technically of great interest.'[1]

When Rea arrived at Sandhurst the RMC was comprised of four companies of cadets (numbered 1, 2, 3 and 5), divided between the Old and New Buildings. Each company contained a mixture of GCs. At the top, there were the Senior Cadets, some of whom were Under Officers and Sergeants; then came the Intermediate Cadets, some of whom were Corporals and Lance-Corporals; finally, there were the newly joined Juniors – the lowest of the low. It was a tough place as Rea would discover, with much of the discipline left to the cadets themselves. This was justified by the fact that the staff considered that they were not running a kindergarten but rather training young men for the dirty business of fighting, so they did not intend to: 'snoop around seeing whether the cadets treat one another like Little Lord Fauntelroys', as one source put it, and worked on the principle that: 'a man's contemporaries are his fairest judges.' Their reasoning for this 'hands-off' approach was that a wild young man could learn wisdom when he grew older (if he survived!) but that a spiritless young man could not learn the dash that wins battles.

Rea Leakey On 30 December, 1915, I was born in Nairobi. My father was a farmer, and like many other white farmers he joined the British Army which drove the Germans out of Tanganyika. It was not an easy task, if only because of the lack of transport – mostly blacks carrying supplies through the bush. Because my father spoke Swahili and Kikuyu, he recruited and looked after these stalwarts, many of whom died of malaria; my father survived several bouts of this disease and was finally invalided out of the Army mainly because he was very deaf.

In 1920 Dad bought a soldier-settler's farm north of Rumuruti, some 150 miles from Nairobi, and in due course the family set forth to this very large stretch of virgin land inhabited by a variety of wild animals. Our transport consisted of three wagons, each drawn by sixteen oxen, and the journey lasted three months. Our mother, née Elizabeth Laing, was some ten years older than my father, of a tough Scots family – and her father was also a farmer. By this time she had produced four children – Nigel, Robert, Rea (me) and Agnes. She was a very brave and competent woman, and for much of the journey was in charge because Dad was ahead with a team of workmen building bridges, then our house and the thorn-tree barricades (*Bomas*) for the cattle.

Rumuruti was, and still is, a small township – in those days an Indian *duka* (shop) and a few farmers. Our farm was some 30 miles north in the middle of nowhere. Well do I remember the house that Dad built – mud floor and grass thatch for the roof. Mother hated cats (her sister, Alice, AA – Aunt Alice, was allergic to them) but had to tolerate them because they dealt with the rats, helped by snakes. The latter were numerous and mainly lived in the roof. However, one breed of snakes, the puff-adder, enjoyed the comfort of our bedrooms. They are killers, and when we went to bed with a candle, a pussy-cat was pushed into the room to check if Mr Puff-adder was 'at home'. If he was Pussy growled, Dad was alerted and he dealt with the snake.

As children, we could not have had a better life. Dad was one of the most honest and straight men I have ever known. The Africans called him *Morrogaru* – the Kikuyu for tall and straight. Our mother was equally loved by all of us – black and white. She was a good teacher and nurse; young as we were, our parents taught us the three Rs and a great deal about the birds and beasts which surrounded us. Nigel and Robert were taught to ride, and they enjoyed the task of chasing the numerous ostriches off the crops of maize.

Quite often at night our parents would wake us up to watch herds of zebra being chased by lions past our house and other buildings. Then we would hear the kill and go back to bed. It was not long before the pride of lions in whose territory we lived decided it was easier to jump into the cattle *boma* and come out with a bullock instead of chasing zebra. Dad discovered their den, a large cave some 10 miles from our house, and this was where they would take their afternoon siesta. They had to be destroyed because there was no other way to stop them devouring the cattle.

Each parent had a twelve-bore shotgun and they were the only ones on the farm who knew how to shoot. They went to the cave and sent the dogs in to awaken the lions and entice them out of their den. Out came five angry beasts. Dad shot the first two, Mum got the next two, and Dad had time to reload and kill the very angry leader of the pride. All of us – staff and family – fed on meat, home-grown vegetables and ground maize (*posho* in Kikuyu). Twice a week Dad saddled his horse and rode out into the veldt and he had to come back with a gazelle or bushbuck. He hated killing animals, but we had to be fed.

Then the rains failed and the river began to dry up. A well was dug, but there was little water, nothing like enough for the cattle. Finally the remaining large pool in the river began to take the toll and it had several dead hippos in it. There was only one answer – pack up, sell the livestock for a pittance and find another job. We traced our steps back to the small town Nyeri, 100 miles from Nairobi. The White Rhino Hotel needed a manager, and this was our next home for a year; my parents disliked the work, especially running the bar, as they were teetotallers.

The next move was to a coffee farm at Ngong, 15 miles from Nairobi. It belonged to Bill Usher – a member of another branch of the Laing family. Mother ran this farm because Bill had other interests. Dad got a job running another farm at Machakos, 30 miles from Ngong. So we did not see much of him. When I was just eight years old, Mother was taken to hospital with a burst appendix and she died. Dad left his job and took over the Usher farm. He could not look after four youngsters. Fortunately the Leakey family came to the rescue and paid for Nigel and Agnes to be sent to England, where they were looked after by uncles and aunts.

Robert and I were sent to the Nairobi School as boarders, and who paid our fees I know not. It was a very tough school, and we boarders were not given much food. Most were day boys and their parents fed them. We soon learned to fend for ourselves; pigeons were plentiful, and it was not too difficult to kill them with a catapult. Fruit was difficult to obtain, but the Arboretum was some 4 miles from the school; there was a small plantation of oranges. Robert and I would frequently get out of bed just before dawn and, each armed with a pillowcase, we would come back with a good supply of fruit.

Unfortunately the staff who looked after the Arboretum discovered the thieves and a team of stalwart Africans were detailed to catch us. Thus it was that when we were gathering oranges, they gave a whoop of joy and went for us. We were off like a pair of scalded cats and escaped into a river which was wide, not deep, and abundant with bulrushes. In due course a team of about thirty Africans set out to find us. We eluded them by holding our noses and remaining under water until they had passed by. It was about 10 a.m. before we dared to sneak out and head back to school. The Headmaster – Captain B.W.L. Nicholson, RN Retired – was waiting for us. Two bedraggled Leakeys received six of the best, and it was a rhinoceros whip. Of course, we were little heroes because the weals were red and bleeding! Such was life at Nairobi School, which changed its name to the Prince of Wales School some years later.

Dad got married again – Bessie or Bully. She was a highly qualified teacher, and neither of us were fond of her, but she did teach us during our holidays, and by this time we had moved to Kiganju, close to Nyeri, where my father had exchanged his Rumuruti farm for one of the most beautiful 1,000 acres of land in Africa. Two rivers, the Thego and Nairobi, flowed down from Mount Kenya, and the farm lay between them. Once again Dad built a house, sheds, and huts for our Kikuyu labour.

He built a road from Kigenju railway station down the steep forest-covered slope to the Nairobi river, then a bridge, and up to the other side to the farm buildings. He and his labourers completed this task using picks, shovels and axes – no such machinery as one would have even in Nairobi. His next task was to clear some 40 acres of forest and plant coffee bushes and build the sheds where the coffee beans were washed and dried. Then he bought tractors and ploughs, and planted 100 acres of wheat. But 'Leakey's Luck' was not on his side. One afternoon I saw a single cloud heading towards the farm and called Dad's attention to it. 'Locusts!' he shouted, and every labourer was sent to the wheatfield armed with empty fuel cans which they beat, in the hope that this would scare them off.

Three hours later the locusts had devoured every wheat plant and they then repaired into the forest. The next morning they moved on and left a devastating sight; such was their weight that most of the trees were stripped of their branches. So much for the wrath of the locusts. But one of the labourers was from a Wanderobo tribe, and locusts were his 'caviare'. So thick were the locusts on the wheatfield that he had no difficulty in stuffing his mouth with them, and when he could eat no more he filled *posho* sacks, and that was his food for weeks.

The next disaster was the coffee: the soil, the climate, and the crop were superb, but the market had dropped. Brazil and other countries were burning their beans and Kenya followed suit. Dad then tried cattle, but that, too, was a disaster. In those days they were rare creatures, and they died of diseases which were then unknown to the vets. This time the Laing family came to the rescue of Dad's remaining children. Robert and I were sent to

Mombasa where we embarked on a German ship named *Ubena*. We had never seen a ship or the sea, and two lads aged fourteen and twelve savoured good food, and plenty of it, on the two-month journey to England.

On a cold winter's evening we arrived at Chichele Cottage, Oxted, Surrey. This was the home of our aunt Alice Laing (A.A.), a spinster who adopted us, and we loved her. Somehow she found the money for us to be educated at Weymouth College – a small public school for boarders and a few day boys. Our educational standard was very low and we were only accepted because Louis and Douglas Leakey, Dad's cousins, had been taught by Mother in Kenya before she was married, and they were scholars who went on to Cambridge University when they left Weymouth.

We were soon in trouble because we went into Evening Chapel not wearing ties; but in Kenya we never wore such items, and, bless her, A.A. had forgotten to teach us how to tie a tie. Our first term at that school was hell, if only because we were bottom of the class and cold baths every morning were compulsory. At the age of sixteen Robert left school and trained as an aeronautical engineer. I left aged seventeen because A.A. had no more money, so I got a job as a farm labourer, employed by a Laing cousin, Joan Little, who was the first woman to get an agricultural degree at Reading University. She lived with her mother, bred large black pigs and a herd of Guernsey cows.

A.A. was in touch with the senior partner of a firm of quantity surveyors in London, and he agreed to accept me as an articled pupil (being paid a pittance) for a five-year course. So I left Joan's farm with much regret, stayed at Chichele Cottage, and in due course went to London to meet the boss and find somewhere to live. The day before I was due to join this firm I decided that living in digs in the slums of London, working at night as a barman, was not for me. A.A. was out shopping, so I borrowed her phone and told the boss that he could find someone else as a pupil. He was not best pleased. Nor was A.A. when I told her what I had done; for the first and last time she was angry, and I don't blame her. 'So what are you going to do?' she asked. 'Join the Army – if they will accept me.' I replied, and off I went to the Oxted Police Station.

The Police Sergeant examined me and produced the document for me to sign on as a private in the East Surrey Infantry Regiment. Just before I signed up he said. 'You speak good, you are very fit, and I think you might do better by taking an examination to become an officer.' I accepted his advice, and he told me I had two months to go to a crammer and work up for the next examination in London which then accepted candidates for special entry as officers in the Navy, Air Force, Royal Military Academy, Woolwich, and the Royal Military College, Sandhurst. Applicants could apply to join any of the Services, and those who did best invariably went to the Navy, the next to the Air Force, then Woolwich where their best went to the Royal Engineers and the remainder became Gunners or Signallers.

Sandhurst accepted the remnants – wealthy Etonians, Harrovians and the like, who followed in their fathers' footsteps and were commissioned into the Brigade of Guards and the Cavalry. Their academic ability mattered little but they had to be wealthy. I wanted to try for the Navy and secondly the Air Force. When I filled in the form A.A. insisted that I apply for Sandhurst because she was sure only Sandhurst would accept duffers like me. For two months I worked like the proverbial slave, cycling 20 miles to the crammer, returning in the evening, and then paying for my keep employed as a labourer.

The results of the examination were published by *The Times* in August. A.A. had very kindly paid for Robert, Agnes and me to join her for a holiday in Germany. So well do I remember leaving early in the morning to buy *The Times*, a two-hour walk to Bonn. Sure enough there was the long list of those who had passed the exam. It was in order of merit and naturally I started at the bottom of the list looking for my name. After scanning through at least four hundred names, I gave up, walked back to our hotel, threw *The Times* on the table and said to A.A. 'That's it, I must go back to Oxted and sign up as a private soldier – I have failed.' I went out and walked for many miles, returning late at night, tired and very hungry. A.A. was waiting for me; she took me in her arms and said, 'You stupid fool, why did you not start looking for your name at the top of the list – you are top of the list – and you could have gone into the Navy, Air Force, Engineers or Artillery!' By God, I loved her.

However, there was a problem. The course at Sandhurst was eighteen months and the cost was £500, excluding payment for the servant who made your bed and cleaned the room. Uncle George (A.A.'s brother) came to the rescue and agreed to lend me £500 – a lot of money in 1934. This time 'Leakey's Luck' was on my side. Because I passed in top, I was awarded a scholarship which covered all my costs – except the servant's tip; that I earned by working on Joan Little's farm during holidays. Sandhurst was tough – certainly for the first six months when you were a Junior and not only under the control of the Guards Regimental Sergeant-Major, but also the Cadet Seniors; they were doing their last six months and, according to their ability, they held ranks from Senior Under Officer, Junior Under Officer, Sergeant and Corporal.

If a Junior misbehaved – late on parade or whatever – the four Senior Cadets gave him a 'puttee parade'. After supper the criminal rushed up to his room, changed out of his Officers' Mess dress into full combat uniform – boots, puttees, plus-fours, jacket and tie, Sam-Browne, scabbard and bayonet, and, last but not least, his .303 rifle. He would then rush downstairs and on to the parade ground. The four Seniors armed with torches, drilled him, each shouting a different command: about turn – slope arms – present arms – double – and on and on until the victim finally collapsed. His junior companions then rushed out and carried him upstairs, undressed him and put him under a shower, and so to bed. If a Junior tried to 'beat the system' and accepted two puttee parades, on the second night his tormentors were more brutal and the Cadet ended up in hospital. One Cadet tried to withstand a third successive puttee parade. He died.

After the first four months the two most promising Juniors were promoted to Lance-Corporal, and normally one of the two would hold the rank of Senior Under Officer and had a very good chance of winning the Sword of Honour. Unfortunately I blotted my copybook. One of the Juniors was a wealthy polo player and he owned two very good polo ponies. An Intermediate Irishman told this Junior that he was going to ride these horses. This caused trouble and the Irishman got his way by using his whip. The Juniors ganged up and warned the Intermediates that the tormentor would be punished by them. They retaliated by providing an escort of four of their Cadets armed with rifles and fixed bayonets. On a Saturday evening, when most of the Cadets went to London or home, some of the Juniors spotted the Irishman going for a walk with his escort. Among others, I joined the gang who went after him. We stripped him, tarred and feathered him and threw him in a lake.

As a Lance-Corporal I was dubbed the leader of the gang and the Senior Under Officers court-martialled me. I was found guilty, suffered two puttee parades, and lost my rank. However, at the end of the day I passed out of Sandhurst as an officer and received a second scholarship. I finished third in the Order of Merit – £50 a year for five years.

The Passing Out Parade at Sandhurst was and still is a great occasion, not only for the Cadets but also for parents and girlfriends. Bless her heart, A.A. came to see me march up the steps of the Old Building, followed by the Assistant Adjutant riding his horse; she was my parent and my 'girlfriend'.

Notes

1.   *The Story of Sandhurst*, Hugh Thomas (Hutchinson, 1961).

CHAPTER TWO

The Western Desert

Editor On commissioning (on 30 January 1936 – so he was just twenty-one), Rea Leakey would spend his first six months at the RTC Training Centre and Depot in Dorset, attending his Young Officers' Course and learning the basics of tanks and tank warfare. By the mid-1930s mechanization was gathering momentum, although Britain still lagged far behind other European armies. For example, the Army Estimates for 1936 included only £2 million in total for mechanization and most of that was to be spent on lorries for the infantry. Brig (later Maj Gen) Percy Hobart, then Commander of the 1st (and only) Tank Brigade, wrote in his annual report in 1936: 'The Royal Tank Corps has now completely lost the lead in the matter of numbers and up-to-date equipment – and now retains superiority, if at all, only in maintenance, organization and tactical methods; and personnel. As to numbers, during these last three years our potential enemies have increased enormously their tank corps. In the RTC no such increase has taken place.' However, despite this gloomy situation, there was a great deal for an enthusiastic young officer to do, within the scope of the RTC, which had six regular tank battalions and numerous independent armoured car/light tank companies, spread over the world in the UK, Egypt and India. As Hobart mentioned in his report, the high standard of efficiency within the RTC gave everyone a tremendous feeling of pride and *esprit de corps*, which undoubtedly made up for the daily problems of having to soldier in 'clapped-out' tanks.

After a few enjoyable months with 4 RTC in North Yorkshire, Rea would find himself on a troopship, bound for Egypt to join 1 RTC, then commanded by Lt Col (later Brig) J.A.L. Caunter. Nicknamed 'Blood', he was a splendid CO of great energy and imagination, constantly encouraging his young officers to get out into the desert, so as to learn the hard way how to live and navigate in some of the most inhospitable conditions on the planet. Like so many other British soldiers who lived and fought there, Rea Leakey clearly found a strange fascination in the barren landscape of 'The Blue' as the soldiers who fought there called it. The world famous explorer of deserts, Wilfred Thesiger, once wrote that no man could live in the desert and not come out unchanged, carrying with him, however faint: 'the imprint of the desert, the brand that marks the nomad; and he will have within him a yearning to return, weak or insistent according to his nature. For this cruel land can cast a spell which no temperate clime can match.'[1]

The Mobile Division. In 1938, the year of the Munich crisis, Percy Hobart, now a Major General, was flown out from England with orders to create an armoured division in Egypt. The enormity of his task can be judged by the fact that the only sizeable British force at his disposal was the Cairo Cavalry Brigade whose equipment was prehistoric! It is, therefore, all the more remarkable that he managed to lay the foundations of one of Great Britain's most famous armoured divisions – the 7th Armoured Division, the 'Desert Rats'. Just before he arrived the Cairo Brigade was sent hurriedly to Mersa Matruh, to form the 'Mersa Matruh Mobile Force' (also known somewhat unkindly as the 'Immobile Farce'!) which was then composed of the following: HQ Cairo Brigade and Signals; 3rd Regiment, RHA, equipped with 3.7in howitzers towed by 'Dragons' (an early type of tracked gun tower); 7th Queen's Own Hussars, with two squadrons of light tanks varying in Marks from III to VIb, but with no ammunition for their heavy machine-guns; 8th King's Royal Irish Hussars with old Ford 15cwt pick-up trucks, mounting Vickers-Berthier guns; 11th Hussars with 1924 pattern Rolls-Royce armoured cars and a few slightly more modern Morrises; 1 RTC, newly arrived from England, complete with fifty-eight light tanks (Lt Mk VIbs), but with worn-out tracks and few new ones available to replace them; 5 Company, RASC; 2/3 Field Ambulance, RAMC. Left behind in Cairo was the 6 RTC, equipped with a mixture of some old Vickers medium tanks and some light tanks of the same vintage as 7H.

After a few exercises around Matruh, the force returned to Cairo, where it was joined by their first infantry unit – the 1st Battalion, KRRC, newly arrived from Burma.

Rea Leakey The next six months were spent at the Tank Corps Schools, Bovington and Lulworth, and for the first time in my life I was solvent and able to buy a bull-nosed Morris for the large sum of £3. Eighteen months later, when I was sent abroad, I sold it to Robert for £5. It never let us down.

Then I was posted to the 4th Battalion, Royal Tank Corps at Catterick, North Yorkshire. We lived in wooden huts – no central heating, but a few coal-burning stoves. It was, and still is, an open and beautiful part of England. Sadly, we were then moved to Aldershot – not as pleasant, but for me it was near the Laing family and my Uncle George, who lived in Limpsfield, close to Chichele Cottage. He had several horses and hunted with the Old Surrey and Burstow hounds.

About 40 per cent of our time at Sandhurst was spent learning to ride a horse, and indeed even in 1963 an Officer joining a Cavalry Regiment was expected to have his own horse and play polo. I was one of the few Tank Corps Officers who had access to riding – Uncle George always lent me one of his horses, and I hunted with him. At the end of the hunting season the hunting fraternity organized amateur point-to-point races and they were very popular. One of Uncle George's horses, Grasshopper, was a very good steeplechaser but had never been entered for a race. As I was young, light and a good rider, my uncle entered me for the amateur Old Surrey and Burstow Races.

I spent most weekends training Grasshopper, staying with my Laing relations and thoroughly enjoying life, but always money was scarce so

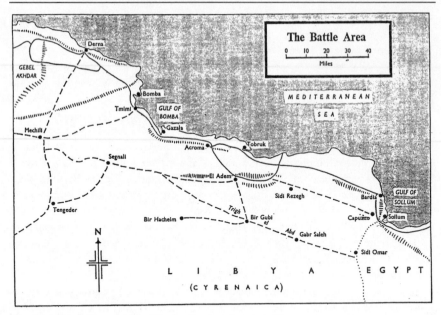

The Battle Area: Egypt and the Western Desert.

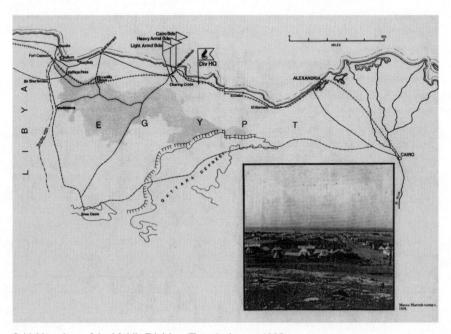

Initial locations of the Mobile Division (Egypt), August 1939.

girlfriends were not interested in me. However, Uncle George's two daughters were and still are most attractive, and, although older than me, they were great companions. Five days before the point-to-point race I was told that I was to board a troopship at Southampton and set sail for Egypt on the day of the race. This was a great disappointment and the one and only chance I had of riding in a race. However, Uncle George rode Grasshopper on the day and he finished second. He wrote and told me that I would have won with ease, and both of us would have taken the bookies to the cleaners because Grasshopper was a rank outsider. As it was, he did very well – God bless him!

That was in March 1938, and three weeks later the Troopship entered Alexandria harbour. I was now one of thirteen young Officers in the lst Battalion Royal Tank Corps. We moved into tented accommodation adjoining a British barracks at Helmeih, some 10 miles outside Cairo, and our outlook was the desert. This was to be our uncomfortable home for the next eighteen months. However, the pay was good, the sports facilities were excellent, and, above all, there was the Gezira Club in the heart of Cairo. This was where we met many of the British residents who welcomed us to their homes. Inter-regimental sports were highly competitive, and I soon found myself involved in most of them – athletics, rugger, cross-country (desert) running, cricket and boxing.

On two occasions brother officers entered me for individual open competitions without my knowing, and only told me when the entrants were published, and certainly, on the first occasion, I did not withdraw my name. I was entered for the Army of Egypt boxing competitions fighting middleweight, and one of the entrants was my batman. I fought my way to the finals, and the arena was packed with soldiers. The fight of the evening was the middleweight, 2/Lt Leakey versus Pte Tyler, and, for all to see written up – his batman. To the delight of the crowd, he won. When he woke me up the next morning with a cup of tea he took a good look at my face, gave me a mirror, and with a grin, said 'Sorry, sir'. I had two black eyes and a broken nose. What neither of us knew was that I had broken a small bone (the schofield) in my wrist for the second time; it never healed and ended my boxing career.

The second occasion was not as bad. I was entered for the Egyptian tennis tournament – in those days more or less the run-up to Wimbledon. I was entered for the Men's Open Singles, and by chance I did see the entry in the local papers. Why not, I said to myself – at least I could boast about my inevitable defeat in that I was the only Army entrant. I got through the first two rounds – how, I know not, except that I had a good first service and it worked well for a change.

The next day I was summoned before our Commanding Officer – Blood Caunter. 'You are playing too many games and overdoing it. Tennis has nothing to do with regimental sports, so you will give that up for a start,' he said.

'But, sir, tomorrow I am playing in the third round of the Men's Singles in the run-up for Wimbledon, and my opponent is the well-known German – Von Cram.'

His reply was final. 'I could not care who you were playing against. You will give up tennis.' I still boast about it.

It was most unusual to see an officer dressed in uniform in the Gezira Club, and here was Derek Thom marching into the lounge. He was doing a week's Orderly Officer for some minor crime. 'Back to camp at once and tell any others you see here,' he said. Nobody took much notice – he had pulled our legs too often. I had been asked out to dinner, and my host's daughter was most attractive. But that was one date I never kept. This was in 1938, and Chamberlain had gone to Munich to meet Hitler, and even in distant Cairo the clouds of war loomed heavy.

Just 24 hours after we had left the Gezira Club we were moving out of Cairo in a train bound for Mersa Matruh, a small harbour town some 100 miles west of Alexandria. Our tanks were unloaded, and we moved out into the desert to await the expected attack by the vast Italian army based in Libya. But Chamberlain succeeded in putting off the war for a year. There are a few who relish the thought of war, and we were no exception, but we were no conscript army, we were proud of our tanks and felt that we could hold our own against our potential foes. Yet there were no grumbles when we were told that we should return to Cairo in three months' time for Christmas.

Our time at Matruh was not wasted. Almost every day parties used to go out on reconnaissance, finding out where the going was good, plotting in each fold in the ground and, above all, learning to navigate. Once away from the sea, there are very few landmarks, no roads or railways which can be used to plot one's position. Each unit had its expert navigator whose task it was to ensure that he could give a map reference of his position whenever asked. He plotted a course as would a mariner and steered his vehicle on that bearing with the aid of a sun compass and noting the distance measured by his speedometer. On his wireless aerial he flew a large black flag. At the end of a 50-mile trip across the desert it was not considered bad if he finished up 2 miles from his destination, but more often than not his destination would be a mere map reference and nobody could dispute his accuracy. There was no quick method of fixing an exact point on a featureless desert.

I did my first long desert trip about a month after my arrival in Cairo. We were fortunate in having Capt Teddy Mitford as a member of the Regiment; he was one of a band of prewar officers who explored the desert for the love of it, and later were to form the famous Long Range Desert Group. Under his expert guidance we learned not only to navigate but, almost as important, how to tell at a glance which bit of the desert would provide good hard-going, and so avoid a soft patch where vehicles would sink in up to their axles.

By the time we left Matruh and returned to Cairo, every officer and many of the NCOs could navigate across any stretch of desert by night or day with complete confidence. I was fortunate in being chosen as one of two young officers whose duty it was to run navigation courses for our own and other regiments; the other officer was Peter Page, who, like me, had learnt to love the desert.

On our return to Cairo, Page and I probably spent more days in the desert than in barracks. We would leave Cairo with about fifteen heavily laden lorries and disappear into the desert. Nobody worried where we went, and from the time we left the Giza Pyramids until we returned, perhaps six weeks later, we were completely out of touch with the outside world. Only when we visited the few oases which lie several hundred miles to the south-west of the Nile Delta did we see other human beings. Whenever possible I used to try and call in on a small oasis called Qara.

It was a difficult place to reach, as on one side the country is very broken, and on the other stretches the Sand Sea which to this day is almost impassable to two-wheel drive vehicles. The sight of this small patch of vivid green, when the last ridge was crossed, was always more than welcome after crossing many weary miles of waterless waste; but even more welcome was the fresh clean water bubbling up out of the ground, and the shade of the date palms. The inhabitants, who numbered about a thousand, lived in caves burrowed into an enormous rock which stood by itself to one side of the oasis. The Sheikh lived in the centre, like a queen bee in a hive, and he was always glad to see me; I spoke Arabic quite well and he liked to hear what was going on in the outside world. I usually brought him some small present and he always insisted on my staying for a special meal – a whole sheep served up on a large copper dish and heaped around with rice in rancid butter. We sat round it on our haunches and pulled chunks off with our hands. But how I dreaded being given the titbit – a sheep's eye! At the conclusion of the meal, it was polite to let off a resounding belch, and the Sheikh always liked Page, because he had the art of producing a monster.

Only once did I get into serious trouble on these long journeys into the desert, and then it was nearly disastrous. I used to read every book I could find on the Western Desert of Egypt, and in one an explorer described a particularly interesting journey he had made by camel across the Qattara Depression and along a secret route that led up the steep escarpment to the west of it. This depression forms a natural obstacle to vehicles, stretching from its northern point 40 miles south of the Mediterranean Sea at El Alamein to the oasis of Siwa, which lies some 200 miles south of Mersa Matruh.

In those days the maps we had gave little detail of the topography of this part of North Africa. To the north was the Mediterranean and to the South the location of the various oases were shown, but little else. So it was not easy to plot the explorer's exact route which led across the depression to the way up the escarpment allegedly impassable to camels – let alone two-wheel drive vehicles. No doubt it had been used by raiding parties and perhaps as a slave-trade route. In June 1939, Page and I, with some thirty soldiers, set out to find it.

The journey from the Pyramids to the Depression was not difficult, but inevitably some inexperienced drivers would get bogged down in the sand, and time would be lost laying down sand-mats to move the two-wheeled drive lorries out of a soft sandbed. Then began the search to find the camel track, and on the second day we found it – at least there were skeletons at intervals leading towards the escarpment to the west of the Depression, which we could see in the dim distance. Much of the way we had to go ahead of the column of vehicles on foot to pick a route across the soft sand, so progress was slow. A week after we had left Cairo we arrived at the foot of the escarpment. We climbed up to the top and on to what appeared to be the usual relatively flat desert stretching away to the west.

That night we leaguered up beneath the pass and decided that at dawn we would try to dig a way for vehicles up the escarpment. If we succeeded, then we calculated that we should have just enough petrol and water to enable us to reach the Mediterranean coast somewhere near Mersa Matruh. But if not, then we had no alternative – we must admit failure and retrace our steps. It took us two days hard digging but we got all fifteen vehicles to the top. It was hard hot work, and we were beginning to run short of water. So, another decision: turn back and hope that we had sufficient petrol to take us to Cairo – 300 miles – or head north for the coast – 150 miles. These were basic calculations because we had no way of knowing exactly where we were. Water could be rationed, and so we went north.

We now found ourselves travelling over a plateau and the going was good until we hit the next obstacle. This was the end of the plateau and there was a drop of some 50 feet. We searched for a way down, but in vain. This was our twelfth day out, and the sun was sinking. We decided to stay where we were and take stock of our situation. We still had enough petrol to retrace our steps to Cairo – it might mean leaving some of the vehicles short of base. If we went down the escarpment we would not be able to get the vehicles back up, so we would have to go north towards the sea, no matter what further obstacles we met. We decided to go on.

By joining two ropes together we were able to use one vehicle as anchor and control the drop of the others down the escarpment. All went well, and we were just discussing how to get the anchor vehicle down when over the top it came. The driver, normally a tank driver, called Maconachie, had decided to take the matter into his own hands. He was a useful soldier to have around. And so started the last leg of our journey to the coast. The first 20 miles was fairly good going, but then the texture of the ground changed, and we found ourselves travelling over an area strewn with large boulders and cut by channels up to a foot deep. It was desperately slow going and the lorries were bouncing about like boats in a choppy sea. It took us some two hours to cover 6 miles, and then we were back in the land of soft sand, wadis and small escarpments. There was no sign of life or of a camel track.

By dusk we estimated that we had covered 30 miles, and we realized that the rough-going had played havoc with the vehicles. Three had petrol tank leaks and another four had radiator leaks, but worse than this, a tap on our water truck had worked loose and not a drop of water remained. When we inspected the loads in the vehicles, we had an even greater shock. Our petrol containers were flimsy 4-gallon tins packed in pairs in wooden cases. Unfortunately, the British Army did not possess the new famous jerrican. On any desert trip a percentage of these tins would get damaged and leak, and we always carried extra to cover this loss. But that 6 miles had wreaked havoc – hardly a gallon of petrol was left.

We were in a jam and we knew it. By draining the petrol from the lorries we would have enough to supply two of the light trucks with sufficient to cover the remaining distance to the coast and on to Mersa Matruh. We could not possibly lift everybody on these two vehicles – we were forty strong. The water situation was serious. There was only one answer. I set off next morning, leaving Peter Page in charge of the remainder of the party, and seldom have I prayed so hard for a safe passage. All that day we toiled in the blazing heat to get our two trucks through the patches of soft sand, up one wadi and down into the next. Each time the vehicle stuck the drill was the same. Jump out, dig the sand away from the rear wheels, put the 8-foot sand-channels in position and then to the back of the vehicle to push. Sometimes the truck would only travel the length of the sand-channel, then sink up to its axle and stop, so the process would have to be repeated. Once it got going the driver would not dare stop until he was on good firm going. The pushers would then run after it carrying the heavy sand-channels. Sweat poured off us, and tempers soon got frayed. Our tongues were hanging out for a drink, and our lips began to swell and crack. But the order was no drink from dawn to dusk – I had left all but a few pints of what remained of our water with Page and his party. That day we covered about 40 miles, which was most disappointing. It was hopeless to travel by night, because even with headlights it was not possible to spot the soft patches or the sharp drops in sufficient time to alter course. Anyhow, we were much too tired.

Next day it was the same again, but already we were beginning to suffer from lack of food and water, and our progress became slower and slower each time we stuck. Then a tyre burst. No sooner had we got going than another went, and then the third. We now had no spares left, and when the next one went, we would have to abandon one truck. On this day we covered 35 miles, and we should have reached the coast track.

After only a few miles travel on the third day, we were on good hard-going, and then we found the track leading us to Mersa Matruh. Our troubles were over, or so I thought, because a squadron of the 11th Hussars was camped by the sea just short of Matruh Bay. I knew the Regiment well because our camp was close to their barracks. The Squadron Commander must have been a little astonished to be confronted by a young Tank Corps Officer who was unshaven and who could hardly speak because his lips were so sore, but nobody could have been more helpful. Yes, he would supply lorries with petrol, water and food, but not until the next day at the earliest, as they had just left for Alexandria to pick up fresh supplies.

It wasn't until about 10 p.m. the next night that we were ready to set out on the return journey to Page and his men. I knew that the sooner I reached them the better because they were going to be short of water, and we made good progress that night. The next morning we found ourselves on the bad-going, and I estimated that we had 80 miles to cover. All went well for about the first 30 miles, and then a dust storm blew up. This was unusual at this time of the year, and fortunately it was a mild one; even so, visibility was reduced to about 5 yards. It lasted 24 hours, and not only did it delay us but it obliterated the tracks of our two vehicles, so making it that much more difficult to reach the abandoned party.

When eventually we had covered the distance, we started the search. The lorries were left in a prominent position, and I moved out in ever increasing circles. In this broken country visibility is limited to no more than a mile. I had suggested to Peter Page that he should find a wadi which would give a little shade from the sun. Neither of us thought of leaving a vehicle on the skyline. After two days of searching I got very worried, and that night I woke my driver and resumed the search. At about 2 a.m. I spotted a light pointing up in the sky. I took a compass bearing on it and drove for it as fast as the vehicle would travel. Another 5 miles and I reached it. Fourteen lorries lay tucked away in a wadi, and one had its headlights shining in the air. The driver thought he heard a vehicle moving and the headlights on this particular lorry were mounted on a bar which enabled them to be tilted. I had found them just in time; they were in a bad state – some could hardly move and lay in the sand crying out for water. The sandstorm had not helped. Another day and I think we would have found some corpses.

The 11th Hussars were returning to Helmieh and I asked the Squadron Commander to tell the Adjutant of my Regiment (Lt H.A. Lascelles) that we were delayed by breakdowns and please not to mention that I had nearly lost some thirty-four men. We moved to a beautiful deserted beach at El Alamein and spent a week there recovering from our experience. We arrived back at our camp in Helmieh after dark, and three of the soldiers were smuggled into the Military Hospital – they were still suffering from the effects of heat and lack of water. The vehicles were in poor shape, and I well remember receiving the sharp end of the tongue of our Regimental Transport Officer – Lt R.M.P. Carver – now FM The Lord Carver. Yet such was the loyalty of those soldiers that neither he, the Commanding Officer, Lt Col Blood Caunter, or the Adjutant, heard a word about the near disaster of that journey.

It was not long after this 'near-disaster' journey was over that I was one of many ordered to Bagush – a few miles east of Mersa Matruh (just the name of a few houses) where the first British Armoured Division was to be formed. It was called the Mobile Division. My appointment was GSO 3 Intelligence, and it was here that I met Maj Gen P.R.C. Hobart, the Divisional Commander. He had flown out to Cairo and then on to Bagush, and he knew nothing about the Western Desert. The only reason I got this important appointment was because of my knowledge of this part of Egypt and its inhabitants, which included the desert rats – *Jerboas*. I had one of these beautiful little animals as a pet, and 'Hobo' asked me what it was, so I explained. 'That is what we will call this Division,' he said: 'The Desert Rats.'[2]

It was not long before the Division Headquarters moved to Cairo where it was named the 7th Armoured Division. Hobo ordered me to take him back to Cairo via the Qattara Depression, a four-day journey. When we dropped down into the Depression he was quick to appreciate its significance in war. I told him that the way I took him down was 40 miles from a small village called El Alamein close by the sea. There was no other way up or down this escarpment for over 170 miles south – deep into the desert. I told him of the journey I had done when I so nearly lost some of my men and my career as a soldier. He examined the map and said it was of such importance that he wanted to examine it himself, and this was to be his next journey into the desert.

So well I remember our arrival back in Cairo. I took Hobo to his luxurious house in Gezira, and he invited me in for a drink – 3 p.m. – hot, filthy and tired. I was introduced to his wife; like him, she was pleasant, but 'business first' as a General's wife should be 'Read this,' she said to him, and handed him a short letter, which he read and then handed to me. 'Lady Gordon Finlayson does not expect Major General and Mrs Hobart to call upon her.' Hobo, a Sapper, had married a brother Officer's wife.

Hobo was dynamic, and it was not long before I was detailed to organize a journey to the Qattara Depression and then up the pass which I had found. By this time I had been sacked as G3 Intelligence because I was too young for such an important appointment, so I was demoted to my correct rank – a Lieutenant in 1 RTC. The General wanted to go in three days' time. For the first and last time in my life I feigned illness and suggested that perhaps the General's ADC, Lt Sir Frederick Coates, might organize this venture. Freddy was one of the thirteen young 1st RTC officers, a great friend of mine, and I felt sorry landing him with this particular job. He came to see me. I was lying in my camp bed, unshaven and pretending to be very ill. I gave him such detailed information that was not on any map and warned him not to expect an easy journey. I suggested that he organize a radio link with the RAF, because it might be necessary to have supplies dropped by air. This he did, and it was the first time this inter-Service link was used.

This Pass up the Qattara Depression was called 'Leakey's Pass' and was kept secret. The Long Range Desert Group and Stirling's SAS used it, particularly in 1942 when they operated behind the German and Italian lines which stretched from El Alamein to the Qattara Depression. We got to know the 11th Hussars and we had a high regard for them. They were the only Cavalry Regiment which had armoured cars, let alone tanks, and we saw little of the other Cavalry Regiments; they rode their horses. However, it was not long before all the Cavalry Regiments – less one, which kept its horses until 1942 – were armed with tanks and a few other light mobile vehicles.

Notes

1.   Taken from the prologue to *Arabian Sands*.
2.   The first Desert Rat for the Division's famous shoulder flash was drawn by Mrs O'More Creagh, wife of Maj Gen O'More Creagh who took over from 'Hobo'. She used a jerboa from the Cairo Zoo as a model and drew its likeness on a sheet of hotel notepaper. It was then transferred in flaming scarlet thread on to the centre of the plain white circle which had been the symbol of the Mobile Division. The resulting shoulder patches were made locally, and it was not until the summer of 1943, while the division was resting in the Homs-Tripoli area, that an attempt was made to get the War Office to agree to an official clothing manufacturer producing an official divisional sign in time to be worn in Normandy. Although this was approved, the resulting animal looked more like kangaroo than a jerboa, while its colour had changed from red-brown to black! To add insult to injury, the War Office refused to sanction any further alterations, so the new 'jerboa' had to be accepted. Later, both 4th and 7th Armoured Brigades produced their own individual 'jerboas', the 4th in black and the 7th in green.

CHAPTER THREE

War

Editor By the middle of 1939 it had become clear that the Italians were contemplating challenging British interests in the Mediterranean area, so there was a vital need to protect our sea and air communications to India and the Far East. The Suez Canal was an obvious target as had been pointed out many times since it had been built[1], and Great Britain was determined to have a centralized command to coordinate the strategic war plans of the whole area of collaboration with France, Greece and Turkey. In June 1939, Lt Gen Sir Archibald Wavell was appointed as GOC in C Middle East, with his HQ in Cairo, and given vast responsibilities but pitifully few resources with which to accomplish them – for example, his total initial staff was just five staff officers, plus his own ADC, while throughout the entire time he was in command he did not even have his own aircraft, so always had to travel in whatever service aircraft just happened to be available! Wavell's own appreciation of the situation, written on 31 July 1939, just two days before he took up his appointment included the following paragraphs: 'The last war was won in the West . . . the next will be won or lost in the Mediterranean, the harder will be the winning of the war. The task of the staff of Middle East Command is therefore to plan, in conjunction with the other Services, not merely the defence of Egypt and our other interests in the Middle East but such measures of offence as will enable us and our Allies to dominate the Mediterranean at the earliest possible moment; and thereafter to take the counter-offensive against Germany in Eastern and SE Europe.'

He then outlined the four steps which he considered were necessary in order to achieve this result. The first was to secure Egypt and the Suez Canal, thus providing a base for the Allies for the rest of the war; the second was to clear the Red Sea and third, the Eastern Mediterranean. Finally, there was the possibility of taking land operations into SE Europe, but this would not be attempted until the other steps had been completed. The initial step – to secure the Egyptian base – included defending the Western Desert along the frontier with Italian-governed Libya, where an estimated 200,000-plus Italian troops, comprising nine metropolitan (i.e., from Italy), four Blackshirt and two Libyan native divisions were stationed. Opposing them were just 36,000 British troops, plus the Egyptian Army which would clearly not be employed outside Egypt. However, as events would soon prove, despite being short on numbers the British were superior, the quality of both men and equipment (in the main the Italians had even more clapped-out weapons of war than we did!) and most importantly, in morale.

Clearly it was essential to train the small force as well as possible. However, as Rea Leakey illustrates, modern armoured tactics which would soon become the 'norm' in the coming desert war were frowned upon by those in charge as being unsporting. The débâcle which directly led to the sacking of Hobo was truly a disgrace. Suffice it to say that the spontaneous display of loyalty and affection shown by the officers and soldiers of the division when Hobo left was evidence of just how far some of the top brass were from reality.

But there was really no time to 'stand and stare'. War was declared first by Germany in September 1939, followed by Italy on 11 June 1940, although Mussolini completely forgot to tell his troops in North Africa that he had done so! GOC 7th Armoured Division had given orders to his leading troops to: 'dominate the frontier between the Italian forts of Capuzzo and Maddalena and to delay any Italian advance . . . to destroy the (frontier) wire wherever possible, penetrate into Italian territory and harass communications along the road from Fort Capuzzo, through Bardia, towards Tobruk.' The orders ended with the phrase which would become all too common at the time: 'Although the utmost aggressiveness will be displayed, it is important to avoid becoming engaged with superior enemy formations.' This was very much the case when, on 13 September 1940, preceded by a tremendous artillery barrage on the deserted village of Musaid, the Italians opened their long-awaited invasion of Egypt. By 20 September, they had advanced some 60 miles at the cost of over 3,500 casualties, including 700 taken prisoner. British losses were just 160. Then they began to build a series of strongly fortified camps, which covered eight main positions: Maktila and Sidi Barrani on the coast; Tummar West and Tummar East and Point 90 to the south of Sidi Barrani; Nibeiwa to the south of the Tummars and Sofafi and Rabia to the southwest of Nibeiwa.

Mussolini was highly delighted with this advance into Egypt, crowing that now Italy had achieved: '. . . the glory that she had been vainly seeking for three centuries', even remarking that he was sorry that the war would be over before he had the chance of winning further victories. 'War,' he told the Crown Princess at the time, 'was the only truly beautiful action that made life worth living.'[2]

Tanks, armoured cars and other vehicles of the Mobile Division are formed up at Mersa Matruh, during one of 'Hobo's' training exercises. (*Editor's collection*)

Rea Leakey In the spring of 1939 we got thirty new tanks, A9s,[3] to name them. They were larger than our light tanks and mounted a gun that fired a 2-pound shell. In addition to the main turret they had two sub-turrets each armed with a machine-gun. And there were other changes. The Royal Armoured Corps[4] was formed, which now incorporated the Cavalry Regiments who were rapidly being turned off their horses and told to become tank soldiers. We, the Tank Corps, had to change our nomenclature; our battalions became regiments, our companies were now called squadrons, and so on. From now on I therefore refer to my unit as 1st Royal Tank Regiment (1 RTR).

When the war started on 3 September 1939, we were once again back in the desert, not far from Mersa Matruh. We were in the 4th Armoured Brigade – part of the 7th Armoured Division. We had been well trained by General Hobart, who was for ever taking us out into the desert. One of the exercises we took part in was of interest. Gen Sir Robert Gordon Finlayson, C in C, British Troops in Egypt, organized one of the largest manoeuvres ever in the Western Desert. The infantry divisions were to defend Mersa Matruh against an enemy attack advancing from the East. The enemy was 7th Armoured Division. A defensive line was built from the coast stretching south into the desert for a distance of some 15 miles. When the infantry had dug in, barbed wire had been erected, and dummy minefields laid, the exercise started.

Gen Hobart ordered his Armoured Car Regiment (the 11th Hussars) to reconnoitre the defences and they soon discovered where they ended. He then moved his Division some 30 miles into the desert, and entered Mersa Matruh by the back door, so winning the battle without 'firing a shot'. I happened to be one of the officers who attended the conference at the early conclusion of this exercise, and I shall never forget it. There must have been some 400 officers assembled at the open-air cinema in Mersa Matruh. On the platform were the senior officers, and the C in C addressed us. He complimented the infantry Divisional Commanders on the layout of their defences, and then described the story of the so-called conflict. 'What happened?: The enemy carried out a manoeuvre which in war would have been quite impossible. Gen Hobart moved his whole division deep into the desert and entered our strongly defended position from the rear.'

Not long after this episode, Gordon Finlayson was posted back to Whitehall into an influential position. Hobo was 'sacked'. I happened to be in Cairo on the evening that he and his wife left Cairo station for Alexandria by train on their way back to England. I was one of the many who came to say goodbye. Outside the station there was chaos; the soldiers of the Desert Rats had taken matters into their own hands and had driven their vehicles into the streets of Cairo, abandoned them and joined the throng on the railway platform. Hobo was demoted to the rank of Lance Corporal in the Home Guard. But he was not forgotten, particularly by the Cavalry

Officers. It was they, I am told, who petitioned His Majesty to have him reinstated as a Divisional Commander. And so he was, but in England.[5]

In March 1940, I was posted to 4th Armoured Brigade Headquarters as Navigator and Intelligence Officer. The Brigade Commander was Brig Blood Caunter whom I knew well, as he had been the CO of 1 RTR. Indeed, as a navigator in the desert I had made a name for myself. With the help of a Professor Cole of Cairo University, I had invented a sun-compass which to this day is known as the 'Cole Universal Sun Compass'. Idiot that I was, I gave the patent rights to a brother officer, Basil Forster, who married an ex-girlfriend of mine, Annette Cole. I had no claim to being 'intelligent!'

Gen Sir Archibald Wavell had become C in C Middle East in 1939. Gen Maitland Wilson commanded the British troops in Egypt. The most immediate danger they faced was the Italian Army on Egypt's western frontier. This was estimated to consist of nine divisions in Tripolitania and five more in Cyrenaica – a total strength of 215,000 men.

War was declared by Italy on 11 June, 1940. Only 7th Armoured Divisional Headquarters and about half the troops were left in the Mersa Matruh area; the rest were back in Cairo. I well remember the night we heard the news that we were to move at dawn, head for Libya and attack the Italians. We listened to the BBC news telling of the German victories in France and of the withdrawal of the British Army towards Dunkirk. I think we were all very depressed. But then Churchill spoke – there was to be no surrender. What a tonic that was, and what a challenge.

Brig Blood Caunter decided that his Headquarters would lead the way and so, as navigator, I had the task of making sure that our column would land up at the right place after a march of 150 miles, which took us two days. Our task was to attack the forts that the Italians had built along the frontier – the main one being Fort Capuzzo. The force under command of the Brigadier was not imposing: the 11th Hussars and some of their armoured cars had fought in the First World War; one armoured regiment – the 7th Hussars – equipped with the A9 cruiser tank; a company of the KRRC and a troop of Royal Engineers.

At dawn on 14 June we crossed the frontier marked by a double-line of barbed-wire entanglements which stretched from the coast across 260 miles of desert to the oasis of Girabub. Unfortunately, few of the 7th Hussars tanks had survived the journey. This was not surprising, because the men had not long been dehorsed and their knowledge of mechanical vehicles was limited. However, Blood's Brigade HQ had a protection troop of two cruiser tanks and three light tanks. They were manned by RTR soldiers. So these five tanks and the company of infantry set forth to capture Fort Capuzzo.

At 9 a.m. three Blenheim bombers swept low across our front and dropped their bombs. They probably frightened the Italians, but failed to break open the fort. Then Blood led the way in one of the cruiser tanks. He took us round to the rear of the fort – just as well, as the front, facing Egypt, was heavily mined, and the battle started. I was in a light tank which should have had two Vickers machine-guns mounted in the turret, but they had not arrived from England. So out of the gaping holes where those guns should have been, my gunner fired his rifle, and I discharged the six rounds from my pistol. After some 30 minutes our tanks had silenced the enemy's machine-guns, and the infantry moved up towards the walls of the fort. By this time Brigadier Blood had his tank positioned some 50 yards from the main entrance to the fort, and he was pumping 2-pound armoured piercing shells through the large metal doors. This was too much for the Italians, and they gave up. The flag that fluttered from the mast in the centre of the fort was lowered, and was exchanged for a white sheet. The doors were flung open, and out marched some sixteen Officers followed by over 200 men. Soon they were on their way to captivity, heading for the small frontier town of Sollum.

For a while all was quiet. Then I heard the drone of aircraft, and looking up I saw five Italian bombers with an escort of eight fighters coming in to bomb us. But I had also noticed the RAF fighter cover for our attack. It consisted of three out-of-date Gladiators. The Italian airmen had not spotted them, and received a rude awakening. Within seconds three of their fighters and a bomber were in flames, and the rest fled, scattering their bombs far and wide. Everybody cheered. Our first battle was over, and it had all been too easy. Two tanks had been blown up on mines, and our total casualties could not have been more than two killed and four wounded.

After blowing up the fort, the tanks and infantry withdrew back behind the wire, leaving the armoured cars to watch for the enemy forces, which we felt sure would soon appear from the east.

But nothing happened to alarm us that day or the next or the next. We were bombed, but our vehicles were widely scattered, and we suffered no casualties. It was five days later that the Italians sent a force of some fifty tanks, thirty guns and a battalion of infantry in lorries to attack us. The armoured cars spotted them soon after they left their base at Sidi Azeiz, some 20 miles across the frontier, and kept us well informed of their movement. They were some 3 miles short of the frontier wire when our tanks met them. The poor devils never had a chance. Their tanks were lightly armoured with only mounted machine-guns. The British cruiser tank with its two-pounder gun was so much superior in every respect, and by this date we had at least fifteen of them. One after another the little Italian tanks went up in flames as the 2-pound solid shot tore through their thin armour plating. In the open desert the Italian gunners took terrible punishment. We could almost hear them screaming as the hail of lead from our guns ripped through their bodies. In less than an hour it was all over. The battlefield was not a pretty sight, and the smell of burning human flesh lingered in my nostrils for many days to come; dead mangled bodies lay in huge heaps beside the guns, and the wounded cried out for water. Thank God the majority had surrendered, including many of the tank crews.

I well remember two small incidents of this engagement. About six months before the war I played in a squash match as a member of the Cairo team against Alexandria. My opponent was a wealthy Italian businessman who lived in Alexandria. After the match he and I sat discussing the international situation over a cooling glass of beer. He told me that he had just returned from Benghazi in Libya, where he had been doing a month's training with the Italian Army. Italy had been calling up her reservists and retraining them. He told me he was a Tank Commander, and then he said, 'And Mamma mia, I hope we never fight you, because your tanks are so much better than ours.' Little did I think that I would see him again.

I was busy bandaging a nasty wound on an Italian soldier's leg when suddenly I heard an excited voice shouting my name. I looked up and there running towards me was my squash opponent. There were tears in this eyes, tears of joy, because, as he said, 'I shall now be able to return to Alexandria, to my wife and children.' I wished him good fortune, and he went on his way with the rest of the prisoners, a happy little man. I called my driver over and told him to hold up the wounded leg, so that I could secure the bandage. He took one look at the bloody mess, and fainted. Before the war he was a butcher!

People have often asked me why we did not venture further into Libya and attack the Italian fortified base of Bardia, which was only some 20 miles beyond the frontier. But the answer was only too obvious; even the few troops we had in this forward area proved a frightful headache to the supply units, and at that time they could not possibly have maintained a larger force, even if additional troops had been available. All we could do was to try and bluff the enormous Italian Army into believing that they faced at least an armoured Division instead of little more than an armoured Regiment. Even at this early stage we built dummy tanks out of old boxes and canvas and trailed chains behind our lorries so that they churned up the dust and would be taken for tanks by the ever vigilant Italian reconnaissance planes. The ruse worked. We learned from prisoners that the Italians estimated our force to be at least three armoured Divisions.

Throughout June and July the situation remained unchanged. But life was not dull. Each day the armoured cars patrolled deeper and deeper into Libya. At night patrols used to sneak down on to the road between Bardia and Tobruk and ambush vehicles; almost every day they brought in a batch of scared Italians prisoners. It was one of my duties to interrogate these prisoners with the aid of an interpreter, as I spoke little Italian. Mostly they were only too willing to talk. Perhaps the best catch was an Italian General and his ladyfriend; he was evacuating her from Bardia when the armoured cars picked him up. I remember her well, because she had a filthy temper and demanded to be taken back to Bardia immediately, but her boyfriend, the General, was determined to take her with him to enliven his days of captivity. We let him have his way!

One day I asked the Brigadier if I might pay a visit to Fort Capuzzo to see if I could find any documents in the various Italian offices. He agreed, little suspecting that my real reason for visiting the place was to loot! When we first captured the Fort, my tank driver had found the Officers' Mess cellar, but had not had the time or opportunity to help himself. Also there was a well in the fort, and our water ration in those days was one pint per man per day for all purposes.

The two of us entered the fort the next morning, as dawn was breaking. We left our truck carefully concealed in a shed, and started to rummage around. It was very eerie. An old bit of corrugated iron creaked, then a half-starved cat let out a screech and fled before us. But the cellar was intact, and we were soon busy loading the truck. I found a brand new Gilera motorbike, and soon had it going. I rode it out of the front gate and got the shock of my life. An Italian plane was circling round and round the fort, only a few hundred feet up. We had been too busy looting to notice it. We decided to get out of the place as soon as the plane disappeared. But round and round it went; after an hour it was relieved by another plane. It would have been suicide to have attempted to make a dash for it, so, like trapped rats, we sat and watched that damned plane. I thought the day would never end, and I just longed for darkness or for that blasted plane to go away.

At long last the sun slowly sank below the horizon, and we got ready to go. 'Listen, sir, do you hear tanks?' said my driver. Sure enough, above the drone of the plane I could hear the distinct clatter of track plates and the hum of engines. What disturbed me was that I knew none of our tanks was out that day, and the noise was coming from the west. I climbed on to a high wall, and looked back towards Bardia. Half a mile away some fifty tanks were slowly creeping across the desert towards the fort, and even at that distance I could clearly see they were not British. Behind them moved columns of large black lorries. And still the plane droned round and round.

With one eye on the approaching tanks and the other on the plane I waited, and the minutes slowly ticked by. The light was fading, so very slowly, I thought. Down below me, my driver had started up the Italian motorbike, and left it ready; he sat at the wheel of the heavily laden truck. He had said nothing, but was obviously determined that I should not leave the bike behind. I had not the courage to tell him that I hardly knew how the gears worked. When the tanks were within 100 yards of the fort, I jumped down, and as they drove in at the back we drove out of the front. Every second I expected to see the dust round me being kicked up as the plane spat lead at me, but our luck held, and that motorbike certainly could move.

It was a very shaken officer who walked into the Brigade command vehicle an hour later and announced that the Italians had reoccupied Fort Capuzzo. Although it would have been ideal to attack Capuzzo again as soon as possible, it was not prudent to do so until we were fairly certain that further Italian forces were not going to venture forth in large numbers. Thus, the inevitable attack was not launched until a week after the Italians had moved back into the fort, and by that time they were well dug in. It was dusk when our tanks once again closed in on the defences, and they got a very hot reception. One of the first tanks to be hit was the CO's, and from then on things did not go well. After only about 20 minutes of hard battle, it was obvious that this was too tough a nut to be cracked by our small force, and the order was given to withdraw. It was the only defeat we suffered at the hands of the Italians.

However, they did not feel confident enough to attack our small force, although they had at least four times as many men in this part of the desert as we did. And we had not the strength to attack them. But Brig 'Blood' did not believe in his protection troop of tanks being idle, and he put me in command. We were given the task of annoying the Italians in Fort Capuzzo. The three light tanks had powerful searchlights and by this time the Vickers guns had arrived. At least twice a week I would lead these three tanks round to the west of Capuzzo, and when darkness fell we would attack the enemy vehicles moving forward from Bardia. We must have inflicted a certain amount of damage, and we certainly made them expend quantities of artillery shells in driving us away. We, in turn, suffered no casualties – the tanks' armour was sufficient to keep out high explosive shell splinters, and the chances of a direct hit were remote.

There must have been a surplus of Senior Officers hanging around Cairo with little to do because 4th Armoured Brigade HQ received a reinforcement of a certain Col Charles Gairdner as Second-in-Command of the Brigade. He was a character! He was tall, well built, and walked with a limp. He was wounded in the First World War serving as a Gunner Officer. I gather that he transferred to the 10th Hussars some time between the two wars. I got to know him well. He told me that soon after joining the 10th, he was boasting about his prowess as a games player. His brother officers bet him that he would not be good enough to play for England at any game of his choice, and the stakes were high. He won, playing in goal at hockey.

Soon after his arrival, he suggested that I take him on one of my tank exploits round Capuzzo but not at night. He felt that in the early afternoon the Italian gunners would be taking a siesta. So, in due course, one hot afternoon, we stopped some 2 miles short of the Bardia–Capuzzo road and watched the large enemy lorries going about their business. 'Let's do a cavalry charge, shoot up a convoy and then away home,' and away we went. I suppose we got within 500 yards of the vehicles before the Italians opened fire, and they had a lot of guns. We had opened fire at about the same time, moving in fast towards the lorries. The Colonel was leading with his head and shoulders looming up out of his tank's turret. In the dust and smoke I saw him wave his hat in the air as his tank turned around and disappeared. As my tank turned to follow him, an anti-tank shell hit us, and we were on fire. We 'baled' out and ran after our gallant Colonel Fortunately the third tank commander, a Corporal, saw us and returned to pick me up. How we got out of that cauldron without a scratch, I do not know, but I guess it was the first of my 'nine lives'.

Living in the desert was tough – we had no beds, no caravans, and water was very scarce. Shaving was forbidden, because in those days we did not have electric razors. There were no mobile laundries, so we never changed our clothes, and did we stink! Bully-beef and biscuits was our fare, and there was no alcohol. But the desert is a clean place, and we were healthy. We were a happy Headquarters, and I never heard a soldier grumble and mean it. It was at this time that Churchill had coined the phrase 'blood, tears, toil and sweat'. And, of course, this is what our four senior officers were called. 'Blood' Caunter (the Brig). 'Tears' – Col Charles Gairdner, because he always looked miserable. 'Toil' was the Staff Captain – Wilfred Rice; yes, he worked harder than any of us. 'Sweat' was the Brigade Major – Charles Ward; he was large and overweight.

As the fighting had died down, leave was started and my turn came up towards the middle of August. The normal way back to Cairo was across the desert to Matruh in the back of a lorry and then train to Cairo – not a pleasant journey. I decided it might be more pleasant to ride my motorbike, and it would be quicker. The ride across the desert was hell, but I arrived back at the Gezira Club at 5 p.m., at least a day ahead of the others, and thus got five days leave instead of four. After a bath and a change of clothes I repaired to the barber's shop, and I requested the removal of my beard. Several of my friends heard I was around and ran me to ground. My beard was about to be removed, and I was sound asleep. They asked the barber just to trim the beard and make sure that I did not see myself in a mirror before leading me back to the bar. Only later in the evening did I discover that I was the owner of a blood-red goatee beard – and in those days my hair was very fair.

Before going on leave I asked Brig 'Blood' if I might return to regimental duty, and he agreed. I rejoined 1 RTR at the end of August 1940, and they had relieved the 7th Hussars so I was back in the desert not far from Fort Capuzzo. I was given command of a troop of cruiser tanks and it was good to be back among men I know well and in a Regiment that I loved.

I had a good crew in my own tank and we were together for many a day. The driver was Tpr Doyle, and he was a typical tank soldier; a good mechanic who took great pride in his vehicle, just as a cavalryman would his horse. He has written a book about this particular tank – T7201, and tells the tale of how on one occasion we had to move into battle at very short notice and he complained that 'Biddy' was missing. This was his chicken who lived in the tank, and on the move sat on his lamp. I told him to get into his seat and get moving. He writes, 'Forlornly I climbed into the driver's seat and started the engine. As I did so, it seemed the skies had opened up and it was snowing. The terrible truth dawned on me. Biddy had the habit of getting into the engine compartment close to the fan. T7201 had made another kill – a chicken.' The wireless operator and loader for the turret guns was a Welshman named Adams, a regular soldier, who, like Doyle, survived the war. Today they live near Cardiff and occasionally we meet to talk of those days in the desert. Tpr Milligan, the main turret gunner, came from Dublin. The two sub-turret gunners were very young. I was the old man of the crew, aged twenty-four.

General Wavell's plan was to hold 7th Armoured Division back in the area of Mersa Matruh, where he hoped to stop the Italian forces when they launched their attack to invade Egypt. A skeleton force was left on the frontier and this included 1 RTR. The great attack started on 13 September 1940 and their forces amounted to six infantry divisions and eight battalions of tanks. I well remember our orders to 'make a fighting withdrawal, but under no circumstances were tanks to be lost in battle'. Yes, in those early days every tank was worth its weight in gold.

The Italians heralded the start of this venture with a heavy artillery bombardment, most of which hit the empty desert, and their bombers gave us a larger dose than usual. When the dust and smoke cleared, we saw the most fantastic spectacle. The Italian Army was advancing towards us led by motor cyclists riding in perfect line – dressed from the right. Then came the tanks, again in parade order, and they were followed by row after row of large black lorries. Adams stared at them for a minute, then turned to me and remarked, 'Bloody hell, Tidworth Tattoo – we can't spoil their march past.'

We had a battery of 25-pounder guns supporting us, and they started dropping their shells into this vast target moving towards us. When our tanks were spotted, the column of vehicles heading for us halted, and in no time they had unloaded guns and the battle was on. We were now given the order to form 'battle line' and race towards the enemy at full speed with all guns blazing. It was certainly an exhilarating ride. We must have frightened the enemy even if we failed to kill them, but when we were some 400 yards from them, the order came to turn tail and get out of the cauldron. Our Commanding Officer obeyed orders – no tanks were to be lost. And indeed on that charge we were lucky, even though most of the tanks had been hit and a number had to be backloaded for major repairs. Credit must be given to our experienced drivers like Doyle. If they missed their gear-change on the turn, the tank would present an easy target to the anti-tank gunners.

And so throughout that day we moved slowly back towards Mersa Matruh, fighting these inconclusive actions but certainly taking a toll of the enemy. When darkness fell we moved a few miles back into the desert, knowing full well that the Italians were as tired as we were, and equally as hungry. It had been a tiring day and we had been bombed and shelled almost continuously from dawn to dusk. Yet it was well after midnight before we got into bed. Each tank crew was kept fully occupied carrying out a variety of tasks to make sure that our machine was ready for another day's battle. Our supply lorries had to find us in the dark, and then the crew had the job of replenishing ammunition, petrol and food with no lights showing.

When all this was done we 'got into bed'. This was a simple process. Each tank was provided with a tarpaulin and two blankets per man. Undressing consisted of removing boots, which were used as pillows, and within seconds five weary men would be lying in a row on the stony desert. The sixth man was sentry, and his first duty was to pull the tarpaulin over his confederates. The nights in the desert were very cold, and there was always a heavy dew.

Half an hour before first light we were on the move, with orders to close in on the enemy before they were fully awake. But they were prepared for us and their guns kept us at bay. It was not long before fighter planes came in on us and gave us a lively time, but they did little damage. We had the misfortune to receive an accurate burst of tracer bullets on the back of the tank, which set fire to the tarpaulin and blankets. Adams and I had an exciting time trying to extinguish the flames, but the smoke attracted more aircraft, and all we could do was throw the lot overboard and dive back into the tank before the next hail of bullets arrived. Over the wireless came a voice offering to sell us blankets at an exorbitant price. Adams was about to rent his wrath on this man, but I managed to stop him. He had a fine flow of language and every word would be heard by every man in the regiment.

For the next three days the pattern of battle was the same – delay the enemy but don't lose tanks. At least one tank was hit and destroyed, and I remember a squadron commander receiving a 'bollocking' for such a crime. The loss of men's lives was not as important as the loss of a tank. When the Americans came into the war, the values were reversed. It takes a long time to train a good tank soldier.

The Italians reached Sidi Barrani, a very small town some 60 miles from the Libyan frontier. Before continuing their advance into Egypt they decided to build up a strong base here and bring forward more troops. They built a series of large fortified camps stretching some 30 miles south from the sea. They also started to build a metal road from Capuzzo to Sidi Barrani. 1 RTR was moved back to an area some 20 miles from Mersa Matruh. We had been 'tried in battle'; we had not lost many men or tanks but we were tired and dirty. Fighting and indeed living in the desert in those early days was tough; we had few creature comforts and the older officers just could not 'take it'. Thus it was that I got command of a squadron and went from lieutenant to major overnight. I was twenty-four years old.

Early in October Col Charles Gairdner came to see me and asked if I would take him to see something of the desert well south of the coast. The 4th Armoured Brigade HQ was out of action, in reserve, awaiting the impending enemy advance – as were 1 RTR, but as there was no sign of this Brigadier Blood had agreed this venture. I decided to take him to Qara oasis because I felt he would be interested to see the Qattara depression and make the acquaintance of the old Sheikh who lived in the middle of the huge rock.

We set off with four trucks and carried a high powered wireless set which would keep us in touch with what was going on while we were away. Three days later I was introducing the Sheikh to the Colonel who, I said, was one of the important officers conducting the war against the Italians. The Sheikh was duly impressed and invited us to an even bigger and better feast than usual. The news had reached him that there was a war, but it meant little to him. The Colonel, being the guest of honour, was presented with the sheep's eye; he screwed up his face in disgust, but I told him he must eat it, otherwise the Sheikh would be highly offended. I am afraid I enjoyed myself at his expense, and he knew it. After the meal we sat on and talked, sipping numerous small cups of mint tea which our host prepared with much ceremony. I could see the Colonel was a little bored, particularly as he did not speak Arabic, and he was obviously longing for a whisky and soda. But the Sheikh was intent on making the most of this great occasion, and I felt we could not leave until the sun had set; in any case, each time either of us tried to make a move, the Sheikh politely but firmly told us to sit down.

At last he rose to his feet, and, adopting an oratorical manner, delivered a long and alarming speech. After expressing his delight at meeting the Colonel, whom he described in glowing terms, he told us that he proposed to bestow upon us a very great honour. Unfortunately, he said, there were at this time only fifteen young virgins available in the oasis; these were now going to be brought in, and we were each to have the honour of selecting three with whom to spend the night under his roof. I beamed and bowed my head in silent mirth, and interpreted to the Colonel. Both of us had caught glimpses of these young girls as they were being assembled in the passage outside the Sheikh's room.

The Colonel looked at me, and said, 'You made me eat the sheep's eye, but now it is your turn. At least one of us must accept this great honour, and this time it will not be me!' I then got to my feet and in my best Arabic expressed our deep gratitude, and went on to explain that we could not possibly deprive him of six of his remaining virgins. But he would hear none of it, and clapped his hands for a servant to march the girls in. I tried to explain that our customs and codes were very different from his, and that we did not indulge in this sort of thing. At this, he got very angry; when in Rome do as the Romans do, was his theme, and if we refused this honour he would be greatly offended. He was fingering his dagger.

I bowed and thanked him and explained that we would not dream of offending him and, as I spoke, I was thinking fast as to how to get out of this difficult situation. I asked if we might have another cup of tea before we had the pleasure of selecting our three girls; this would take at least ten minutes and I needed time. He agreed, and I told him that while he was making the tea I would go out to see that our soldiers with the trucks were all right; I also explained about our wireless set. By this time the trucks were unpacked and the men were about to turn in for the night. I got hold of a corporal who was intelligent and I hoped a good actor, and gave him detailed instructions. Then I returned to the Sheikh's quarters, where I again sat on the floor and made polite conversation, stalling for time.

Ten minutes later in rushed the corporal, looking most agitated and brandishing a piece of paper. I took it from him, and as I read it my face grew longer – at least, I hoped that it looked as if it did. Handing the paper to the Colonel, I stood up and told the Sheikh that over the wireless had come news that the Italians had launched a heavy attack, and his distinguished guest was urgently requested to take command of the situation; it meant we had to leave immediately, not a minute could be spared. On the paper I had explained my plan for the Colonel's benefit. We got away with no further trouble, but neither Colonel Charles nor the soldiers were particularly pleased at having to pack up the vehicles and drive some 40 miles in the dark. I have never had the courage or the opportunity to visit Qara oasis again!

Notes

1.   Ernest Renan had remarked in 1884, when the builder of the Suez Canal, Ferdinand de Lesseps, had been elected to the French Academy: 'Hitherto the Bosphorous has provided the world with embarrassment enough, now you have created a second, more serious source of anxiety. For this defile not only connects two inland seas, but it acts as a channel of communication to the oceans of the world. So great is its importance that in a maritime war everyone will strive to occupy it. You have thus marked the site of a future great battle.' (As quoted in *The Mediterranean and Middle East*, vol 1, Maj Gen Playfair).

2.   Quoted in *Mussolini*, Denis Mack Smith, (Weidenfeld & Nicolson, 1981).

3.   See Appendix at the end of this book for details on this and the other tanks in which Rea Leakey served or has mentioned.

4.   The Royal Armoured Corps came into existence on 4 April 1939, when the Secretary of State for War (Leslie Hore-Belisha) announced in Parliament that the newly mechanized cavalry regiments would combine with the battalions of the RTC to form the RAC.

5.   Maj Gen Sir Percy Hobart would go on to form and train two more remarkable armoured Divisions – the 11th which he did not command in battle (they said he was too old!), then the 79th – 'Hobo's Funnies' as they were called – whose strange AFVs had such a tremendous impact on the success of D-Day.

CHAPTER FOUR

Operation Compass

Editor The total Axis forces now manning the line of fortified positions 60 miles inside Egypt comprised some 60,000 Italian and Libyan troops, but despite much huffing and puffing, they made no move to advance any further. The commander of the Italian forces in North Africa, Marshal Rodolfo Graziani, the cowardly and inept 'Butcher of the Desert', had much to say about his future intended advances but actually had no real intention of making any further forward moves. Wavell's reply to this inaction was to plan Operation Compass, initially proposed as just a 'five-day raid' to deal with the Italian incursion into Egypt, timed to start on 9 December 1940. It was to be undertaken by the Western Desert Force, under the leadership of the charismatic Lt Gen Sir Richard O'Connor. His force basically comprised just two divisions – the 7th Armoured and the 4th (Indian) Infantry, which together with Corps troops amounted to some 32,000 men, so they were outnumbered two to one by the defenders in their well-protected and well-prepared positions. However, the British did possess a 'secret weapon' in the shape of 7 RTR, which was equipped with the Matilda Mk II heavy infantry tank, soon to earn the nickname: 'Queen of the Desert'. At 26.5 tons, with armour 13-78 mm thick, it was impervious to practically every weapon the Italians possessed (one Matilda tank commander told me that during the battle for Bardia in January 1941, he had been hit forty-six times without a single penetration!).

Because of the complexity and strength of the Italian fortified positions, O'Connor decided to hold a full-scale dress rehearsal which Rea Leakey attended, not knowing what it was all in aid of because of tight security – Cairo was as always full of spies. Known as Training Exercise No. 1, it took place on 26 November and was to be followed by Training Exercise No. 2 scheduled for the second week in December. This would be the real attack, but nobody guessed. The rehearsal took place using an extremely accurate model of the Italian forts which had been built by the Sappers.

O'Connor's plan was to send 4th Indian Division, plus 7 RTR through the gap between the forts at Sofafi and Nibeiwa, then to assault Nibeiwa and Tummar camps from the rear. Meanwhile, 7th Armoured Division and the Matruh garrison would screen this movement and prevent the Italians at Sofafi and Buq Buq from interfering, while the Navy bombarded Sidi Barrani and the RAF attacked Italian airfields to keep their planes grounded (this sea and air bombardment began on the night 8/9 December and was highly effective). The ground attack began at 0715 hours and three and a half hours later the Matildas had broken through the rear of the Nibeiwa camp, knocking out a number of enemy tanks, while the infantry assaulted with fixed bayonets. The Italian garrison fought bravely, the commander, Gen Pietro Maletti, being shot dead while firing a machine-gun at the attackers. That afternoon, Tummar West and East were attacked and by the evening, both had been captured, while 7th Armoured had captured Azzaziya and cut the Sidi Barrani to Buq Buq road. The next phase of O'Connor's plan came into operation on the following day, namely the capture of Sidi Barrani by 16th Indian Infantry Brigade. It began with a fierce artillery duel which lasted all day, but by evening it was all over and large numbers of prisoners and booty had been taken.

O'Connor now decided to pursue the retreating Italians with the faster tanks of 7th Armoured Division, sending 4th Armoured Brigade due westwards above the escarpment, whilst 7th Armoured Brigade harried them along the coast road. Despite bad weather and supply difficulties, they pushed the Italians back steadily, capturing Sollum on 16 December and at almost the same time taking Fort Capuzzo. The 'five-day raid' had fulfilled all its expectations and the invading army had been comprehensively destroyed in a brilliant operation which had gone almost like clockwork. It would have been easy, therefore, for the Western Desert Force to have 'rested on its laurels' having achieved its aim so quickly and so painlessly – but this would not be allowed to happen! There were still even greater prizes to be won and the Aussies of 6th Australian Infantry Division, who had, somewhat unexpectedly[1], just replaced 4th Indian Division, were desperately anxious to have a go, so there would be no respite for the already demoralized Italians.

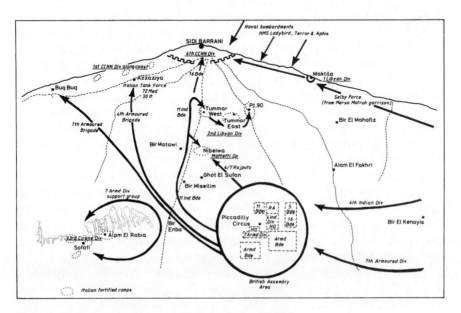

Operation Compass: opening moves, 7–11 December 1940.

Rea Leakey It was surprising how little the Regimental Officer was told about future plans, and perhaps just as well, because Cairo was full of enemy agents. About the middle of November I was detailed as an umpire in an exercise which was to be held some 20 miles south of Mersa Matruh. An exact replica of one of the Italian fortified camps had been built and it included dummy anti-tank minefields. A brigade of 4th Indian Division was given the task of attacking this camp supported by artillery and tanks. The plan was to carry out a frontal attack with the infantry and tanks advancing behind an artillery barrage, the task being to break through the frontal defences on a narrow front. The exercise took place. No live rounds were fired and the tanks were represented by trucks flying red and yellow flags.

To me it was all rather boring and typical of any prewar exercise, but the conference which was held afterwards did interest me. The Chief Umpire made his comments and recommendations, and these and the plan were accepted by the Commander of 4th Indian Division and the Commander of the Western Desert Force, Lt Gen O'Connor. The C in C, Gen Wavell, then gave his blessing, and said, 'Before I return to Cairo, has any Officer any comments?' To his astonishment, an RTR lieutenant colonel stood up and stated that the task of clearing the anti-tank mines which surrounded the camp would be difficult and delay the advance. Wavell told him to 'shut up' and do what he was told by his superior commander, and then he departed. General O'Connor recalled the dispersing officers and asked Lt Col Roy Jerram (CO of 7 RTR) to explain his alternative plan. He suggested that, instead of his tanks accompanying the infantry, they should drive round to the rear of the camp and come in by the back door, which, if surprise were achieved, would not be mined. This was accepted.

FM Wavell (as he became) had, like all of us, his weaknesses. In 1947 I was commanding a company at the RMA Sandhurst, and at a dinner I found myself sitting next to this 'silent man'. I had met him on several occasions, and I am sure he knew me, but he said not a word to me. Towards the end of the meal I confronted him and asked why he disliked the RTR He turned his back on me. Maybe it was because our Officers are alleged to have dirty fingernails, but I suspect it was because, like a number of our senior officers in the Second World War, he had little knowledge of tanks and preferred horses.

Towards the end of November the Regiment moved west and took over the task of patrolling the desert south of Sidi Barrani. Each of the squadrons was detailed to watch one or more of the fortified camps. It was an interesting role, but never did the Italians venture out of their camps in our direction, and if we came too close to them we were heavily shelled. On the morning of 8 December 1940 we were ordered to move east and concentrate 10 miles from Nibeiwa camp, which lay 20 miles south of Sidi Barrani. We arrived in this area in the late evening and found ourselves close to the camouflaged tanks of 7 RTR. These were the famous Matilda tanks, and this was their first appearance in the Western Desert.

Gen Wavell realized that before long the Italians would have built up sufficient supplies in the Sidi Barrani area to enable them to continue their advance into Egypt. It was also obvious that very soon he would have to send troops to both Greece and the Sudan, and the forces at his disposal were not even of sufficient strength to guarantee the safety of Cairo. He therefore decided to retard the Italians' preparations by attacking the fortified camps and destroying the supplies which they had already dumped in this area.

Later that evening we were put in the picture. It was estimated that the Italians had some six divisions disposed along the line of camps which stretched from Sidi Barrani on the coast, to Sofafi, which lay some 35 miles to the south. Our patrols had discovered a gap 10 miles wide between the camps of Nibeiwa and Sofafi, and at night there appeared to be no difficulty in getting through this gap. Wavell's plan was to put in a major raid against those camps with two divisions, 7th Armoured Division and 4th Indian Division. Apart from elements of 7th Armoured Division who were already in the forward area, these two Divisions moved forward some 70 miles on the night of 7 December and lay up the next day carefully camouflaged. The Italian Air Force failed to spot them.

Before first light on 9 December, 7 RTR was to move through the gap and enter Nibeiwa Camp from the rear. Meanwhile, an Indian Brigade was to launch an attack against the front of the camp. 7 RTR was then to move north, and the next camp was to be dealt with in a similar manner, and so on up the line of camps. Meanwhile, the Sidi Barrani camp was to be bombarded by the Navy, bombed by the RAF and invested by a force who normally manned the Matruh defences.

As soon as 7 RTR was through the gap they were to be followed by 7th Armoured Division. Their task was to advance well inside the line of camps and prevent the Italian reserve formations, including their tanks, from interfering with attacks on the camps. They were also to try and get through to the coast road to the rear of Sidi Barrani. It was an ambitious plan and if things did not go well 7th Armoured Division might have difficulty in getting back through the gap. That night I asked the Padre to come up and hold a short service for my squadron; soon after the sun had set we collected round his truck, and dressed in all his robes he conducted one of the most moving services I have ever attended.

We were awakened before dawn by the clatter of the Matilda tanks as they moved forward to the gap. Far to the north we could hear the rumble of large guns. The Navy had started the bombardment of Sidi Barrani. Then it was our turn to go through the gap, and beyond into the heart of the enemy territory. As we passed through, the battle for Nibeiwa Camp was as its height. We could clearly see the Indian soldiers in extended order moving across the desert towards the low stone walls of the camp. A few shells burst among them, but not many. There was no sign of the Matilda tanks, so we concluded they must already be inside the camp, which by this time was shrouded in a pall of smoke and dust.

Cpl Adams had got hold of the wireless frequency being used by 7 RTR and had netted in one of our tanks on this frequency. I signalled this tank to come up close to mine, and I jumped on to it and put on the headphones. I could not have timed it better. Over the air came the voice of Maj Henry Rew, who was in command of their leading squadron, and this is what he said, 'I am surrounded by at least five hundred Italians all with their heads in the air. Can you send somebody to collect them, because they are hindering my progress and are of considerable embarrassment to me.' And shortly afterwards he came on the air with the announcement that in his opinion the battle was over, and asking permission to replenish with ammunition in readiness for the next battle.

Later we heard that the Italians had been taken completely by surprise, and received their first shock at being woken up by tanks shooting at them from the middle of their heavily fortified camp. Their second shock was when their gunners saw their shells bouncing off the thick armour of the Matildas. But to many of us the news of Henry Rew's death was a sad blow. At the conclusion of the attack on the second camp, he was again surrounded by prisoners; he opened his turret and put his head and shoulders out, and an Italian shot him in the back. Henry had played rugger for England, and his massive figure was well known to many officers and men in the Royal Tank Regiment, and that day they lost a great friend.

Our passage through the gap was uneventful and we advanced some 12 miles before making contact with the enemy. As we came over a small ridge we saw about twenty Italian tanks cutting across our front to the north. They were M13 tanks, which were about the same size as our cruisers and mounted a similar gun. Over the air I gave out orders to my squadron: 'Enemy tanks ahead, form battle line on me and stand by to engage.' My eight cruiser tanks raced forward to their battle positions, while the light tanks, who were in the lead, moved across to either flank of the cruisers. They could do no good in this battle. The squadron on my right performed a similar manoeuvre, and the stage was set for a battle which must have borne a marked resemblance to a battle at sea. The Italians spotted us and turned to engage us, and in no time the air was alive with the scream of high velocity shells.

Milligan was a good shot, but only if he had a cigarette dangling from the corner of his mouth. Before the war it was a court-martial offence for a man to smoke inside a tank, but in war many of us found that smoking helped to stave off sleep; even in a moving tank I have known tank commanders to sleep heavily after several days and nights of action. My orders to Milligan were not quite according to the book. 'Gunner, AP action, traverse right, traverse right, steady, on. Enemy tanks, eight hundred, and here's your cigarette. Now, for goodness sake, shoot straight.' Milligan's first shot was over the top of the Italian tank. I had over-estimated the range. 'Drop half a target,' I shouted to Milligan, but as I did so, the next shot sped on its way, and this time it was a hit.

'Loaded,' yelled Adams, and Milligan fired again. On target again, and this time a telling hit, because the enemy crew were baling out, and their tank was on fire. Soon the next tank was in flames, and then the action was over. The Italians had had enough, and were fast disappearing over the horizon, leaving behind them eight of their number. We followed after them and bagged one more, but they were moving fast, and we had not the speed to catch them.

Their gunnery had not been good; two of our tanks were hit, but neither suffered serious damage. By midday we had penetrated some 20 miles behind the Italian camps and we were now ordered to halt and take up hull-down positions if we could find them. Our task was to counter any enemy attempt to send forces to the relief of the camps. Meanwhile, other units of 7th Armoured Division were heading north to cut off Sidi Barrani. The third Italian camp was about to capitulate. So far the raid could not have gone better.

Late in the afternoon we received orders to continue the advance, and we started to edge towards the north. As we moved forward, we came upon more and more Italian lorries moving slowly across the desert; there was no need to waste ammunition on them, we merely rounded them up and told the startled occupants to throw away their weapons. At dusk we had a sharp engagement with some Italian gunners, but when they found our light tanks were working round behind their position they threw in the sponge. We had now collected at least 400 prisoners, and it was a problem to know what to do with them. In the end we packed them into their own lorries and sent them back the way we had come, escorted by two light tanks. We were now running short of petrol and ammunition, and orders were given to halt for the night.

It was bitterly cold that night and we were very glad of a rum issue. In one of the Italian lorries we had found a supply of tinned fruit and spaghetti, so we were able to have a really good meal for once in a while. All night long aircraft droned over our heads, and in the distance we could hear the dull thuds of their bombs. The RAF was giving the Italians no respite.

Early next morning we were on the move, and this time heading north towards a place called Buq Buq, which was nothing more than a salt marsh a mile from the coast. Reports had been received that there was an Italian division in this area, and one brigade of 7th Armoured Division was to go and deal with it.

I was a little relieved that we were going north and not west, because not even the CO had a map which went further west than Buq Buq. We had come on a raid, and even Divisional Headquarters had not bothered to bring up maps of the country further to the west.

As we approached the coast we saw before us a mass of men, lorries, guns, and a few tanks, and we were on them before they knew what had hit them. There were so many targets I hardly knew which to engage first. Milligan was having the time of his life, and even the young sub-turret gunners with their machine-guns were getting rid of belts of ammunition at an alarming rate. For a while the Italians fought back, but then white handkerchiefs and scarves began to appear in all directions. We stopped firing and closed in on them.

The regiment on our left was not so fortunate. They ran into a battery of guns and the Italian gunners were their best soldiers, they did fight. The tanks tried to charge them, but ran into the salt marsh and stuck. At point-blank range the gunners soon had a number of these tanks in flames. This seemed to give heart to the Italians in this area, and they started to fight back hard. Leaving a few tanks to round up prisoners, we moved across to join in the battle. It was difficult broken ground beyond the salt marsh, and the Italians were holding firm. For several hours we manoeuvred round, gradually closing in on them and knocking out each gun in turn. It was late evening when finally the last Italian was 'in the bag', and we must have collected over 6,000 of them. Until well into the night we were busy sorting them out and making sure that there was no chance of their grabbing weapons to resume the fight in the dark. Our supply lorries did not reach us until dawn; they had many miles of bad-going to cover, and we knew they were bound to be late.

This was the third day of Wavell's raid, and I doubt if even he had expected it to go so well. While we were busy getting rid of our prisoners and waiting for further orders, the news came through that Sidi Barrani and the camps around it were being attacked by 4th Indian Division, while to the south the only remaining Italian camp, Sofafi, was being evacuated. We now got orders to move south and try and cut off these Italians. This involved a move of 30 miles across very rough going, and we would then come up against a steep escarpment that ran from Sofafi to Sollum, the little Egyptian frontier town. Apart from the road which ran up from Sollum and over the escarpment to Capuzzo, there was only one other way up, Halfaya Pass. It was obvious that the Italians would destroy the Sollum Pass, so we made for Halfaya, and this was no easy task when we had no maps of this area.

But we still had to fight our way forward, not that the opposition was strong, but it all took time, and at dusk we estimated we were at least 6 miles from the pass. As we were running very short of petrol, we were forced to stop for the night. Sidi Barrani had fallen and some 20,000 Italians were captured. That night we got no petrol, and at dawn we got orders to push on until we ran dry. Some of us reached the top of the escarpment before exhausting the last drop of petrol, but there was nothing more we could do until our lorries caught up with us. It was an anxious day, and we were bombed several times, suffering a few casualties.

It was late evening before the lorries came up, and as soon as we could, we moved forward. Our orders were to make for the frontier wire and go through, several miles to the south of Capuzzo. Still we had no maps, but most of us knew this area only too well, and orders would come over the wireless in this manner:

'Do you remember where Sgt Brown was "Brewed up"? Over.'

'Yes, isn't it near that "bir" where we always found scorpions? Over.'

'That is correct. Well, I want you to move on a course of 280 degrees from there for 5 miles, Over.'

'OK. Moving now. Out.'

We tried going on at night, but being unable to see the few landmarks there was a danger of getting hopelessly lost, and so we gave it up and waited for the dawn. We also needed time to carry out maintenance on the tanks and guns, and we got no sleep that night. Few people realize how much work has to be done on a tank at the conclusion of a day's fighting.

An hour after dawn on the fourth day of this great raid, we were through Mussolini's wire fence, and once again in Libya, and still we had no maps. The Italians were holding Fort Capuzzo in strength, and another defended position at Sidi Omar, 10 miles to the south. We passed through the gaps between these two positions, and received orders to deploy and prevent any enemy force from reaching Sidi Omar, which was about to be attacked. It was a bitterly cold day, and we were still clothed in nothing more than khaki shirts and shorts. Battle-dress had not yet reached the Middle East. By midday we still had not been able to pause for a hot meal, which made us feel all the more cold. All that day we were on the move rounding up prisoners and fighting a few minor battles. The one important event was the receipt of the long-awaited maps of Libya.

As dusk was falling, I was ordered to move north and cut the roads which connected Fort Capuzzo with Sidi Azeiz and Bardia. Capuzzo was still in enemy hands, and both roads were being used to capacity by the fleeing Italians. I knew we were in for an interesting night. In pitch darkness we nosed our tank forward towards the first of these roads, moving in line ahead. Every few minutes I would ask Doyle, the driver, how many miles we had covered, and slowly we crept up to the distance I had made it on the map. 'Speedo reading 7½ miles, sir.' That was it, yet there was no sign of the road. I jumped out, ran forward of the tank, and listened. Vehicles seemed to be moving all round me, and it was hopeless to try and guess how far off they were. After checking on the general direction of advance with my compass, I got back into the tank, and on we moved. I could not have been more than 30 yards away, when suddenly I saw the outline of the road and the vehicles moving up it.

I ordered the tanks to form line on either side of my tank, and warned them about the closeness of the enemy. When all reported that they were in position and had identified their targets, I gave the order to open fire. In a second the darkness was cut by line after line of tracer bullets, and each line found its mark in an Italian lorry. The poor devils never stood a chance; as each lorry burst into flames the survivors could be seen clambering over the back and disappearing into the darkness. Not a shot came back at us, and within a minute all guns were silent. Only the groans of wounded Italians and the crackle of the fires disturbed the stillness of the night. We had certainly closed that road, but for many months afterwards I used to dream of that terrible scene, and I felt ashamed of myself. At the time we were too busy and too tired to think about this; we did what we could for the wounded, gave them some of our precious water, and asked for ambulances to be sent, but we knew only too well that they would have to wait until dawn before help could reach them.

We then moved on towards the Bardia–Capuzzo road. But this time the Italians had been warned of what to expect. When we were still a mile short of the road, two searchlights shone out and picked us up. We tried to extinguish them with our guns, but they were well off to the flanks, and soon we were being heavily shelled. I gave the order to close range towards the road, and as we moved forward the shelling increased. Now anti-tank shells started screaming over, and then one of the flank tanks reported enemy tanks coming in against us. This tank commander said he thought there were at least thirty, and I remember telling him that he was seeing double. Nobody had ever heard of Italian tanks moving around at night. But I got no reply from him, and looking across I saw what must have been his tank in flames. Then another of the light tanks was hit, and the gunner killed. All this happened in the space of a few seconds, and it is at times like this that a tank officer has got to think and act very quickly. If only I had not been so desperately tired; I gave the order to the remaining light tanks to withdraw while the cruisers were to engage the enemy tanks, and, sure enough, there were at least thirty of them bearing down on us. I had six cruisers, and as it would have been madness to try and fight it out we, too, pulled back, and we were lucky not to lose any more tanks. The Italians followed us for about half a mile and then halted, or, at least, we saw them no more.

During this withdrawal, carried out in the black of night, it was only to be expected that tanks got separated, and although I had given a bearing on which to move back, navigation under shellfire is not easy. Over an hour went by before I had gathered my flock together. As we were getting very short of both ammunition and petrol, I decided to pull back to where our supply lorries were waiting. I was out of touch with Regimental Headquarters, who were some 15 miles away. In the desert at night the wireless was very poor. It was already beginning to get light when we had finished our replenishment, and I decided to allow the crews to light fires and at least 'brew up'. The CO had by this time got through to me and told me that a squadron from another regiment had moved out towards the area where we had last seen the enemy tanks, and that we were to go to their assistance if they required it. We sincerely hoped we should be left in peace.

Trooper Doyle was preparing one of his famous 'burgee' porridges[2] and had just brought it to the boil, when Adams called to me and told me I was wanted on 'the set'. Over the air came the CO's voice: 'Move at once. Our friends have met the enemy tanks and are having to withdraw due to lack of ammunition.' The rest of the Regiment was coming up fast, but had 15 miles to go, and my squadron was only about 3 miles away. I thought Doyle was going to burst into tears when I told him to throw his porridge away and start up his tank. But at least we had managed to get a cup of tea laced with rum, and I felt fully revived, anyway for the moment. We were on the move within two minutes.

When we came up to this squadron we found that the Italian tanks had halted, and were showing little fight. With our arrival they started to withdraw towards the scene of our night battle. We followed them, but with caution, as we were outnumbered by at least three to one. Soon we reached our burnt-out tank, and then we were on to the Bardia–Capuzzo road. This was my third attempt to reach it, and it was a great moment for me. The Italian tanks were pulling back fast towards Bardia, but we now found we were running into pockets of enemy infantry, and these had to be dealt with. They showed little fight, and soon each tank was surrounded by a group of prisoners clamouring to be sent back to Egypt.

At about this time I noticed an extraordinary performance taking place in front of one of my light tanks, and I drove across to see what was wrong. The scene that I witnessed as I reached this tank was a little unusual, to say the least of it. The tank commander and the operator, armed only with revolvers, were some 200 yards away jumping in and out of a series of trenches and collecting more and more prisoners. The driver was my old friend, Maconachie; he was sitting back in his driving seat with his legs dangling out of the front of the tank. He had removed one of his boots and exposed a very dirty sock, which exuded a none too pleasant aroma. A line of Italian prisoners filed past the tank, and each in turn would kneel down and kiss Maconachie's foot. Needless to say, my crew were crying with laughter, and I am afraid my face was not altogether devoid of mirth when I demanded an explanation.

'Sir,' said Maconachie in his broad Scots accent, 'before the war I received twenty-eight days punishment in the Glasshouse and lost my pay merely for hitting an Italian. Now I am being paid to kill the b——ds. I am demanding recompense from those that are not dead.' I well remembered him being punished for hitting the Italian; this man was a photographer and used to charge exorbitant prices for his prints. One night in a Cairo dance hall, he made the mistake of taking a picture of Maconachie when the latter was none too sober, and then demanded a high fee for the compromising photograph. His large box camera mounted on a tripod was handy, and Maconachie hit him with it.

Leaving the prisoners to find their own way to captivity, we pushed on in pursuit of the tanks, and we now found ourselves deployed either side of the road leading to Bardia. As we came over a rise I could see the Italian tanks moving on to the road and in turn passing through the heavily fortified defences that surrounded Bardia. These stretched from shore to shore round the town and harbour. The barbed wire, concrete pill-boxes and anti-tank ditch remain to this day.

With each passing second we drew closer to the defences, and what an opportunity this was to penetrate them before the 'gate' was closed. I gave the order to advance with all speed and as my tank was on the road, I was soon well in the lead. We could not have been more than half a mile from the barrier when the whole desert seemed to erupt about me. Every gun in Bardia fortress which could bring fire to bear on this area was now in action, and it was quite clear to me that we were not going to win this battle. I gave the order to 'about turn' and get to hell out of the area as fast as possible.

As my tank turned off the road, a shell exploded beneath one of the tracks and we were immobilized. As Doyle and the two sub-turret gunners were now serving no useful purpose by staying in the tank, I told them to 'bale out'. Through the dust and smoke I could see two tanks inside the barrier shooting at us. I got Milligan on to them, and he fired one shell, and that was all. At that moment Adams shouted 'She's on fire', and I saw the flames spreading across the bottom of the turret. We were out before the ammunition exploded and I dashed round to the front of the tank to check that the other three had got away. One sub-turret hatch was half-open, and a glance was enough to convince me that this young soldier was dead. An anti-tank shell had pierced the armour and hit him square in the face. He was not a pretty sight.

A ditch along the side of the road saved our lives, and 15 minutes later we were back with the rest of the squadron. We had lost most of our belongings, but not our most treasured possession – no, not a bottle of rum; several months previously Doyle had found a half-starved kitten and it lived in the driving compartment amongst the various tools or on his lap. That afternoon we moved south of the Bardia defences and stopped for the night 10 miles west of the defences and 7 miles south of the Bardia–Tobruk road. It had been a long, hard day, and I was not best pleased at being woken up at 10 p.m., 5 minutes after I had fallen asleep. 'Move at once north and cut the Bardia–Tobruk road.' There was no moon but the sky was clear, as was the North Star. A steep escarpment cut across our route, but we found a track down and moved on towards the road. As we got near it, we could see several large black objects, but there was no movement – they were burnt-out lorries.

It was a bitterly cold night and time passed so very slowly; there was not a sound to be heard, and how I longed to close my eyes. At about 4 a.m. one of the tank commanders reported that he could hear vehicles moving towards us from the Bardia direction. Then I, too, heard them, and there could be no mistake – they were tanks. We waited for them in silence. When they were about 300 yards from us, they halted; we could not see them, and now the only noise was the low hum of their engines. I saw two soldiers coming towards us. They spotted my tank at the same moment, and they took to their heels. We opened fire and the enemy retreated at speed.

As dawn broke, I asked for orders, and the reply was what I expected: 'Stay where you are.' The first wave of bombers came over just as we finished breakfast. They were flying in perfect formation and released their bombs at the same instant. Then out of the sun came the fighters.

I had just got out of the tank, armed with a shovel to answer nature's call, when Adams pointed to the next lot of bombers and fighters, and I was back inside just in time. This was to be the pattern throughout the day. Their aim was to make life for us so unpleasant that we would move away and give their ground forces a chance to see this vital road. It was a terrible day, yet not one tank received a direct hit from a bomb, and fortunately the fighter aircraft's guns did not penetrate our armour. As darkness fell and we knew that we had won the day, a cheer echoed across the silent desert when orders came through that we were to be relieved that night.

Bardia was isolated. Before the advance could be continued, this fortress would have to be taken, and we knew it would take time to build up the necessary forces. Once again Wavell was going to use only two divisions. The 7th Armoured Division was to contain the garrison while the untried 6th Australian Division moved forward from Cairo and prepared itself for the assault. Bardia contained a garrison of 30,000 soldiers.

There was less than a week to go before Christmas, not that many of us realized this, because in the desert it is only too easy to lose track of time. The tempo of the battle had now died down. Even Italian bombers were scarce, since the RAF had received its first consignment of Hurricane fighters. Almost daily we would watch these new fighters tearing into a formation of bombers, and they had not got the speed to get away. Soon it was not uncommon to see the bomber baling out merely at the sight of a Hurricane. No enemy tanks came out of either Bardia or Tobruk, so for a while we saw no fighting. We had time to write letters, and when enough water had been saved, we washed ourselves and our clothes. Except for desert sores we were very fit.

Christmas Day 1940, was the same as any other day, except that each man received a tin of bully-beef to himself, and there was a double rum ration that night. Wavell sent us his greetings, but there was insufficient transport to send us turkeys and Christmas puddings. It would be wrong to say that we did not miss the usual luxuries and celebrations, yet nobody complained or grumbled. It would have taken much more than a few trifles like these to shake the high morale of this small desert force.

Notes

1. The change of divisions also came as a complete surprise to O'Connor, as Wavell had told no one, not even Churchill, of his intention to move the Indians, the reason being that he wanted them to fight in the Sudan. The most important factor was the availability of shipping and this entirely influenced the date they had to leave. Wavell did not tell O'Connor until after the war when he concluded his explanation with the words: '. . . with my limited

resources I had to decide either to remain entirely on the defensive in the Sudan for some time to come, or to accept the delay in the pursuit in the Western Desert while the Australian Division relieved the Indian. My decision was a difficult one, but I am sure it was right.' (Quoted in John Baynes, *The Forgotten Victor*)

2. 'Burgee porridge', also known as 'Biscoo', was a biscuit porridge made out of the large, otherwise inedible Army biscuits, which were first put into a sandbag and then pounded to powder against a stone. The powder was then mixed with a small quantity of boiling water to make a quite satisfying porridge. However, if you were lucky enough to have some Red Carnation tinned milk and some sugar, then nothing could have tasted more delicious than this mixture on a cold morning in the desert!

CHAPTER FIVE

'Fox Killed in the Open'

Editor After such a swift and easy victory, Wavell and O'Connor were determined
to keep up the pressure and to push the Italians back into Cyrenaica. As Rea Leakey
explains, this was achieved most successfully: the coastal strongholds of Bardia and
Tobruk were captured on 5 and 22 January respectively, by the newly arrived
Australians, supported by the heavy Matilda tanks of 7 RTR, so that by 23 January,
the Western Desert Force (now known as XIII Corps) was within 20 miles of the
coastal town of Derna. In Tobruk alone, some 25,000 prisoners had been taken, plus
208 guns and 87 tanks.

It was by now clear to O'Connor that the Italians intended to pull back right out
of Cyrenaica, so he decided upon a daring plan, which entailed establishing an
armoured roadblock behind the retreating enemy, well southwest of Benghazi in the
Beda Fomm-Sidi Saleh area. To achieve this block, 7th Armoured Division was
ordered to send a flying column through the virtually unmapped desert, while the
rest of XIII Corps kept up pressure along the coastal route. This force, known as
Combe Force after the CO of 11th Hussars who commanded it, was despatched
and, despite the terrible going and several enemy air attacks en route, they managed
to reach the coast at Sidi Saleh and to cut off the Italian retreat on the morning of
5 February. Combe Force contained just one squadron of the 11th Hussars and one
of the King's Dragoon Guards, together with the 2nd Battalion, Rifle Brigade
(motorized infantry), plus nine Bofors guns – less than 2,000 men in total, without
any tanks or artillery. Meanwhile, the 4th Armoured Brigade was following up fast,
the leading elements of 7th Hussars and 2 RTR reaching Beda Fomm that
afternoon. The rough-going had played havoc with the AFVs and they had just
twenty cruisers and thirty-six light tanks still motoring. Both groups established
themselves in commanding positions.

The two blocks had a paralysing effect upon the Italians, who had never expected
to find the enemy so far behind them. Instead of trying to outflank the tiny British
forces, they launched a series of frantic, uncoordinated frontal attacks, all of which
were beaten off with heavy losses.

It was a remarkable battle which lasted until the early hours of 9 February, when
the Italians finally surrendered. The small British force had by then captured 20,000
men, including six Italian generals, 216 guns, 112 tanks, 1,500 lorries and immense
quantities of arms, equipment and stores of all kinds, not to mention all the enemy
they had killed and the vehicles and equipment they had destroyed. All this was
achieved at a cost to 7th Armoured Division of just nine killed and fifteen wounded.
O'Connor, who visited the battlefield immediately after the Italian surrender, sent a

message to Wavell telling him of the success and beginning with the words: 'Fox killed in the open', a hunting phrase which Wavell would have undoubtedly appreciated, but one which was probably completely unintelligible to the 'Fox'!

Operation Compass and the subsequent follow-on advance by O'Connor's small, well-trained and brilliantly led force which ended in the defeat of the entire 10th Italian Army, must rank as one of the greatest feats of arms of the Second World War Thanks to O'Connor's unorthodox but highly effective command, two divisions, one armoured and one infantry, plus a battalion of heavy tanks, had completely destroyed an entire Army of ten Divisions. Total British casualties were under 2,000 while they took over 130,000 prisoners. The well-known British historian and armoured warfare 'guru', Sir Basil Liddell Hart, later described the victory as being: 'one of the most daring ventures and breathless races in the annals of the British Army', while Anthony Eden coined a new version of Winston Churchill's famous Battle of Britain phrase, saying, 'Never has so much been surrendered by so many to so few!'

Undoubtedly O'Connor and his Western Desert Force had left their mark upon the desert war, but soon they would be up against a new and far more dangerous opponent. However, that was still in the future, so let us now look at this action from the eyes of someone who was right up at the 'sharp end'.

Rea Leakey On the evening of 2 January, 1941, my squadron moved back to within a few miles of Bardia Fortress, and we had a grandstand view of the Navy and RAF plastering the defences with high explosives.

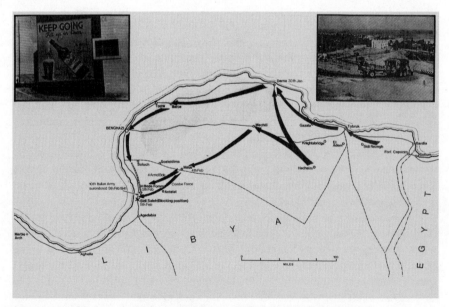

Movement of 7th Armoured Division in Libya up to Beda Fomm, February 1941.

Throughout that night the rumble of bombs and shells hardly ceased, and many areas glowed red. At dawn the next morning the Australians, supported by the Matilda tanks of 7 RTR, moved forward to attack the Fortress. We were some miles to the west of where they were attacking, and we could see little of what was happening.

Our task was to drive our tanks to within a few hundred yards of the perimeter and cause a diversion. It was hoped that we would draw the fire of Italian guns, which would otherwise be free to shell the Australians. We were on the move half an hour before dawn and, while visibility was still more than 200 yards, the tanks formed battle-line, and we closed with the defences. On this first charge we got within a few yards of the anti-tank ditch before turning and going back the way we had come. When the shelling slackened off, I gave the order to about turn, and once again we raced forward with guns blazing. This time we did not get quite so close; I had been told not to lose any tanks. Back and forth we went, like a lot of terriers worrying an animal at bay. As the shelling increased, so each tank jinked and dodged about to give the enemy a difficult target. Every man in the squadron knew that if their tank broke down when close to the defences, their chances of survival were slender. We were told to keep up this diversion game for 2 hours and then to rejoin the rest of the Regiment. They were already moving fast towards Tobruk, which lay some 70 miles to the west.

When tanks are in action and are being shelled, it is usually left to the discretion of the individual tank commander as to whether or not he 'closes down'. This simply means closing the two hatches on the top of the turret. By doing so the crew is safe even from a direct hit there; on the other hand, the commander's visibility is reduced to what he can see through a periscope. In this respect a tank bears a slight similarity to a submarine. In this particular action I noticed that a number of the tank commanders had closed down, and I did not blame them, as we were receiving more than our fair quota of shells.

In the last run that we made, one of the light tanks got a little too close to an anti-tank gun and received several direct hits which penetrated the armour. Of the crew of three the driver was killed by the first shot, and the commander, our newest young officer, had one of his hands shattered. The driver's foot still rested on the accelerator and the tank continued to motor in towards the enemy. All this the young commander told us over the air, and we were powerless to help him.

He was still talking on the wireless when suddenly he yelled, 'the tank's on fire.' He must have then dropped his microphone, but the wireless was switched to 'send', and it broadcast to the rest of the squadron the happenings inside that turret. The tank was closed down, and before the two in the turret could bale out they had to open up the hatches. We heard the gunner yelling to his officer to help him because by this time he had evidently been wounded, while the commander shouted that both hatches were stuck fast. Then all we heard were the most terrible screams of agony; they were being burnt alive while their tomb of fire still drove on towards the enemy. This was one of the worst experiences I have had, and even after many years I wake up in a cold sweat and realize that I have been haunted by that so vivid scene.

For the rest of that day we drove steadily west. Late in the afternoon we reached the Italian aerodrome of El Adem, which lies 10 miles south of the Tobruk perimeter. The Italians had evacuated the place in a great hurry, and had left most of their belongings. We stopped here for an hour and had time to look round the buildings. I was amazed at the comfort in which these Italians lived, but even more so by the quantity of scent, hair grease and other effeminate toilet articles that were to be found in every man's room; they must have spent much of their day beautifying themselves for the benefit of the ladies of the brothel which occupied the best building in the place. We laughed at all this, and it was good to have something to laugh at that day.

This time we were not given the doubtful honour of cutting the coast road to the west of Tobruk, and we were not sorry. With the rest of the Regiment our task was to patrol the desert to the south-west. After Tobruk, the next Italian line of defence was established southward from the area of Derna to the desert outpost of Mechili. Here the pattern of the country changed, and deep wadis, rocky heights and very bad-going made for easy defence. At Mechili the Italians had a strong garrison including a number of tanks. Once again we had to wait until the Australians and the remaining Matilda tanks moved forward and attacked Tobruk.

By this time 7th Armoured Division had lost almost half its tanks, mainly through breakdowns due to excessive mileage, and two of the armoured units were withdrawn to Cairo. What tanks they had were shared out among those of us who remained with the Division. Within the Regiment we reorganized. I handed over my cruiser tanks to the other two squadrons, and took over ten light tanks from another regiment. My squadron then consisted of light tanks only. Unfortunately, my crew went with their tank, except for Adams, and I was very sorry to see them go. There was only one officer in the squadron besides myself. All this took place late one afternoon some 20 miles west of Tobruk, and that night I was ordered to move north on to the coast road and reconnoitre westwards towards Gazala and Bomba. By dawn we found ourselves driving along the best surfaced road we had seen for years. A mile to the north of us was the sea, and the country on either side was very rough and cut by deep wadis. There was no sign of the enemy; in fact, the whole area was deserted and depressingly silent. The Regiment must have been covering a vast frontage; the nearest squadron to me was 30 miles to the south. Wireless speech with Headquarters was impossible, and for the next week all messages were passed by Morse code. We felt, and we were, very much out in the blue on our own.

That night we halted near Bomba, which had been an important Italian seaplane base, and we leaguered for the night astride the road close by the sea. Far to the east we could see a red glow in the sky, which grew in brightness as the hours passed by. Tobruk was being subjected to harsh punishment at the hands of the Navy and RAF. At dawn we were told the Australians had opened their attack on this fortress. The date was 20 January.

We took no part in this attack, and, in fact, we were some 50 miles to the west. Our orders were to continue going west until we were stopped by the enemy. Because of the nature of the country and in order to make rapid progress, we all moved on the road strung out one behind the other. In an advance of this nature one of the most difficult problems was to decide who was to lead, and in later years I had to face this decision time and time again. The leader's chances of survival were slender, but never once did I have a tank commander complain when ordered to lead. It was, however, never a subject that we discussed.

Our first encounter was with an armoured car, but it disappeared rapidly down the road at the sight of our leading tank. A few miles further on, the leading tank was fired on by a light anti-tank gun. This was a small rearguard party which had been left to delay our advance, but as soon as our tanks deployed off the road and started closing in on them, they slipped away. For the next 5 miles we saw no sign of the enemy, and then, as we rounded a bend in the road, we came upon some half-dozen little, neat, white houses. We could hardly believe our eyes. They were obviously civilian houses and each had a small garden. They were deserted. I had gone ahead of the squadron with two tanks; the rest of the squadron was some miles behind refuelling. I sent one of the tanks a few hundred yards beyond the houses to keep a lookout while we investigated the area.

In one of the gardens I found a bed of spring onions, and my mouth watered; we had not tasted fresh vegetables or fruit for many months, and for all I could care, the war could stop until I had gathered enough to add flavour to a bully-stew. But once again it was Adams who shouted the bad news. The lookout tank reported at least six Italian tanks coming along the road towards us, and they were getting very close. They were M13 tanks, and we were powerless against them. I shouted to Adams to tell the other tanks to withdraw, and I started pulling up onions like a madman. 'Come on, sir, they are nearly up to us,' shouted Adams, and so they were. But I got my onions, and we were away. By this time I knew the Italian tanks never fired when on the move, so we were quite safe, but for once Adam's London wit deserted him; he forgave me when later he tasted the onion stew.

Had these Italian tanks really shown fight there was nothing to stop them driving to Tobruk and joining up with their confederates, who were at that moment being defeated by the Australians; my fifteen light tanks had no gun that could penetrate their armour, and we were entirely on our own. But fortunately for us, these tank men had little fight in them, and the moment they started moving forward our bullets would patter against their armour. When they stopped and swung their guns towards one of our tanks, it would disappear, only to reappear somewhere different. It was a game of hide-and-seek, and we enjoyed it. Then they stopped for good, and took up hull-down positions covering our line of advance. We tried getting round them, but the country was too difficult, and there was considerable danger of being cut off if they advanced. So for the rest of the day we sat and looked at each other, occasionally exchanging shots, but otherwise minding our own business.

At dusk the Italians withdrew to the west, so we settled down to spend a peaceful night, knowing full well that we would be unmolested. We could not maintain touch with the Regiment because atmospherics were very bad, so even the wireless watch was closed down. Before first light we were on the move, and as dawn broke we were once again in the area of the little white houses. There was no sign of the enemy and we continued along the road, getting closer and closer to Derna. But long before we even came in sight of this beautiful little seaside town, we hit the defended position, which the Italians had established, and which ran from the coast to the desert outpost of Mechili. Not only did we now meet the fire from their tanks, but also from heavier guns, and we could make out a line of defence posts that were strongly held. We could go no further on our own, and we asked for assistance, if only to prevent the Italian tanks chasing us back.

Only two events enlivened our day; an Italian bomber flew low over us, and we set it on fire. It crashed close to Derna. Just before dusk a truck from our Headquarters appeared, bringing two young Officer reinforcements, but perhaps even more gratifying, there was a large mail, the first we had received for weeks. When one of these young officers told me his name, I exclaimed in surprise 'But that's my name!' 'I know, sir,' he said, 'I am a cousin of yours.' Adams, who was nearby and had obviously heard this conversation, turned to a neighbour, and thinking I was not listening, said, 'Blimey, another of the same name! He, too, probably values onions more than his life. Gawd 'elp us.' That night we moved back about 4 miles, as we did not want enemy infantry creeping up on us in the dark, and nobody disturbed our sleep.

Next day we received reinforcements. They consisted of three artillerymen, and they owned a small anti-tank gun mounted on the back of a truck. The sergeant, who was as keen as mustard, explained that they had yet to fire their gun in action, and were most anxious to do so. We drove forward to the Italian defended posts, and then started the amusing sport of trying to induce the Italian tanks to advance from behind their defences and follow us down the road. We tried sending only two tanks forward which retired rapidly when shelled; we tried waving coloured flags at them; we even sent several men on foot along the road towards them, but they would not move. The sergeant volunteered to drive his unarmoured truck well forward to where he could get a shot at one of the tanks, but I would not let him as he would have been too easy a target even for the Italians.

Next day Major H.A. Lascelles arrived, and took over command of the squadron. He was several years senior to me, and it was good to see him again – we were, and still are, great friends. That day the Italians did send tanks forward, and our gallant artillerymen went into action. One shot from their gun was enough to induce the enemy to beat a hasty retreat, and that was the last we saw of them. In the meantime, Tobruk had fallen and the Australians were ordered to capture Derna. The 7th Armoured Division's task was to operate in the desert to the South and capture Mechili.

We were ordered to rejoin the Regiment, which was already heading for Mechili. This we did late that afternoon, 30 miles east of this place, and our task was to reconnoitre the area to the north. The maps were not good, and I was told to remain with the Regiment until the supply lorries arrived and hopefully lead them to the squadron in the dark. At 9 p.m. I set off on a 25-mile journey across unknown country, and it started to rain. Navigation became a nightmare; every half mile or so the column would halt, and I would run forward to take a bearing – not that there was anything on which to take a bearing, but at least I made sure that we were travelling more or less in the correct direction. The going got worse and worse, and we found ourselves crossing deep wadis.

At about 2 a.m. we had covered the distance, and I was not surprised at not meeting up with the squadron. Tony Lascelles suggested I continue on the same bearing for 3 more miles, so on we went. Still no sign of them, and they dare not show a light as there was an enemy camp in this area. 'Go North,' he suggested over the air. The going got worse, it was still raining and we had been on the move for over 12 hours, with only one short stop. Each time I got back into the tank after taking a bearing, I had to wake up the driver. Then we found ourselves in a deep wadi, and I gave up. Tony agreed we should wait for dawn. We were too tired to unroll the tarpaulin – I fell asleep under the tank soaked to the skin.

At dawn I set off on foot to find a viewpoint. Less than a mile away was a large Italian camp, and I could see several tanks. This was another occasion when I missed my breakfast. We had no trouble in finding the squadron, which was just as well, as they had stopped because some of the tanks were almost out of fuel. For the next two days we patrolled north of Mechili and then rejoined the Regiment. The Division was meanwhile preparing for an attack on this position, and our task was to move south and then west so as to cut off escapers. This entailed a 70-mile march across unmapped country. It was the first time for many weeks that the Regiment moved together. Hoisting my black navigator's flag, I led the way.

The sun was shining, so I could use the sun compass, but the going was very rough and the light tanks did not give us a comfortable ride. At about 3 p.m. I reported that we had reached our destination. Nobody argued with me – one bit of desert looks much the same as any other. An hour later the news came through that the Italians had started evacuating Mechili, and we were ordered to close in on them. We headed north-east as fast as we could, but we were too late, they had fled. What now? we wondered.

The Australians had made good progress along the coast road. They had a tough fight to overcome the positions which had held us up, but they had little difficulty in capturing Derna and then Barce. This town lies in the heart of the Gebel country, and was the centre of the prosperous Italian farming community.

This beautiful green country was not for the 'Desert Rats': our route was to take us many miles to the south. On 3 February we got our orders. The 7th Armoured Division was to move with all speed across the unmapped desert from Mechili to cut the coast road at Beda Fomm, some 70 miles west of Benghazi.

This march of 150 miles was a complete nightmare, and I remember little about it because most of the time I was too tired and bruised by my bucking tank. It was bitterly cold and for much of the way it was either raining or blowing a sandstorm. We were leading the most southerly column, and by day the squadron was deployed on a very wide front with the task of finding the easiest passage through the rough and rocky countryside. If a tank broke down, and many did, the crew reported its position, and they stayed with it until the Divisional recovery teams towed it back to Tobruk. One of these was my cousin's tank, and his was the most southerly vehicle in the Division. He was working under my direction, and I duly reported the map reference of his position, then forgot about him and his crew.

It took us just over 36 hours to reach the coast road, and by this time the Australians were already entering Benghazi. Not more than forty-five British tanks survived this terrible journey, and together with the divisional artillery and infantry we found ourselves up against over 20,000 Italian soldiers who were well equipped and determined to fight their way through to Tripoli. When we came up to this enormous column of guns and lorries, we were not a little disturbed to find that it included 120 new M13 tanks, which we later discovered had only arrived in Benghazi by sea a few weeks before. There were endless targets, and on the first day of this battle my tank ran out of ammunition twice. Our cruiser tanks were in constant battle with the Italian tanks, and on several occasions they were forced to give ground. That night the enemy made a desperate effort to break through to the west, but our infantry held firm and none escaped. Next morning the battle raged again all along the 10-mile column, and now we were beginning to close in on them. Late in the afternoon the first few white flags appeared, and we knew the end was close; by the last light prisoners were coming in by the hundreds, but all that night we were kept busy mopping up the last few pockets of resistance.

Then it was all over, and for the first time in four days I was able to relax – in the back seat of some Italian General's car. The amount of equipment, lorries, guns and even tanks, that were left lying by the roadside had to be seen to be believed. Yet even more remarkable was the amount of paper that was lying about the battlefield. We thought that our Army was sufficiently 'bumf'-minded, but the Italians appeared to carry about a greater weight of paper than ammunition. We also found lorry loads of food and wine, and we certainly made merry, and so ended the great Wavell raid.

The day after the battle ended, the CO ordered me to take leave, and I did not object. With Derek Thom and two others I set off to cover the 500 miles back to Cairo in an Italian car. Passing through Benghazi I saw an RAF pilot whom I knew well, and we stopped to have a word with him. As luck would have it, he was flying back to Cairo in an hour's time, and he said he had room for one passenger in his bomber. None of us relished the thought of a 500-mile journey by road and desert track to Cairo, so we drew lots for the seat, and I won. That evening I was lying in a hot bath in the famous Shepherds Hotel. What bliss it was to feel clean, to wear clean clothes, to have a full stomach, and to kiss a pretty girl.

My four days went all too rapidly, and I dreaded the thought of the journey back to Beda Fomm, possibly travelling most of the way in the back of a lorry loaded with petrol or ammunition. The Italian car had broken down, and, in any case, Derek Thom only started his four days leave the day I was due to return. Jimmy Cruickshank, also of my Regiment, was due back at the same time as myself, and we decided to avoid the desert route by lorry at all costs. The RAF would not help, so we thought of the Navy. We travelled by train to Alexandria and booked in at the Cecil Hotel. We then telephoned Naval Headquarters, and said that two important high-ranking Army Officers wanted to reach Beda Fomm as quickly as possible. Could they help? The Officer at the other end said he would find out, and where could he contact us? We gave him the hotel phone number, and he promised to ring us in an hour or two. We retired to the bar, hoping for the best.

'Report to HMS *Peony* at 1500 hours. You will find her in Dock No. 13.' That was the message we received, and we wondered what kind of ship HMS *Peony* was. An Egyptian taxi dropped us at the dock gate, and with our bedrolls on our backs we set off to find HMS *Peony*. Our morale dropped a little when we found her, and saw that a little guard of honour was waiting to welcome the high-ranking officer passengers. When two young captains, carrying their bedrolls, tried to sneak round the back of the guard and climb aboard, they were not politely received! However, the little matter was explained, and we were glad to find that Naval officers have a good sense of humour. I was soon well established in the Captain's cabin and we were at sea.

Our ship was a small Corvette which was being used to sweep for magnetic mines. When operating, she towed a long rubber-encased cable, which was electrically charged and would set off these mines if the ship survived the first passage over the mine. We could hardly imagine a more unpleasant occupation, and our spirits did not rise when we were told that the ship's destination was Benghazi harbour, and that her task was to sweep the harbour in preparation for the first British cargo ships.

Apart from the fact that for the first 24 hours the sea was so rough that even the Navy were at times a little alarmed, we had a most pleasant and uneventful journey. As the ship entered Benghazi harbour all hands were at action stations. The harbour was deserted and looked very forbidding. As it was getting late, the captain of the ship decided to tie up to the mole at the outer end of the harbour and start sweeping operations next morning.

Hardly had the ship's engines stopped than we received our first shock. In the clear water some 10 yards from the ship a large green parachute was visible. I was informed that beneath that parachute there was certain to be a magnetic mine, and the Captain had already given orders to move. Our bedrolls were thrown on to the mole, and we followed them. As we did, so the first bomb crashed down into the sea not far from the bows of the ship. We had all been so occupied that nobody noticed the dozen dive-bombers coming in at us out of the sinking sun. The attack could not have lasted more than three minutes but it was a vicious affair, and how HMS *Peony* escaped, I do not know. I believe she did suffer slight damage from near misses, but that was the last I saw of her. One bomb hit the mole about five feet from where we were lying, but fortunately a low buttress protected us from certain death. It left us stunned and slightly deaf, and I got a splinter in my bottom which caused a certain amount of merriment amongst my brother officers when I rejoined them later that night. The Medical Officer removed it with a knife and fork in the Officers' Mess.

During my absence 7th Armoured Division had advanced as far as El Agheila, some 50 miles west of Beda Fomm. But only elements of the Division went forward; the main part halted in the area of Beda Fomm, and was engaged in salvaging valuable Italian equipment which was urgently needed in Greece. In fact, Greece had asked for more than arms to help them in their struggle against the Italians in Albania, and troops that were urgently needed in the desert were sent to the assistance of this gallant country.

It was impossible for the British forces to continue their advance against the fleeing Italians. Most of the tanks and other vehicles were worn out and would need workshop overhauling; petrol, food and ammunition still had to come forward from Tobruk by road, and transport was very short. Benghazi harbour could not be used because it was heavily mined and was constantly bombed by the German Air Force. The Italians had been swept from the skies and the Germans had come to their assistance.

A new Armoured Division[1] had recently arrived in Egypt and now started to arrive in the desert, although several of its tank units had been sent to Greece. The bulk of 7th Armoured Division was to be sent back to Cairo to refit. Needless to say, we were delighted with the news and were only too glad to hand over our few remaining serviceable vehicles to the newly arrived units. Some seventy of the Italian M13 tanks were found to be in fair working order, and because the British Army was so short of tanks, these were to be used by our troops. 6 RTR, who had left the battle at Tobruk, were sent forward and ordered to take over these tanks. A few weeks later they were in action against German tanks and they suffered many casualties. Among these was Maj 'Tinny' Dean, another famous rugger international. He lost a leg and was captured.

Tank workshops had been set up in Tobruk, and it was here that we handed in our worn-out vehicles. As I was leaving the workshops, I noticed a familiar light tank being towed in, and I went across to see if I knew any of the crew. 'Well, you are a nice sort of cousin to have around. I break down and you leave me in the desert to starve!' I must admit that, what with leave, the thought of returning to Cairo, and the general rush of the previous fortnight, I had forgotten about the tanks which had broken down during the mad rush from Mechili to Beda Fomm. We had been told that they had all been recovered, and the crews were already back in Cairo; I had not bothered to check up.

Edward Leakey's tank had broken down in the middle of a hard mud-flat which lay well to the south of the route taken by the main Divisional column. I have a suspicion that when the recovery teams plotted the position from the map reference I had sent, they must have thought somebody had made an error, and they were too busy to check on it. But whatever the cause of the error, my cousin and his crew spent three lonely weeks in the desert before being rescued. In order to keep themselves occupied they dug out the word 'HELP' in large letters, and on the day they finished the 'P' an aircraft, which was flying off its course, saw this word and landed. It was fortunate that every vehicle operating in the desert had to carry three days supply of food and water for the crew. I gave my cousin full marks for making his supplies last three weeks.

And so by way of Bardia, Capuzzo, Sollum and Mersa Matruh, we drove to Cairo, and there were not many of us who had any desire to return to that barren battlefield. I heard one soldier make the old comment that if he were to win the Derby Sweep he would buy the desert and put it out of bounds to British troops!

Notes

1.   The 'new Armoured Division' was the British 2nd Armoured Division, commanded by Maj Gen Gambier-Perry. They were having all sorts of problems with their new cruiser tanks, which comprised just one effective armoured brigade and half a support group (in those days the 'Support Group' contained all the division's infantry and artillery), while their reconnaissance regiment had only just converted from horses to armoured cars. To cap it all, none had any desert battle experience. Fresh out of England, unacclimatized and commanded by an officer with virtually no armoured knowledge, they would prove easy meat for the 'Desert Fox'.

CHAPTER SIX

Enter Rommel

Editor With the surrender of the 10th Italian Army complete, the whole of Cyrenaica was now in British hands and the road to Tripoli lay wide open. Yet, just two months later, the enemy were once again back on the Egyptian border and the victor of Operation Compass was a prisoner of war. There have been many explanations given for this sudden reversal of fortunes the most important of which I will explain. However, first and foremost, the main reason for the debacle which followed our stunning victory is made obvious by writing just one name – 'Rommel'. The arrival on the scene of Lt Gen Erwin Johannes Eugen Rommel, whose personal success in the 'France 1940' campaign had catapulted him to stardom, would soon write another chapter in the unfolding saga of the desert war. However, the newly arriving German forces did have some major advantages over the unfortunate Italians whom they had come to assist, as well as a brilliant commander. The principal obstacle to a further British advance was quite simply a lack of troops. Churchill had decided that it was essential to send troops to aid Greece. His senior advisors had endeavoured to get him to change his mind, but he was adamant. The then Chief of the Imperial General Staff (Dill) tried, as he later explained: 'I gave it as my view that all troops in the Middle East were fully employed and that none were available for Greece. The Prime Minister lost his temper with me. I could see the blood coming up in his great neck and his eyes began to flash. He said, "What you need out there is a Court Martial and a firing squad. Wavell has 300,000 men, etc., etc." I should have said: "Whom do you want to shoot exactly?" But I did not think of it till afterwards.' (Quoted in *Against Great Odds* by Brig C.N. Barclay: Sifton Praed & Co Ltd, 1955). Churchill later explained that he did not go to the aid of Greece simply in order to save the Greeks or to avoid loss of face with the Americans: rather, he wanted to form a Balkan front to delay the coming German invasion of Russia. His actions certainly achieved this – Alfred Jodl, Hitler's personal chief of staff, later stated that Germany lost the war because she had been obliged to divert divisions to meet the British landing in Greece. This meant that she had lost six precious weeks: '. . . she lost time – and with time she lost Moscow, Stalingrad and the war'.

The pressure to send German troops to North Africa had begun as early as June 1940, when the then Governor of Libya (Air Marshal Italo Balbo), had asked Marshal Pietro Badoglio, Chief of the Italian Supreme General Staff, to get some German assistance. 'Now that the French campaign is going to end,' he wrote on 20 June, 'could you obtain from the Germans about fifty of their magnificent tanks, plus the same number of their armoured cars for Libya?' He was killed a few days later, so the request was never followed up. Whether Hitler ever heard of Balbo's request is not clear. He and his high command (OKW) were driven to the decision to send armoured forces to help their ally simply because they were worried that the inept Italians were going to lose their hold on North Africa in the same way as they had begun to lose it in East Africa. So Operation Sunflower (Sonnenblume) was put into action and Rommel was soon on his way. His new force, which began to arrive in Tripoli on 14 February 1941, was soon to be known as the Deutsches Afrika Korps (DAK) and, like the British and Commonwealth forces, would quickly prove extremely good at adapting to this new environment.

The DAK was a small force, initially just comprising 5th Light (leichte) Division (later to be reorganized as 21st Panzer Division), together with various Corps troops such as a recconaissance company, an anti-tank battalion, an AA battalion, a signals battalion, etc. Until the arrival of the second panzer division the total tank strength of Panzer Regt 5 of 5 leichte was only some 155 tanks, as thirteen (10 x PzKpfw IIIs and 3 x PzKpfw IVs) had been lost during loading in Naples, when the 'Leverkusen' caught fire. Additionally, many of these (seventy in total) were the small PzKpfw Is and IIs, while seven were command tanks (3 kl.Pz Bef Wg and 4 gr.Pz Bef Wg). This meant that they only had 61 Mk IIIs and 17 Mk IVs. Nevertheless, these powerful tanks – more powerful than anything the British could field – would have a similar impact on the battlefield as had the now battle-scarred Matilda Mk IIs of 7 RTR.

Rommel held a number of military parades in Tripoli as each element of his force arrived. He even made the tanks of 5 leichte's panzer regiment drive around the town several times, so as to keep the British guessing on the true strength of the DAK. He also had his pioneers make a large number of dummy tanks out of wood and blankets, mounted on little Volkswagen staff cars, to deceive British air reconnaissance. His orders were to use the DAK as a blocking force to bolster the shattered Italians and prevent the British from advancing any farther into Tripolitania. However, merely sitting in a blocking position was definitely not Rommel's style, so he was determined from the outset to disobey the German High Command's direct orders not to advance, gambling on surprise and speed to win the day. And he was right. When he attacked at Mersa Brega on 31 March, just a few short weeks after setting foot in North Africa, 5 leichte, went through the enemy like a hot knife through butter, causing the British to make a general withdrawl. Agedabia was captured on 2 April and a supremely confident Rommel moved his HQ forward there the following day. The Germans were advancing so quickly that they were soon short of both fuel and ammunition. Gen Johannes Streich, who was the commander of 5 leichte then said that he needed a four-day halt to replenish fuel and ammunition. One can imagine Rommel's reaction! He immediately ordered them to unload all their lorries and to send convoys back to the divisional dump at Arco dei Fileni (known by the British as 'Marble Arch' – it marked the frontier between Tripolitania and Cyrenaica on the coast road), taking with them spare crews (found from the tank crews) for a round-the-clock refuelling trip. Streich protested that Rommel was grounding his division but was told that this was the way to conquer Cyrenaica quickly and thus save lives – another black mark against the unfortunate Streich who would be sacked a few months later.

The advance continued on the night 4/5 April, Rommel dividing his forces into four 'Blitzkrieg-type' columns and sending them up the coast with orders to keep going at all costs. The panzers quickly spread confusion far and wide, being well supported by the Luftwaffe, who had fifty Stukas and twenty Me 110s on call, plus access to long range Ju 88s and He 111s from Sicily. The 3rd Armoured Brigade and the Indian motorized brigade were, for example, caught near Mechili and practically wiped out. And so it went on. By 11 April, Tobruk was cut off and surrounded, and the British and Commonwealth formations were all back behind the Egyptian frontier wire, except for the small, stubborn force of two Australian brigades and the remnants of 3rd Armoured Brigade, holed up in the battered fortress of Tobruk, ready to defend it against all comers. And where else might one have expected Rea Leakey to be, but inside Tobruk, ready as always to take on all that Rommel could throw against them!

Rea Leakey By this stage of the war all the barracks in Cairo were occupied by base units or had been converted into hospitals, and in consequence we found ourselves occupying a tented camp which had been set up in the desert not far from the Great Pyramids. It was not a comfortable camp, and when the winds blew the whole area was enveloped in a cloud of fine sand which got into everything, including our food. But these trials were nothing after our last year's experiences, and we were more than content merely to be within reach of civilization.

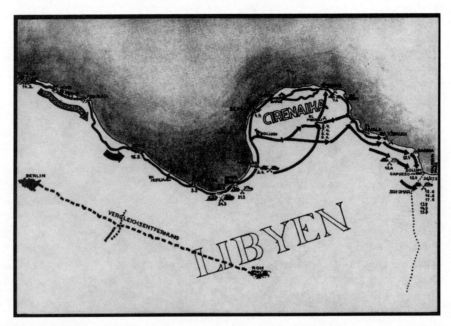

Rommel's initial advance.

We had no tanks to maintain or with which to carry out training, so we sent as many as possible on short spells of leave. Every evening lorry loads of soldiers would enter Cairo, where the Egyptians were only too willing to help them spend their money, and they had plenty of money saved up. It was interesting to meet and talk with the Australian, New Zealand and other Dominion troops, and there was very seldom any trouble or fighting. There were, of course, odd incidents, but usually they ended up by the parties concerned treating each other to numerous pints of beer. On one occasion, some of our soldiers entered a bar and found themselves next to some New Zealanders who were wearing their bush hats. Our lads made the slight error of greeting these men with the words: 'Good evening, Boy Scouts.'

Most of us were too occupied enjoying the fleshpots to worry much about how the war was progressing. We heard that German soldiers had made their appearance in the desert, but that did not disturb us back in Cairo. We trusted that the Armoured Division which had relieved us could look after them. Anyhow, we had no tanks, so there was nothing much we could do. Of the original thirteen subalterns, not many of us remained with the Regiment, although our battle casualties had been light. Peter Page went to Greece, and I never saw him again. He returned to the desert and was killed in his tank fighting with 3 RTR. Gus Holliman, another great friend, had joined the Long Range Desert Group and only on very rare occasions was he in Cairo. Of the six of us who remained, three got married during the period in Cairo. Derek Thom, Dennis Coulson and myself remained single, possibly not through the lack of girlfriends, but because we were always too 'broke'. We still had many good friends in Cairo, and we were still able to play all the games we wanted at Gezira Club.

About a week after we arrived in Cairo, one of our squadrons was sent to the area of Ismalia, where they were to be taught the drill of assault landings, and they spent much of their time driving a tank on and off a tank-landing craft. In time the whole Regiment was to receive this training, and much later in the war we learned that the object of the training was to prepare us for an attack on the island of Rhodes. The appearance of General Rommel in the desert put an end to this plan.

Once again, I was in command of my old squadron, and, as we were due to receive our assault training last, I decided to take a few days leave in Alexandria. We had now been in Cairo about a fortnight, and I felt that a little sea air would do me good. I always kept a small car in Cairo, and now, accompanied by our QM, Jimmy Noel, I drove the 120 miles to Alexandria. The date was 4 April 1941. Jimmy Noel had a brother who was captain of a Naval Depot ship, which rarely moved out Alexandria. We stayed in this ship and spent much of our time sailing in the harbour. I had met two attractive Scottish nursing sisters, who were also on leave from Cairo, and they were pleasant sailing companions.

On the evening of 7 April, as we approached the landing stage in our boat, I noticed a soldier walking along the quay wearing a black beret. In those days the only soldiers who wore the black beret were members of the Royal Tank Regiment. I hailed the man, and, to my surprise, he turned out to be one of my own squadron. I asked him what he was doing, and he replied, 'I am just going to get on board ship,' and continued to walk along the quay towards an old merchant ship that was laying alongside close by. I thought he must be out of his senses. We sailed towards this ship and received a nasty shock: looking down at the four of us – and we were clad in bathing costumes – was the majority of our Regiment, and there was much laughter and cheering. Then the CO poked his face over the side of the ship and asked where the hell we had been in the last 24 hours. I had forgotten to give our address when we left Cairo. 'Well, never mind where you have been, get moving. Go back to Cairo immediately and collect the truck we have left there for you. You will then drive to Tobruk and you have not a minute to spare.' He had hardly finished speaking, when the captain of the ship yelled at us to get our b——y boat out of his way, as he was already moving.

Yes, we had looked at the odd newspaper, but, for security reasons, the true situation in the Western Desert was not given. Rommel had launched an attack against our slender forces at El Agheila, and his powerful tanks had turned the scale against us. In a short space of time he had retaken Benghazi, and was already approaching Tobruk, driving all before him. Wavell was faced with a very difficult situation. He had sent all the troops he could possibly spare to Greece, and there was little left with which to meet this new threat. The 7th Armoured Division had not been re-equipped as all available equipment had also been sent to Greece. However, in the base workshops quite a number of the old tanks had been partially overhauled and others were at least able to move. These would have to be used.

On the afternoon of 6 April 1941, my Regiment got orders to call in every available man and draw up these tanks from workshops. That evening Officers visited the cafés, bars and hotels of Cairo, and ordered members of the 7th Armoured Division to return to their units. Cinemas were stopped, and the same announcement made, 'Return to your units immediately.' The next day was one mad rush for every man, except for the two of us, and we were peacefully sailing round Alexandria harbour with two attractive girls. Many of the tanks were in a very poor state, but so long as they could move, they were driven to the station, and put on flats which took them to Alexandria. In no time they were hoisted on board the ship, and that same evening she sailed for Tobruk, the captain ordering a little sailing boat to get out of her way.

It was not long before we were on the road driving hard for our old camp near the Pyramids. We arrived at about 10 p.m., and were met by Derek Thom, whose squadron had been left behind as there were insufficient tanks for them. He had packed our kit and loaded it on to an old Morris truck, which he thought might reach Tobruk before breaking down. There was no other vehicle available, and he took over my little car, as otherwise he would have no transport. In less than half an hour we were once again driving down the desert road towards Alexandria. At midnight, just before turning west along the desert track that led to Mersa Matruh, we called at an airfield to try and get some petrol. All they could give us was aviation fuel, which would probably blow the head off our old engine, but it was better than nothing. Taking turns, we drove through the night and never stopped.

By dawn the next day we were past Mersa Matruh, and fast approaching Libya. We now started meeting a constant stream of vehicles of every description, driving in the opposite direction. As we came through Bardia, we saw dumps of petrol and other stores burning, and the number of vehicles that passed us had diminished considerably. A few miles to the west of Bardia we were stopped by a Military Policeman, who said that the road to Tobruk had been cut and that we could go no further. As the odd truck was still coming past, we decided to go on, and we had the road to ourselves. Several times we saw armoured cars in the desert to the south of us, but we did not stop to find out whether they were friend or foe.

At about noon we saw the Tobruk perimeter wire, and the gateway across the road, was still open. But as we drove towards it, we saw soldiers hurriedly start to push the heavy wooden beams across the gap, and a burst of machine-gunfire drew our attention to some German armoured cars which were approaching from the south. 'Come on in, you Pommy bastards,' shouted the Australian soldiers, and pulled back the beams. We drove through, and once again Tobruk was surrounded. The tables were turned, and this time we were inside with the Germans and Italians outside.

In the desert there was chaos; the Armoured Division that had relieved us had taken terrible punishment from Rommel's tanks, and there had been no time for them to get acclimatized to desert warfare. They were driven back to Mechili and here their headquarters was surrounded and captured. They ceased to exist.[1] To the north on the coast road which ran from Tobruk to Benghazi, an untried Australian Division, the 9th, was driven back into Tobruk perimeter and these were the men who opened up the barrier for our truck. In the months to come, I got to know many of the officers and men of this Division, and they were second to none. Noel and I drove our battered old truck down to the harbour, and there we found the Regiment busy disembarking and still working like beavers on the tanks. When they had collected them from workshops in Cairo, they found that no wireless sets were fitted, guns were still in crates and covered in grease, and many other items of vital equipment were lying in the bottom of the turrets. While the ship was at sea, the crews had gone down to the hold and started on the task of getting the tanks fit for action. There was no time to lose; as each tank was hoisted off the ship the crew seized upon it, and the work went on.

As squadron commander, I went back to a cruiser tank, with two of my old crew. Everybody was now telling us to hurry up and get moving, and we needed little encouragement as Tobruk harbour was not a healthy place; the German aircraft were already putting in raid after raid against the shipping and dock installations. While we were getting ready to move we saw two ships sunk. It was very noisy.

To the west the Germans were attacking the perimeter defences that lay either side of the road, and the Australian infantry were crying out for tank support. We were the only operational regiment in Tobruk, and even we were not really in a fit state to go to battle. But at about 4 p.m. those tanks that were more or less fit were in action. As we drove up to the battle area we could see very little through the dust and smoke, but the Australian infantrymen came back and guided us forward. They showed us where the Germans were, and we opened fire. A few German tanks appeared, but our artillerymen drove them back, and towards dusk the Germans withdrew. They had failed to get into Tobruk, but only just. Rommel had received his first check.

The main part of 7th Armoured Division was soon back in the desert in the area of the frontier, and here again Rommel was forced to halt. But he had isolated Tobruk, and captured Bardia. He was very short of supplies which had to come by road either from Tripoli or Benghazi, and Benghazi was a poor harbour. Before he could continue his advance into Egypt, he had to capture Tobruk; not only was this fine harbour essential to him, but he could not afford to leave an enemy force behind him which was capable of harassing his lines of communication. Also his transport vehicles had to make a detour round Tobruk perimeter, which involved a journey of some 30 miles across very bad-going. He was determined to take this fortress town.

Tobruk was full of soldiers, but many were base personnel who had been trapped there by Rommel's rapid advance. The 9th Australian Division, commanded by General Morshead,[2] formed the main bulk of the Garrison. They were supported by British artillery, and my Regiment provided the main tank support. There was also a British infantry battalion, and, in fact, almost as many British as Australian troops. The perimeter was 30 miles in length, and, unlike Bardia, the anti-tank ditch was shallow and provided little or no obstacle to tanks. Fortunately, the Italian pill-boxes and dugouts were in a fair state of repair, and the Australians made full use of them.

We got little sleep that night. The Germans were closing in all round the perimeter trying to find a weak spot, and, as the night wore on, more and more enemy guns moved into position and opened fire. Several times during the night we received orders to move from one part of the front to another as reports came through of the Germans' probing attacks which might be successful in getting through the perimeter defences. We did little shooting, as the mere presence of tanks moving about in the dark was usually sufficient to make the enemy pull back. But it was tiring work, and we longed for a chance to sleep.

At dawn we were told that several enemy tanks had broken through the perimeter at a place called Acroma. Off we went to deal with them and we were delighted to find that they were the little Italian two-man tanks[3] which had not been seen for many months. They were now being used as flame-throwing tanks, and we soon disposed of them. We were just about to 'brew up' when we were ordered to move east to the area of the Tobruk–El Adem road. Enemy tanks were closing in on the perimeter, and the Australians in this area had no anti-tank guns.

Here, for the first time, my Regiment fought against German tanks. There were about fifteen of them, and we had about the same number of cruisers. But we had an equal number of light tanks, which, although useless in a tank fight, could be used to distract the enemy and make him believe we were stronger than was in fact the case. We opened fire on them when they were within 800 yards of us, and we were disturbed to see our 2-pounder solid shots bouncing off their armour. But some of our shots found soft spots and the crew of their leading tank baled out. Then they opened fire on us, and the battle was on.

We were one side of the perimeter defences, and the Germans were the other; the Australians were in the middle, and we could hear them cheering us on. We were very relieved to see the Germans start to withdraw as already they had brewed up three of our tanks, and we had only accounted for one of theirs. It was painfully obvious that we were out-gunned by these tanks. When the action was over, I heard Milligan telling the other members of the crew that he had failed to brew up a single tank, and yet he thought he was shooting as accurately as ever before. He had not seen his shots bouncing off the targets and I did not enlighten him. In the afternoon we went back to the Acroma area and spent the rest of that day hull down behind a low ridge firing at enemy tanks that attempted to come forward towards the perimeter. And all day long German aircraft kept passing over on their way to bomb the harbour. They had many successes.

That evening my squadron was ordered back to a place called Fort Pilastrino, which lay some 3 miles inside the perimeter, and it was dark by the time we arrived there. After refuelling, we settled down for our first sleep for two days and nights. An hour later, we discovered the identity of our neighbours. It was the British Battery sergeant-major's voice yelling orders to his gun crews that woke me up, and then eight guns started firing as hard as they could go. I turned over and went to sleep, despite the noise and the stone sticking into the small of my back.

At midnight the duty wireless operator woke me. I was wanted on the set. I knew what to expect, and all I had to be told was where the threat had now developed. It was a long move, at least 7 miles, to the east and close to the Bardia road block. I called up the tank commanders, and gave out my orders, and then we were on the move, slowly picking our way across the rough ground in the darkness. There was nothing we could do until dawn, but we had to keep moving about as the noise of our tanks always had an adverse effect on the enemy. Once again the Australian infantry had stood firm, and the enemy withdrew, leaving a number of dead behind him. All that day we were in action at one point or another, and we lost another tank.

Whenever we showed ourselves to the enemy, we were heavily shelled, and several of our men were wounded. That night was the same as the previous night, except that we got even less sleep, and again next day we were seldom out of action.

So it went on day after day and night after night, but the perimeter held. Most of the enemy tank advances had been in the nature of probing attacks, trying to find a weak hole in the defences, but we knew that very soon a major assault would be launched. It came on 14 April. At 1.30 a.m. I was called to the set, and the CO gave me the news. The Germans had launched a very heavy attack against the perimeter in the south astride to the El Adem road, and had made a breach in the defensive line. Tanks could be heard moving about in this area, and it was anticipated that at dawn they would advance north towards the town and harbour. My orders were to move east and be prepared to engage the tanks as they attempted to get down an escarpment, which ran east and west 3 miles south of the town.

I called up the tank commanders and gave them their orders. It was very cold and dark, and we were desperately tired; I had an empty feeling in the pit of my stomach. When I gave the order to the commanders to go back to their tanks and 'start up', one of my two officers broke down and cried out that he could not go into action as he knew he would be killed. He was very young and had not been long with the Regiment. I had noticed that, like quite a number of the tank commanders, he was beginning to feel the strain. All might have been well if we could have given each man a day off, but we had no men to spare, and on this occasion one tank could not go into action as it had no tank commander. I grabbed the young officer, and pulled him aside; he was shivering and whimpering like a child. I tried to calm him down, and told him that as an officer he must set an example to the men. But he went on repeating 'I can't go into this action because I know I will be killed.' Time was slipping by, and I knew only too well the effect on the men if this officer did not go into action; they, too, were just as tired and frightened. I gave him a drink of neat rum, but it had little effect. I tried being gentle and kind to him, but this made him worse. It was a most unpleasant incident, and I knew I had to settle it there and then. I tried the last resort, and it worked. I drew my revolver, cocked it, and pointed it at his temple. 'All right,' I said, in a very stern voice, 'either you get into your tank or I shoot you for cowardice in the face of the enemy.' He turned and went back to his tank, and I heard him giving his orders. Even after all these years I have nightmares connected with this incident.

We moved off into the darkness, and even the rumble of our tanks could not drown the roar of the Tobruk artillery. The harbour was being bombed incessantly. It was dawn before we reached the road running up the escarpment and the air was crystal clear. High overhead there was an air battle in progress, and we could hear the scream of the aircraft engines as they climbed and dived in mortal combat. As my tank reached the junction of the El Adem and Bardia roads I happened to look up and saw a fighter plane diving straight for me with his throttle wide open, and he was descending vertically at a tremendous speed. It was a Hurricane, and obviously the pilot was already dead; it plunged into the ground only 6 feet from my tank and seemed to shake the whole earth. Then a lorry drove across towards me; an artillery officer jumped out and shouted at me, 'For goodness sake, turn right and come to our help. My battery is being attacked by enemy tanks and the guns are being over-run. Look! they are only 500 yards away.'

He was right, some forty German tanks were now clearly visible, and they were indeed busily engaged in destroying these guns. There would be nothing to stop them driving down to Tobruk harbour, only 3 miles away. We swung right into battle line. I handed Milligan his cigarette, and told him to start shooting. There was no need for me to indicate the target to him. 'Loaded,' yelled Adams, and away went another solid shot, tearing at the thick enemy armour. The fumes of burning cordite made us cough, and our eyes water, and soon the turret was so thick with smoke that I could only just make out the figure of Adams as he loaded shell after shell into the breach. We were firing faster than ever before, and so were my other four cruiser tanks.

It must have been a minute before the Germans spotted us, and by then their tanks had received many hits from our shells. They appeared to panic, because they started to turn in all directions, many of them turned about and started moving back the way they had come. But then they were on to us, and we could clearly see the flash of their guns. The tank to my left was hit several times, and 'brewed up'. I saw some of the crew bale out. Then another of my valuable cruisers went up in flames, and there were only three of us left. I noticed one man of this crew dragging himself along the ground, badly wounded, and machine-gun bullets were hitting all round him. I felt I had to give him cover.

'Driver advance, turn slightly left.' My tank moved across to give this man protection. It was a stupid move, because by turning I presented the German tank gunners with a larger target, and they took full advantage of it. As we were turning back head-on to the enemy, the engine cut out, and we were left slightly 'broadside on'. 'She's on fire, sir!' shouted Adams, but he went on loading shells. At the same moment Milligan's head fell back against my knees, and looking down I saw that a shell had pierced the armour and removed most of his chest. He was dead. 'Bale out,' I yelled, and, as I pulled myself out of the turret, what few shells we had left in the turret started exploding, and the flames were already licking round my feet. I saw Adams get out safely, and we dashed round to the front of the tank to check up on the others. As we got round, the driver flopped out of his hatch, and Adams grabbed him and helped him back. I opened up the first sub-turret gunner's hatch, and looked in, but I knew what I should see, as there was a neat hole through the armour just opposite where this gunner's head would be. He was dead, and already his clothing was burning fiercely.

The other sub-turret gunner was laying by the side of the tank, and he looked up at me and smiled; his right leg was shot off just below the knee, and the useless limb was attached by one small piece of skin. He was a big lad, and how he had got out of his small hatch unaided and with only one leg has always remained a mystery to me. We were being machine-gunned. Somehow I got him over my shoulder and carried him back to where I found a shallow trench. The other two were there, and we laid him down, but he straightened up, looked at his leg, and said, 'Cut it off, sir, it's no use to me.' I did so, and he then lay back smiling. At that moment up drove an ambulance driven by a large Australian. Within a few minutes this lad was in Tobruk hospital; I saw him a year later at a base hospital, and he was as cheerful as ever, walking about on crutches.

The two remaining cruisers survived this battle, and the Germans fled back out of Tobruk perimeter. Only one of their tanks was left burning on the battlefield, but much later we learned that many others were put out of action for several months. Once again we were made conscious of our inferior gun and armour plating.[4] A battalion of German infantry had accompanied these tanks, and they were now left behind manning an old anti-tank ditch well inside the perimeter. A company of Australian Army Service Corps lorry drivers were ordered to go and deal with them. Their commander came over and asked if we could lend them the support of a tank. I detailed one of the light tanks, commanded by Cpl Hulme, to carry out this task. Having nothing better to do, I followed the tank on foot to see this little action carried out. Cpl Hulme positioned his tank so that he could fire his machine-gun down the line of the trench which the Germans occupied. He gave them one burst of fire and they all put their hands up; meanwhile, the Australians moved in extended order towards the trench with bayonets fixed.

As the Germans had surrendered, Hulme decided it was sufficiently safe for him to emerge from the turret of his tank. A German soldier put seven bullets into his heart, but that soldier paid the penalty for his treachery. He had evidently not noticed the Australians coming up; they saw his action, and they saw red. He let out a squeal like a pig as three long bayonets squelched into his stomach. There was no more trouble from those Germans.

That day Rommel's soldiers received their first real defeat, and for a few days the Tobruk garrison had a comparatively quiet time. That evening I felt very tired and depressed. I mourned the loss of many good men and I felt very guilty at having ordered that young officer into his tank. His was the first to get brewed up, and he was killed. Then came the difficult task of writing to the next-of-kin of those who had been killed. Yet there was one pleasant surprise that evening: a great friend rejoined the squadron. Adams had gone to workshops to see if there were any tanks repaired and fit for action. To his delight he found a cruiser, and there was Doyle's kitten asleep on the driver's seat.

Our next major action started on 1 May. The day before I handed over command of my squadron to Maj Walter Benzie. He was several years senior to me and this was to be his first time in action. There was considerable enemy activity to the west of the perimeter and we moved to a place called Acroma. It was a day move and German dive bombers were much in evidence. The RAF had been swept from the skies in the Tobruk area and these bombers were based at El Adem, only 10 miles south of the Tobruk outer defensive line.

German infantry and some seventy tanks had been seen assembling for an attack, and as we approached the area an artillery duel was in progress. We could see nothing for the dust and smoke. As the sun was setting the attack was launched. This was to be the favourite time for the enemy to attack. They looked east while we looked west into the sun. We could see little through the dust and smoke, but at least we stopped the enemy tanks closing in on the Australian pill-boxes. When darkness fell, we were of little use and pulled back a mile. All that night the attack raged, and the Germans captured 4 miles of the perimeter. There was no second line of defence. Every man in the garrison who could be spared was now brought up, given a spade and a rifle and told to dig himself in. Cooks, clerks, lorry drivers, and even skilled mechanics, were pushed into the line and the line held, but only just. All that day we moved about from place to place and fought back enemy tanks that were trying to probe forward.

That evening the Australians counter-attacked with a battalion of infantry that had been taken out of a quiet sector of the line. They were supported by eight Matilda tanks which had been repaired in workshops. But the Matildas met their match in the German tanks and anti-tank guns, and only two returned. The infantry won back a few of the perimeter posts, but at a terrible cost. Yet this attack did prevent the Germans pushing forward that night, and gave the Australians more time to strengthen their new line of defence. For four days and nights this battle raged, and both sides suffered heavy casualties. The Germans held on to the ground they had gained, but could get no further. At places the opposing infantry trenches were no more than 150 yards apart, and this part of the front settled down to a state of deadlock which must have resembled the Western Front of the 1914–18 war.

Apart from the incident when Cpl Hulme was shot, I never witnessed or heard a of a case of foul fighting by the German Afrika Korps. On the whole they fought very hard, but they fought clean and they treated prisoners and wounded well. During this battle I saw a scene that was typical of the spirit of the forces that fought at Tobruk. At one place there were a large number of Australian wounded lying out in 'no man's land' close to the German line. An Australian padre walked forward and up to the German line. A German Officer came out and guided him through their minefield. After a while he returned to our own lines, and led out several ambulances. While the wounded were being collected, the German took the Padre into his dugout and gave him coffee. German soldiers helped to collect the wounded and load them on to the ambulances, and during the whole time not a shot was fired by either side.

Rommel had found Tobruk too tough a nut to crack, and there was nothing he could do but wait until he had built up a sufficiently strong force to launch a major assault. This was to take him a long time, and during this time he was to find that the Tobruk garrison was like a running ulcer in his side.

Notes

1.   In addition to losing the 2nd Armoured Divisional commander (Gambier-Parry) when his entire HQ was captured at Mechili, the British also lost their best field commander – Gen Sir Richard O'Connor together with newly arrived Lt Gen Neame, VC. They had been up in the forward area reconnoitering and, on the night of 6 April, had been travelling back to XIII Corps HQ at Timimi, in a staff car without an escort. Both generals were exhausted and had fallen fast asleep in the back of the car. They were intercepted by a motorcycle patrol from 5 leichte and captured after a brief exchange of fire.

2.   Maj Gen Leslie Morshead was a tough, somewhat irascible commander, who earned the nickname 'Ming the Merciless' from his admiring troops. When some newspaper wrote an article on Tobruk headed 'Tobruk can take it' he was furious, retorting that his garrison was not there to 'take it' but rather to 'dish it out' by aggressive defensive action!

3.   The little Italian tankettes were CV 33/L35s (carro lanciaflamme), based upon prewar British Vickers Carden Loyd Mk VI tankettes which the Italians had purchased in the 1920s. They were fitted with a long-barrelled, hooded flamethrower instead of the usual machine-guns and towed a 500-litre armoured trailer of flame fuel.

4.   I have already described this particular battle from both sides, in another book entitled: *Tank Action*, also published by Sutton Publishing Ltd, in 1995.

CHAPTER SEVEN

Locked up in Tobruk

Editor This was to become one of the longest sieges in British military history. Initially it involved mainly the Australian 9th Infantry Division, who, supported by some British armour and artillery, successfully defended the fortress against Rommel's DAK and their Italian allies. Six months later, the British 70th Infantry Division took over the defence and the Aussies were withdrawn by sea. However, Rea Leakey's period of incarceration had also ended by then, so it is this first Australian period that concerns us here.[1]

The importance of capturing Tobruk cannot be overemphasized. Although it was only a small port of some 4,000 plus inhabitants, it was, apart from Benghazi, the only safe, accessible port for more than 1,000 miles between Sfax in Tunisia and Alexandria. Thus its capture would have greatly shortened Rommel's supply lines. In addition, of course, its continued defiance had a tremendous morale-boosting effect on the Allies at a time when there was a shortage of victories everywhere.

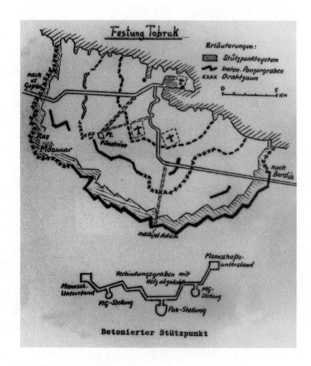

Fortress Tobruk

Nevertheless, Rommel was ecstatic. In just over two weeks he had captured all the territory the British had won from the Italians. In the same short weeks, his magnetic personality had imbued his 'Afrikaners' with such confidence that they felt there was nothing they could not do, so it must have been all the more infuriating that they were unable to deal with with Tobruk. There would be continual 'hard pounding' against the stubborn defenders and more black marks against Streich's 5 leichte for not getting the job done quickly enough.

Rea Leakey When I think back on those six long months I spent locked up in Tobruk fortress, I feel a sense of pride and achievement at having been a member of that garrison. I learned what is meant by comradeship, what it is like to be short of food, to live without any of the normal amenities of civilization, and I gained a lasting affection for the Australian soldiers.

About the only clean thing in Tobruk was the sea that licked the shores of this barren desert fortress. Every house in the little town which lay by the side of the harbour had been hit by either bombs or shells, and was filled with dust and rubble. Then beyond the town stretched the many square miles of desert enclosed by the perimeter defences, but it was a filthy bit of desert. Men had camped here for many years and had left their rubbish behind them; tanks and lorries had churned up almost every square yard of the ground, and when the winds blew the fine dust covered everything. There were fleas and flies, and, in many areas, a constant smell of burning cordite.

By day it was not possible to use the harbour, because the enemy had complete control of the air. What few supplies of food and ammunition we received were brought in by destroyers of the Royal Navy. Those ships would sail from Alexandria laden with stores on their decks and face the constant threat of enemy bombers, submarines and mines, to reach Tobruk at midnight. As soon as they dropped anchor a fleet of small craft would come alongside, and with amazing speed and hardly a word spoken, they would be relieved of their cargo, and the wounded would be lifted on board. Half an hour after their arrival, the ships would be stealing out of the pitch black harbour and heading back for Alexandria. The Navy kept Tobruk alive, but paid a heavy penalty.

With Walter Benzie in command, my squadron moved to an area that was to be its base for the next eight months. We occupied a series of underground caves which the Italians had once used as a prison camp; they were filthy and full of flies, but they did provide protection against the constant shelling and bombing which we received. Instead of feeding by tank crews, we started a squadron cookhouse, and our cooks had a difficult task trying to provide three meals a day out of the meagre rations. Often breakfast consisted of a cup of tea and a dry biscuit.

We used one of the caves as an officers' mess, and the four of us soon loathed the place. It was always dark, smelled of sweat and was full of fleas, and at this time of the year it was desperately stuffy at night. But after dark we could at least sit down and read or write by the light of a small electric bulb, which was run off an old tank battery. It was the fleas that finally drove us out and forced us to sleep in the open on top of the cave. We preferred to be shelled rather than be bitten to death.

Towards the middle of May our squadron was re-equipped with a new type of cruiser tank, the A13 (See details at end of the book). These tanks, and there were only twelve of them, had been left behind in Tobruk workshops by the Armoured Division which relieved us at Beda Fomm. Although they had the same armour and gun as our previous cruisers, they were much faster. Their speed was governed down to a maximum of 30 mph, but if the governors were removed, they would exceed 50 mph, which is fast for a vehicle weighing over 15 tons. But they were mechanically unsound and were constantly breaking down.

Throughout the month of May we were called out to fight about every third day, but they were inconclusive battles, and we seldom got the chance of knocking out enemy tanks. All these actions took place inside the perimeter. Now the scene changed. We were told we could go out of the perimeter and attack those who were containing us. There was nothing Benzie liked more than to have a crack at the enemy, and he used to go round the various Australian battalions holding the perimeter offering the services of his tanks. We could only operate successfully by day, and the infantry did most of their fighting at night. However, on several occasions we were asked to go out and shoot up some enemy position that was causing trouble. Normally only four tanks would be used on these raids, and Benzie and I took turns in leading them.

In an effort to stop these raids, the Germans were forced to keep tanks constantly alerted at strategic points some 3 or 4 miles from the perimeter. They also laid many minefields which the Australians would lift for their own use. When they were located we used to attack these tanks. The mines blocking our route to their location would be lifted and when the sun was at its hottest we would move out of the perimeter and drive slowly towards them. At this time of the day most soldiers were asleep, and with luck we would close to within 500 yards before our presence was noticed. For a short time we would create havoc and then, outnumbered by at least ten to one, we would turn tail heading for home at 40 mph.

Benzie and I had attacked one particular group of tanks guarding the main road leading to El Adem on two occasions. On the third occasion it was my turn to lead the raid. The mines had been lifted the night before, and all went well until I started to speed up for the final run in towards the target. An anti-tank ditch had been dug. I ordered the driver to go on at maximum speed and warned the crew to hold on to something solid in the tank. All three vehicles jumped the gap and in seconds we were charging in among the enemy. We did a lot of damage in a short time before returning the way we came without a casualty. It says much for the skill of the drivers and fitters of the RTR that we never lost a tank on these raids. Yet it was not all plain sailing; on one occasion we were doing the final check on the vehicles before leaving the perimeter, and a driver showed me oil leaking out of the engine compartment. I was quite sure that he had deliberately caused this fault – it is inevitable that some men crack earlier than others.

Then came another change of policy. Supplies of petrol in Tobruk were running so low that we were forbidden to move our tanks unless there was an emergency. Once a week we were allowed to start up the engines just to make sure they were still in working order. As the weeks went by, there was seldom an emergency, and we got very bored.

Benzie and I had become the greatest of friends, and I learned a great deal about him. Just before the war, he had married a very beautiful girl, and they were a devoted couple; but she was delicate, and two years after their marriage, she contacted tuberculosis and died. Benzie never really recovered from this loss, and often used to tell me that his one desire was to join his Joan wherever she might be. In some ways he almost courted death, and he certainly did not know what the word fear meant. He had an infectious laugh, and I never knew him lose his temper; the men almost worshipped him. Neither of us could stand inaction, and we were constantly looking round for something to do to keep us amused. We were not the only ones.

The caves where we lived were at the top of a fairly deep wadi. Some 400 yards down the wadi an Australian Engineer Unit had taken up residence. On a hot afternoon, when there were no enemy aircraft flying over at which to shoot, these Aussies used to amuse themselves by taking pot shots at us as we walked across from one cave to another; the game was to see how close they could shoot with hitting us. We never really objected, until they started shooting with machine-guns. This was inclined to be a little frightening, especially as they employed two or three guns at the same time. One would fire immediately ahead of the victim and the other behind him. Benzie and I went down and had a word or two with these neighbours of ours, but we got little change. Among other tasks these engineers used to repair vehicles, and there were always about a dozen lorry radiators propped up on the side of the wadi; they were evidently put up to dry out after holes had been sealed. We started using these as targets for our tank machine-guns, and in so doing ruined many hours of work which the Aussies had put into them. A truce was signed, and before long we were all the greatest of friends. We discovered they used to run short courses on mines and explosives for the infantry, and Benzie and I attended the next course.

We learned how to disarm the most complicated mine, and even how to set the unpleasant booby-traps which were almost impossible to detect. Each set of students was made to go out into the German minefields and bring back a definite number of anti-tank mines. This was not too bad, but the final test really did take a little nerve. In the Acroma area, no man's land, between the German and Australian lines, had been sown with every known type of mine and booby-trap, and was one of the most unhealthy places imaginable. The Australian infantry, always anxious to get at their opponents, used to ask the Engineers to clear safe lanes through these minefields, and it was not a pleasant task. What better idea than to make the students do it, and this then became the passing-out test. It was one test that I am never likely to forget!

As soon as it was dark, we were led up to the front-line trenches and shown where the safe lane was wanted. Equipped with a roll of white tape, a pair of wire-cutters and a pocketful of nails, we would climb out of the trench and start our dangerous work. No sooner was I out of the trench than a flare went up from the German lines, only 200 yards away, and a machine-gun sent a stream of bullets over my head. I lay still until all was quiet on my immediate front. Then crawling forward inch by inch, I searched the ground with my fingers, and before long I found my first mine. It was a German 'S' mine, which we called 'Jumping Jack', and this was the size of a large jam jar. It was made in two parts: an outer container, which held a slightly smaller container inside. Beneath this inner container was a small charge of explosive, just sufficient to throw this container about 4 feet in the air. Once in the air a second charge exploded and scattered about 350 solid metal balls in every direction. When laid, the mine was buried in the ground, and only the firing mechanism showed above the ground. This consisted of either three little prongs about an inch long, or a single projection of the same length, but about the thickness of a pencil, and to this would be attached a very thin trip wire. To tread on the three little prongs or to disturb the trip-wire was certain death, and anybody within a radius of 40 yards of the mines was lucky if he escaped alive. I have known one of these mines to kill twenty and wound about twenty-five soldiers.

The one I found was one with the three prongs, and once found they were easy to make safe by the use of a small nail. I found a trip-wire two yards further on, and it took me some time to locate the mine to which it was attached. I then got two more normal 'Jumping Jacks' and felt I was doing very well. I had advanced at least 30 yards, and had cut through two lots of barbed wire. Then over to my right I heard the soft first bang of a 'Jumping Jack' followed by the much louder bang as it exploded in the air, and the metal balls flew past me. My next-door neighbour had failed his test, and paid the price – death. With even greater caution I continued to work my way forward. But the Germans were obviously aware that we were out because flare after flare went up from their lines, and whilst the whole area was lit up it would have been suicide to have moved or looked up. Dawn was not far off, so I started working my way back, and as I went I carefully covered up white tape with earth so that it should not betray my path to the Germans. It was a great relief to get back safely to the trench, and there was a hot cup of tea ready for me in an Aussie dugout. But unless we were to spend the day in the forward trenches, we had to get away before first light, so Benzie and I hastened.

We spent the day with our squadron, but slept most of the afternoon. That night we again went forward and continued our task. We both made good progress and felt sure that another night would see us through. But on that third night I was disturbed by a German who must have been laying mines in no man's land, and he was working only a few yards away from my lane. I was worried that he might see my white tape and then follow it towards his own trenches, where he would stumble over me. As soon as I could, I crawled back past him and got the Aussies to fire into the area where I had last seen him. It was then too late to continue work, and so I had a fourth night of excitement. Benzie was very pleased with himself, as he got through and even looked down into a German trench.

It was certainly a night of excitement: the German must have found my tape, and he prepared a series of booby traps to test my skill. I found the first some 20 yards from where I had left off work the previous night, and I silently thanked my instructor for warning me to go very carefully even over the area I had already cleared. It was an unpleasant booby-trap to play about with in the dark, and soon my fingers were clammy and felt like a lot of thumbs. Although it was cool I was sweating all over. I did something wrong because I heard the metallic click of the firing-pin strike forward, and I knew the thing would explode in about three seconds. Fortunately, it was nothing larger than an ordinary British hand grenade and I managed to wrench it clear of the wires that held it in position, and flung it towards the German trenches. It exploded in the air several yards from me and I was fortunate to receive no more than a few small splinters into my flesh.

The next second the whole area was a blaze of light from illuminating flares, and I felt very naked lying out in no man's land. Two German machine-guns sprayed the area with bullets and several hand grenades were thrown in my direction. I had certainly courted excitement, but I never bargained for the amount I received on this occasion. There was nothing I could do but lie perfectly still and hope for the best. It seemed an age before the noise died down, and I remember having plenty of time to think of the peace of a trout stream in Scotland, of a hot bath and a good meal. I wondered if I would ever know these joys again.

Although it was still comparatively early on in the night, I felt too tired and frightened to go on forward that night, so I came back. As I flopped down into the trench, an Australian voice said, 'It is the Pommie bastard, he's not dead, after all,' and I was soon sitting in a dugout drinking tea. I felt very ashamed at having failed in my task and apologized to the Australians, saying that I would finish it the next night. But wisely they considered that my lane could not be used for a raid, even if it were completed, as the Germans obviously knew only too well where it would finish up at their end. They kindly told me that I had done enough to pass the test and need do no more. I did not volunteer to try and clear another lane for them, and I hoped that I would never see a minefield again.

Meanwhile, 100 miles to the east, on the frontier, Wavell had been building up sufficient forces to launch an attack and relieve Tobruk. This attack started on 15 June, and we in Tobruk stood ready to break out of the perimeter when the relieving forces were near at hand. But the Germans were too strong on the frontier and very little progress was made. At the end of about a week's fighting our forces pulled back to their original positions, and in Tobruk we sank back to our life of waiting for something to happen.

Life in Tobruk was, I suppose, no better than that of a prisoner-of-war, except that we were our own masters. Food and drinking water were short and alcohol was unobtainable. I relate two incidents connected with the latter. Not far from our caves was the Australian equivalent of the British NAAFI. The manager was a friend of mine, and one morning when I called in to see him I found him confronted by a British Commando Officer who was being highly abusive and demanding whisky. My friend was insisting that he had none. 'My name is Randolph Churchill, and my father is Prime Minister – I demand whisky.' I hit him with my fist, and we dumped him in his truck and told the driver to 'get lost'. He was who he said he was.

Then we did receive an issue of alcohol, a small bottle of beer per Other Rank, and half a bottle of whisky between four officers. There were four of us in our squadron mess and Benzie was the only one who liked whisky, so we said he could have the lot. That night he said to me, 'Rea, please, I cannot drink alone – join me.' After several 'nips', he suggested we play an old army game with pistols called 'Are you there, Moriarty?' We lay on the floor at either end of the cave with pistols at the ready. 'Are you there, Moriarty?' he called.

'Yes,' I replied, and moved sideways. He fired and the bullet smacked against the wall. The light was out. Then it was my turn. 'Are you there, Moriarty?'

'Yes,' he said, and I fired. And so it went on until each of us had fired six shots. A very stupid game to play, but we were bored, and I knew that Walter Benzie somehow courted death. As it was, we each 'drew blood', but fortunately minor injuries. Perhaps it was just as well that was the only issue of whisky we received while I was in Tobruk.

In contrast to us, the Australian infantry manning the 35-mile perimeter were forever twisting Jerry's tail. Night after night patrols would seek out the enemy strongholds that contained the Tobruk Garrison, inflict casualties, remove mines and generally make life unpleasant for them. In several sectors of the front these activities forced the enemy to move his defensive positions further and further away from the perimeter. Searchlights and dogs were used to stop these aggressive Aussies.

As life for us without petrol and alcohol was so dull, Benzie and I decided to join the infantry. Our superiors agreed to me joining an Australian Battalion as a private soldier for three months or until I was wanted back in the Regiment; Benzie stayed with the Squadron. I had made friends with Lt-Col Evans commanding the 2/23 Australian Infantry Battalion. Besides bringing in supplies, the Naval destroyers ferried in reinforcements. Evans told me when he was to receive a draft and, as they moved away from the harbour soon after midnight, I joined their ranks.

I had been equipped with Australian uniform, a Sydney address and an indifferent Aussie accent.

In the morning the Regimental Sergeant-Major marched the six of us before the CO. Only Evans and his Adjutant knew of my true identity. I duly joined C Company, and tried hard to behave as Pte Leakey, a Sydney publisher's son. But it was no good. Within 24 hours my cobbers knew that I was no more than a 'Pommie bastard'. They were amused that an Englishman should join their ranks just to see how Aussies fought, and they promised me plenty of action. They certainly kept their promise. The next night I went out on my first patrol into no man's land. From the time we left until the time we got back, they hardly stopped cursing me for my clumsiness and for my slow reactions. I was more frightened of the Aussies than of any enemy who might have been around.

Each patrol was very carefully planned and given a particular task to carry out. The route was drawn out on a map and bearings and distances noted. The patrol leader would search each man to make sure he carried no incriminating papers; watches and other objects that might glint in the dark were removed; weapons were examined and care was taken to ensure that there were no loose bits of metal that might make even the slightest sound if jerked. There was no need to blacken our hands and faces as we were all heavily suntanned. As a tank man, I had never worn a tin hat in action and asked if I might wear my beret, but this was refused. Every man was given a particular task and, while the patrol was out, nobody spoke.

Once clear of the perimeter, the patrol leader set his compass on the correct bearing and off we went. Two men counted the paces, so we knew how far we had travelled. Clad in gym shoes, the patrol could move almost as quietly as a pride of lions. Every so often the patrol would stop, lie down, look and listen. The Germans patrolled the same areas and on two occasions we encountered them. Both times we saw them first, and they never even suspected we were close at hand.

To start with, the patrols I accompanied were merely sent out on reconnaissance, and our orders were to fight only if we were attacked. Our task was to get information about the defences round a particular post which was to be attacked. We would crawl to within a few yards of the enemy sentries and then lie for several hours just watching. The dogs were our greatest enemies, as they were well trained and seemed able to detect the slightest movement. The searchlights were of little trouble. The second the beam appeared we would drop flat on our faces and wait until it had passed away from our particular area.

Very soon I was considered up to the required standard and graduated to fighting patrols. These were always fun, as a patrol would never dream of coming back without having had some sort of a fight. Surprise was, of course, essential if any success was to be achieved, and if one could possibly get inside the wire perimeter of a post without being detected, then success was certain. The Italian posts were the easiest to 'beat up' because they panicked and quite often would be willing to surrender. The Germans knew this, and kept a proportion of their troops holding positions in the Italian units areas. One of the tasks of the reconnaissance patrols was to find out which post was which – not very difficult, especially as the Italian soldier had a smell of his own.

Sometimes a patrol would be told to bring back a prisoner from a particular area. Early on I accompanied a patrol with such a mission, and I was already familiar with the area. While out on a reconnaissance patrol I had noticed a hole outside one of the posts which was used as a latrine. I suggested that we should lie up close to this hole and hope that some soldier would be caught short during the hours of darkness.

We had no trouble in finding the hole, mainly because of its smell, and three of us lay up a few yards from it. After about an hour's wait, our victim appeared. When he was well settled with his trousers down we acted quickly but quietly. While one person stuffed a pad over and into his mouth to prevent his shouting, the other two lifted him off his perch and carried him into the desert darkness. Not a shot was fired and not a sound was made. Later we found that escorts were provided for those who visited outside latrines at night.

Because I was sent out almost every night I became good at this game, and I was often picked for particularly difficult tasks. One of the most interesting I did was with the Battalion Intelligence Officer and a large tough Sergeant. Our task was to investigate some diggings astride the Bardia road, and try to discover the exact layout of the defences in this area.

We set out as soon as it was dark, as we had to cover some 5,000 yards and still allow time for investigation. Our navigation had to be very accurate, as our aim was to get between two lines of trenches that were only 100 yards apart, the exact locations having been plotted on the map from air photographs. We decided to make for a crashed aircraft on our first leg, as we knew its exact position. It was well known that German patrols also used this obvious landmark, but we thought that with a patrol of three we were unlikely to be spotted. However, as we approached it we moved with extreme caution, and it was as well we did. The moment we saw the aircraft we lay down, and almost at the same moment an enemy patrol got up from beside it and walked towards us. There were ten of them and we had a good chance of dealing with them, but, as usual, our orders were quite clear – on a reconnaissance patrol, avoid a fight. It was a tense moment and it needed a great deal of self-control to restrain from even cocking a pistol in readiness. One man passed within a yard of my head; at one moment I thought he was going to tread on me as he was coming straight for me, but three or four paces from me he moved across to one side. We were lying in a small patch of desert scrub and this saved us from detection.

There was no moon that night and as time went by a bank of clouds obscured the stars, which not only made navigation more difficult, but reduced visibility to a few yards. When we estimated that we were about to move between the two lines of trenches a lorry started up, its side lights were switched on, and it moved slowly down the Bardia road in an easterly direction. The pinpoint lights were sufficient to show us that a large gang of men were working in this area, and now we could hear their picks and shovels. We moved slowly forward towards them, and soon we could hear them talking softly to each other. They were Italians, so we moved closer still. We got so close that we were able to examine their work, but it was so dark that we could not really tell what they were digging. At that moment another lorry started to move, and we could clearly see a man walking in front, who was guiding it. He came straight towards us, so we crawled out of his way. The lorry passed within a few feet of us. I thought what fun it would be to throw a few hand grenades in among the workers. 'Perhaps another night, but not tonight,' was the reply I got when I whispered my thoughts to the other two.

I suppose we must have crawled around for about an hour, then we moved back the way we had come. We had discovered little useful information, and the Intelligence Officer decided we should lie up close to this position and spend the day in watch. He had thought this might be necessary and had brought a large groundsheet, which was carefully painted so as to fit in with the colouring of the desert. We searched around for a suitable hiding place, but all we could find was a pit 6 inches deep and just wide enough for the three of us to lie in. We lay down, pulled the sheet over us and, while one kept awake, the other two slept.

Even in August the nights in the desert are cold, and I was glad of the warmth given out by the bodies of my companions. None of us slept much, because we were so closely huddled together in the narrow trench that it was a case of 'when father turns we all turn'. We had no idea exactly how close we were to the enemy positions, but felt we were safe enough as we could not hear a sound, and we awaited the dawn with interest. It was therefore not a little disturbing to find ourselves within 300 yards of a series of trenches and dugouts which were fully manned. However, there was nothing we could do about it, as even the Italians could not fail to see us if we started crawling back. There was nothing for it but to lie perfectly still throughout the hours of daylight, and hope that our camouflaged sheet would hide us.

It was fascinating to lie and watch these enemy soldiers carry out their usual daily routine and compare it with ours. We were amazed to see the quantity of blankets and even white sheets that were brought out and aired, and they hardly seemed to bother about cleaning their weapons. Their food had obviously been brought up to the position at night ready cooked, because we saw no fires. They looked a scruffy lot.

Lying in our trench covered by a groundsheet was no picnic. The sun blazed down on us and the sweat poured off us; soon our clothing was soaked, and I got the worst time as I was in the middle. Then the flies started attacking us and we longed to be able to swat them. We talked in whispers about our families and girlfriends, and my companions told me of their country, of the blue gum-trees and of the surf-bathing. And all the time we watched the enemy soldiers we made notes and sketches of their positions, the location of gun positions, gaps through the wire and many other details that would be invaluable to a raiding party. We gained an immense amount of information.

At about midday a large dog started hunting around, and he was working his way towards us. He came within 100 yards of where we were lying, and then fortunately his master called him back. We breathed a sigh of relief. The heat was unbearable and I longed for a drink of water. Nature called, and there was nothing for it but to wet ourselves and the stench added to our miseries. So the long day wore on, but so very slowly, until at last the sun sunk below the horizon and the welcome darkness closed in on us. What a relief it was to stand up, stretch our cramped limbs and feel the cool air blowing over our bodies. Our return to Tobruk perimeter was uneventful, and there could be no doubt as to the success of our reconnaissance. Several nights later that post was attacked and its garrison was wiped out. I was sorry to have missed that attack, but I was out on another job.

The idea of lying out close to the enemy positions by day caught on, and soon there were a number of permanent watching lairs in no man's land. Most had telephone lines linking them to Tobruk. I was given the honorary rank of lance corporal, and spent many a day with two privates in these posts. I was also given the task of establishing new posts, and it was on one of these expeditions that I was nearly captured.

In the area east of the El Adem road some of the enemy positions were 7,000 yards from the Tobruk perimeter, and even from the watch towers it was not possible to see them. Many years ago the Romans had dug a number of water cisterns in the Western Desert, and even today the mounds of earth above each cistern provide some of the best landmarks in this featureless desert. There was one of these marked on our maps just over 7,000 yards from the perimeter, and it was chosen as a possible site for an observation post. I was told to go and try it out.

My party numbered about ten men, and we set out from the perimeter as soon as it was dark, laying a telephone cable as we went. We had no trouble in finding the mound, and we estimated that it was about 500 yards from the nearest enemy position. It stood some 8 feet high, and must have covered an area of 10 square yards. It had obviously been used as an observation post before, because there was a shallow trench dug in the top. We enlarged this by scooping away the soft sand, and made a depression in which three men could lie. It would do.

The telephone was connected and I spoke to the Battalion Commander back in Tobruk, telling him that I intended to occupy the post. Two privates stayed with me while the rest of the men went back, and they left us well equipped. We had a good supply of water and bully-beef, a small sack full of hand grenades, a Bren machine-gun, a Thompson submachine-gun, my pistol and an ample supply of ammunition. The three of us lay down in our shallow hole and pulled the painted groundsheet over us.[2]

It was always exciting to see what the dawn revealed from a new position, and this was no exception. Appreciating that the mound we now occupied was an obvious landmark and therefore a likely artillery target, the enemy had kept clear of it. However, there were a series of defensive positions almost all round it; in fact, only to the north of us along the route which we had taken from Tobruk was it possible to approach the place without running into an enemy position. The nearest position to us was 400 yards away, which was not too bad. But what did disturb us was a watch tower 300 yards north of our mound. It consisted of a platform erected on the top of telegraph poles, and must have been some 30 feet high.

At about 9 a.m. when the sun was well up, three Germans walked across from one of the enemy posts and climbed on to the platform, and throughout the day they took turns in watching to the north through a pair of binoculars. They probably could just see Tobruk perimeter. So long as they did not turn round and look south, we felt we were safe. We, too, had a grandstand view from our 8-feet high mound. On all three sides of us there was a great deal of activity. Lorries drove up to the various positions and unloaded stores, parades were held, and long lines of men queued up at the cookhouse for their meals. I kept up a running commentary to Tobruk, and soon an artillery officer came on the line – he said he had moved some guns up to the perimeter from where he could shell these enemy positions. Using my compass and judging the distance, I was able to give him fairly accurate locations of these groups of men. Soon the shells were landing in among them.

Two mobile canteen lorries drove up and stopped close to one of the positions. Through my binoculars I could clearly see the salesman open up his shutters and prepare for business. I plotted the position, passed on the information to the gunners, and suggested that they wait until I gave the word to open fire. It was not long before a crowd of soldiers gathered round, and I could see that business was brisk. Then down came the shells and the crowd scattered back to their dugouts. But the lorry stayed on. When the shelling stopped an ambulance drove up, and I saw several bodies hoisted aboard. Then the crowd started collecting again and business was resumed. Three times I spoiled that man's trade, and in the end he gave up and drove away. His windscreen had been smashed by a shell.

Not far to the south of our mound, I could see the bypass road which the enemy had built round Tobruk perimeter, and which his vehicles now used on their journeys to and from Bardia and the frontier. It was a busy road and it was normally free from interference by the Tobruk Garrison, being well out of view. However, on this day, any collection of vehicles that were either travelling close together or happened to halt on the sector of road which I could see, received rough treatment from the Tobruk artillery. All day long I kept our artillery supplied with targets, and I was enjoying myself at the expense of the enemy. I hardly noticed the heat, the flies or even the slight dust storm that blew for about an hour at midday. I was so busy that I had no time to bother about food or even a drink.

About 3 o'clock in the afternoon one of the Aussies with me called my attention to the three men on the watch tower. It must have been painfully obvious to them that this area, which was normally never shelled, was now under close observation, and they in their turn were looking round for the observers. They must have examined every bit of scrub and every stone to the north of their tower, and they found nothing. Then they searched east and west, but still with no result. Now we could see them looking south, and we lay very still. One of them pointed down to where we lay, and the men with the binoculars focused them on us. Then the three of them climbed down from their perch and ran across to the nearest line of trenches. I phoned the artillery officer, and asked him to be prepared to give us a little support when we were attacked, and he wished us luck.

We saw them the moment they left their trenches, and there must have been about fifty of them. They moved across the desert in extended order, and their bayonets glinted in the afternoon sun. Our shells fell close to them, but on they came, and soon I had to tell the artillery to stop firing as the shells were beginning to land close to our mound. The two Aussie privates were itching to open fire, and I had a difficult time restraining them. Then the enemy party split up into four groups and surrounded the mound. We lay very still and waited. Closer and closer they came, and there was no sound except for the occasional sharp word of command given by one of their officers.

When the nearest group was within 15 yards of our position. I gave the order to open fire. The effect was like a damp squib going off. The Tommy-gun fired about six rounds, then stopped. The Bren gun fired one round, and stopped. The dust storm which had blown up earlier on had filled the working parts with fine sand. But these few shots were sufficient to make these soldiers drop to the ground, and I heard one man cry out in agony. Then the fun really started. Each enemy group had at least one machine-gun, and these and the rifles sent a hail of bullets in our direction. For some reason I was not wearing my tin hat, and one of the Australians noticed. 'For heaven's sake, put your tin hat on,' he yelled. 'If you hold your finger up, you will get it shot off, the bullets are coming so thick and fast.' And to illustrate the point, he poked one finger up in the sky, only to pull it down with an oath less than a second later; the tip was shot off.

Although the trench in which we were lying was less than 6 inches deep, it was just sufficient to give us shelter from the ever increasing stream of bullets that came at us from every direction, and we knew we were safe from a bayonet charge so long as these idiots continued to fire from all round our position. I ordered the two Australians to lie on their backs and start tossing hand grenades over the side of our trench. With the sack between them, they were soon busy pulling out the safety-pins and deftly flicking these deadly grenades over the side, and each one rolled down the slope and burst among the enemy. Meanwhile, I worked like a madman cleaning up our two guns. I got the Tommy-gun going, and handed it back to its owner, who now set about the task of killing off the enemy one by one. Then both guns were working.

Some instinct made me turn my head and look in the direction from where we thought the enemy were all dead. One bold man was charging up alone with his rifle at the ready, and the bayonet at the end of it was aimed at my stomach. I grabbed my revolver and fired at him. It was the best shot of my life; I hit him between the eyes and he fell back dead, not two yards from me.

All was then quiet. I picked up the telephone and Lt Col Evans answered me. He told me that he had sent three Bren gun carriers to our assistance. I thanked him, but told him that they would not last long in our present area, as every enemy soldier was by this time on the alert. Sure enough, as the three little tracked vehicles came charging down towards us, every gun that could bring fire to bear on them opened up. But on they came, and the three of us raised a hoarse cheer. They did not dare stop for a second, and we were relieved when they circled round a few hundred yards from us and disappeared back towards Tobruk. They were lucky not to be hit, and there are not many soldiers who would drive a vehicle through a barrage of fire such as these men faced that afternoon.

Then the enemy turned his guns on to us, and shell after shell exploded round us. If any of the fifty men were still alive, this shelling must have killed them, because they did not have even the protection of a shallow trench. About 1,000 yards to the south of us I could just make out a large number of the enemy moving slowly in our direction, and behind them was a tank. As the smoke and dust from the enemy shells closed in on us, we could see very little. Therefore we, too, would not be seen if we got out of our hole. By this time our telephone wire was cut, and later I was told that it was considered we would not be seen or heard of again after the damage we had caused.

Carrying our weapons and the telephone, we rolled down the little hill and joined the dead at the bottom. Here we exchanged our shallow steel helmets for the coal-scuttle type worn by the enemy. By this time the shelling had eased off, and in comparative safety we got to our feet and started staggering off in the general direction of Tobruk. We limped and held our heads and did what we could to convince the thousand eyes that were watching our every movement that we were survivors from the fifty-strong attacking party.

The shelling stopped and we walked on across the silent desert. As we passed beneath the watch tower, somebody shouted at us in a foreign language, and glancing to my right I could see two soldiers standing on top of a trench beckoning to us. I pretended not to see and limped on. My greatest desire was to start running, and one of the Australians suggested that we should do so, but I knew that once we started to run every gun would be turned on us. So very slowly, it seemed, we moved past one after another enemy post, and all the time we could hear the shouts as the occupants tried to attract our attention. I hope I never again have to experience the nervous strain of that walk.

We must have been about 500 yards north of the last enemy post when the first few bullets kicked up the sand around us, and only then did we start to run. Soon there were a number of machine-guns firing at us, then they shelled us. Every pace took us closer to Tobruk and safety, but we had over 6,000 yards to cover and soon my lungs felt as if they were about to burst. At last the shelling stopped, and we were beyond the range of the machine-guns. But still we ran. I knew there was still danger, and my fears were confirmed by the sound of clattering tracks and the steady hum of an engine. I shouted the word 'Tank', and tried to increase speed. Then I heard the scream of shells and the dull thud as they burst behind us. The Tobruk artillery was engaging our pursuer.

Just as the sun was setting, we saw the perimeter wire and heard the cheering of the men of our battalion. They walked forward to meet us, and helped us over the shallow anti-tank ditch. Somebody thrust a bottle neck between my parched lips, and I drank greedily. It was neat rum, and I had not had an alcoholic drink for many weeks. My knees sagged, and I crumbled to the ground drunk. To this day I detest even the smell of rum.

I spent the next few nights in more or less the same area trying to find another lying-up position which would give us the same field of vision, but one that was not so close to a watch tower as the last. In the end we did select a position that seemed eminently suitable, and we spent the whole of one night preparing it. The next night five of us occupied it, and anxiously awaited the daylight. As the Germans were now using tanks to hunt us out of these daylight hides, we included an anti-tank gun in our armoury. We spent an interesting day, but our view was nothing like as good as from the mound position; however, we were able to direct the artillery on to several juicy targets, and we were certainly not bored.

At about 3 p.m. the telephone tinkled, and the operator back in Tobruk told me he had a call for me from Divisional Headquarters. Most unusual, I thought. 'Where the hell have you been? I have been trying to get in touch with you for the last two hours.' He was one of the staff officers, and I knew he was sitting in comfort in one of the deep dugouts which Headquarters occupied. I did not like staff officers!

Before I had a chance to tell him where I was, he went on to say that I was to report back to Cairo as soon as possible; I was to proceed immediately to his office to collect my documents and then go down to the harbour and await the destroyers which would arrive at midnight. 'But I can't move from my position until dark,' I explained, and then he really did get angry, and ordered me to do what I was told.

At that moment one of the Australians nudged me, and pointed across the desert. A German tank was slowly moving forward towards our position. I twisted the handle of the phone and got the operator to cut out the irate staff officer and connect me to the artillery. The tank stopped about 1,000 yards short of our position, and started shooting at a pile of rocks some 20 yards from us. As it was doing us no harm, we took no retaliatory action, and after about an hour it turned round and went away. The only damage it did was to cut our telephone line with one of its shells, and it would have been madness to have ventured out to repair the line. I remembered the staff officer and laughed to myself. Yet I wondered why I was wanted back in Cairo so urgently.

We were due to be relieved that night, and our orders were to wait until the relief party arrived. They turned up about an hour after dark, and I was told to get back to the perimeter as fast as possible. Here I was met by a truck and I was bustled into it, and off it set bouncing across the dark desert. Then we were on the road and I told the driver he must stop when we were near the squadron caves, but his instructions were to take me to the harbour as fast as possible, and not to stop. I was too tired, cold and thirsty to argue.

I suppose I arrived at the quayside a few minutes before midnight, and here again there was no time to argue or ask questions. I was led off to a boat, and as I stepped on board Walter Benzie ran down the steps after me. I did not even have a chance to shake his hand, but we shouted good luck to each other across the water, and I felt very lonely. I wondered how many of my friends I would see again, and I did not like the thought of leaving Tobruk.

The destroyer was already under way when the small craft that carried me out from the quay reached her, and I had a few anxious moments climbing aboard – it was just as well I had no luggage, not even a toothbrush. I was shown down into the ward room where about a dozen army officers were being looked after by the ship's doctor. They all stared at me as I walked in, and it was only later that I realized what a sight I presented. I was covered in dust from head to foot, I was unshaven, and my clothes consisted of a filthy khaki shirt, a pair of shorts that were even worse, and a pair of brown gym shoes. The doctor gave me a pint of beer, and I was so thirsty that I even forgot to thank him. It was gone in a few seconds, and he gave me another. This went the same way, and for the second time in a week, I collapsed drunk to the world.

Notes

1.   For a full and comprehensive account of the siege I can recommend: *Tobruk, the Great Siege Reassessed*, Frank Harrison, Arms & Armour Press, 1996.

2.   Rea Leakey's escapades with the Australians were the subject of a picture-script story in *Victor* magazine.

CHAPTER EIGHT

A Break from the Desert

Editor After many months 'Up the Blue', Rea Leakey was about to have his first real break from the desert war, having been selected, much against his personal wishes, to attend the Staff College at Haifa in Palestine. There were three Army Staff Colleges operating during the Second World War – one in the UK at Camberley, Surrey; which had originally opened in April 1858 in the buildings of the RMC, then four years later (1862) moved to another fine building close by; secondly, at Quetta, India (now in Pakistan), which opened in July 1905 for officers of the Indian and British Armies serving in India and the Far East; finally, the temporary wartime college for officers serving in the Middle East, at Haifa. All were charged with the provision of command and staff courses intended to teach the rudiments of staff work – vital in wartime just as in peacetime, but as we have already seen, staff officers and the workings of the 'gilded staff', were an anathema to Rea. However, despite all his attempts to frustrate them, the 'powers that be' had eventually captured this reluctant embryo staff officer and would train him accordingly.

Brevity. While he was thus engaged being staff-trained, the desert war had continued, with the defenders of Tobruk continuing to do their job so well that Berlin forbade Rommel to make any more attacks. Gen Franz Halder's deputy, Lt Gen Freidrich Paulus, was sent out to make an on-the-spot report and Rommel was summarily told to regard the holding of Cyrenaica as being his primary mission, regardless of whether or not he took Tobruk. The OKH (Oberkommando des Heeres – the Army High Command) had rightly appreciated that the British were about to attack very soon. Churchill was insistent that Wavell should start an offensive to win back Cyrenaica and relieve Tobruk. This led to two badly conceived operations, named 'Brevity' and 'Battleaxe'. The first was launched on 15 May in three places: at Halfaya Pass; at Sollum and Fort Capuzzo; and on the desert left flank. The Pass was quickly taken and so was Fort Capuzzo but only after heavy fighting. Rommel thought this was the start of a major offensive and sent in an immediate counter-attack which recaptured the Fort. However, when the DAK probed further forward they found that the British had withdrawn to the Pass and, ten days later, 8 Pz Div recaptured it, outflanking the British positions and forcing the defenders to withdraw.

Battleaxe. Although 'Brevity' had had to be abandoned, the arrival of the 'Tiger' convoy, bringing some 240 new tanks to Alexandria on 24 May, encouraged Wavell to mount another offensive, codenamed 'Battleaxe'. 'The Tiger now only needs to grow claws' signalled Wavell to Churchill on 25 May and three days later he was confirming that he was ready to attack again. However, the Germans had also received reinforcements, namely 15 Panzer Division. The second division for the DAK had arrived in three convoys on 24 April, 2 and 6 May, with a total of 146 tanks, of which 71 were the highly effective PzKpfw IIIs and 20 the even more powerful PzKpfw IVs. The Halfaya Pass garrison now comprised some 900 German and Italian troops, with considerable anti-tank and artillery weapons, including five of the dreaded 88mm AA guns which had proved so devastating in the ground anti-tank role. The Pass was under the command of a remarkable soldier, Capt (ex-pastor) Wilhelm Bach, who would later win glory defending it against all comers. The intention behind 'Battleaxe' was to break through the German-Italian defences on the Egyptian/Libyan border, drive to Tobruk and then exploit to Derna and Mechili. A major frontal attack would be made on Halfaya Pass, using the newly arrived Matilda Mk II tanks, plus part of 4th Indian Infantry Division, while a rebuilt 7th Armoured Division swept around on the desert flank and 4th Armd Bde, plus elements of 4th Indian Div went for Fort Capuzzo and Point 206. This would be followed by a second phase, moving on Sollum the coast. Rommel was, however, prepared for all these eventualities.

The offensive began on 15 June and initially the British did well. However, on the following day the progress slowed and the enemy began to counter-attack. Heavy tank battles followed, with severe casualties to both sides and two days later, on 17 June, losses were so bad that the offensive had to be called off. The British had lost nearly half of the tanks committed. The German's skilful use of their own armour to draw enemy tanks on to the anti-tank screens was well demonstrated, especially at Halfaya Pass, where Pastor Wilhelm Bach knocked out eleven Matildas on 15 June alone.[1] Having blunted the British attack, Rommel then went on to the offensive, so that by 17 June they were back at Halfaya Pass, and, although the bulk of the British armour had made its escape, losses on both sides were considerable, final figures being: British losses – 220 tanks (although only 87 were complete write-offs the rest were repairable); German losses – 100 (this was the British claim although Rommel put his losses at 25). The 'Desert Fox' was once again triumphant, writing home on 23 June: 'I've been three days on the road, going round the battlefield. The joy of the Afrika troops over this latest victory is tremendous. The British thought they could overwhelm us with their 400 tanks. We couldn't put that amount of armour against them, but our grouping and the stubborn resistance of German and Italian troops who were surrounded for days together, enabled us to make the decisive operation with all the forces we still had mobile. Now the enemy can come, he'll get an even bigger beating.'

Crusader. One of the immediate results of the failure of 'Brevity' and 'Battleaxe' was the replacement of Wavell by Gen Sir Claude Auchinleck, while the British and Empire troops in the desert were grouped together to form the Eighth Army under Lt Gen Sir Alan Cunningham. Almost immediately Auchinleck found himself under pressure from Churchill to launch another offensive, which led to Operation 'Crusader' being launched on 18 November. Its aims were to relieve Tobruk and, at the same time, destroy as much enemy armour as possible, thus forcing Rommel to withdraw. The most important result was the major tank battle of Sidi Rezegh, in which both sides fought themselves to a standstill, with extremely heavy casualties.

1 Rea Leakey's parents, Gray and Elizabeth. (*A.R. Leakey*)

2 The four Leakey children in Kenya in 1923. *Left to right*: Nigel (aged 11), Robert (aged 9), Rea (aged 8) and Agnes (aged 7). (*A.R. Leakey*)

3 Visiting the Palace. Batch 'N', comprising nine immaculately dressed, newly commissioned RTC Young Officers, leaving the gates of Buckingham Palace, after attending a levee held there in 1936. They were accompanied by the redoubtable Maj Gen Sir Ernest Swinton, KBE, CB, DSO, then Representative Colonel Commandant of the Regiment which he had played such a major role in forming during the First World War. (*A.R. Leakey*)

4 On board HMT Nevasa just before sailing to Egypt, 18 March 1938. Rea is seen here with Basil Forster (in uniform) and F.L. Gates (another YO of Batch 'N'). The lady is Mrs Forster. (*A.R. Leakey*)

5 Lt Col 'Blood' Caunter was Rea's CO in 1 RTC. He is seen here briefing officers and NCOs of the 1st (Light) Battalion, RTC, during a prewar exercise held on Salisbury Plain in 1937. (*Tank Magazine, May 1982*).

6 Vickers Light Mk VIBs of 1 RTC on manoeuvres near the Pyramids, 24 January 1939. (*Editor's collection*)

Topee flash 1939-41 and Vehicle sign 1939-45

7 The original 7th Armd Div sign with the Desert Rat superimosed on top of the Mobile Division white circle. (*Editor's collection*)

8 War imminent! 1 RTR crews being briefed, 24 August 1939. Note that they wear black denims, some carry respirators and wear solar topees, while the sergeant-major in KD has black hosetops. (*Editor's collection*)

9 The battered walls of Fort Capuzzo, which constantly changed hands during the war in the desert and was the scene of one of Rea's lucky escapes. (*Editor's collection*)

10 The delights of Cairo, such as Groppi's tea gardens seen here, were always there ready to refresh desert-weary warriors! (*Editor's collection*)

11 The architects of Op Compass, O'Connor and Wavell. (*IWM – E 1549*)

12 Col Birks briefing members of the garrison of Tobruk on plans for their aggressive defence posture, using an ad hoc sand table model. In the middle of the group of five RTR soldiers appears to be the familiar face of Rea Leakey. (*IWM – E 6854*)

13 Red Flag Corner, junction of Tobruk, Derna and Bardia roads. The flag was hoisted during air raids to warn MT drivers who were unable to hear the noise of the aircraft above their own engine noises. A POL issuing point can just be seen in the background below the sign. (*Editor's collection*)

14 Outside Tobruk, the Germans take a breather before mounting another assault on the fortress, while their artillery hammers away at the defences. (*Editor's collection*)

15 There was no let up in the desert war while Rea was in Haifa. Here a German panzer burns on a desert battlefield. (*Editor's collection*)

16 451 Sqn, RAAF. A.R.L. in a dugout at Sidi Azeiz, Libya, 1941. (*A.R. Leakey*)

17 The new 'player' on the British side was Lt Gen Bernard Montgomery – seen here in his Grant tank – who arrived to take command of the Eighth Army. His charismatic, dedicated approach would breathe new life into the British troops. (*Tank Museum*)

18 'The Dustman', Rea Leakey's batman, who started badly but rapidly became indispensable to him. However, he sadly had to leave him behind at Shaiba on 1 April 1943. (*A.R. Leakey*)

19 A.R.L. skiing on Mount Lebanon. (*A.R. Leakey*)

20 Shermans of the Eighth Army break through at Gabes Gap in early April 1943, about the same time as Rea joined 3 RTR. (*IWM – BNA 1812*)

21 Excellent shot of a Sherman belonging to 44 RTR in Italy. The snow-capped mountains and winter wear of the tank crew show that Christmas will soon be here. However, the Regiment will be home in February 1944, to prepare for the invasion of Normandy. (*Tank Museum*)

22 A waterproofed Sherman landing from a Landing Craft Tank (LCT) on to the beach in Normandy. Note the waterproofing around the gun and the engine breather towers sticking up through the back decks. On this occasion there was no need for the waterproofing as the tank could easily wade through the shallows. (*Tank Museum*)

23 44 RTR Sherman M4A1s and a half-track, passing through a French village. (*Tank Museum*)

24 Before Dunkirk came the assault on Le Havre in which the 'Funnies' of 79th Armd Div played a major part. Here are some of their specialized armour 'marrying up' with the infantry. They include a Sherman 'Crab' mine flail followed by a bridgelayer. The Crab was the most successful of all flail type mine-clearing devices, with 43 flailing chains on a rotor which was driven via a power take-off from the main engine. (*Tank Museum*)

25 Rea Leakey with Maj Gen Alois Lishka and other Czech officers after receiving the Czech Military Cross, at an Investiture Parade on 6 May 1945. (*A.R. Leakey*)

26 Tanks of RHQ 5 RTR, near Hamburg. (*A.R. Leakey*)

27 Signboard indicating the last location of RHQ 5 RTR at the end of the war. (*A.R. Leakey*)

28 Rea Leakey in his RHQ tank 'Long John Silver II', on his way past the saluting base at the Victory Parade, held in Berlin, on 21 July 1945. (*A.R. Leakey*)

29 The Leakey family attend a very special ceremony at Buckingham Palace, in June 1946, when they received Nigel Leakey's posthumous Victoria Cross. Album caption reads: *L to R*: Dr Buchman (*Oxford Group MRA*) C. Gillbrand, Agnes, Bremer, Dad, self. (*A.R. Leakey*)

30 Rea Leakey accompanying HM King Hussein, during a visit to his armoured car regiment. (*A.R. Leakey*)

31 Rea Leakey, GOC Malta and Libya, with his ADC, Capt Roger Meares. (*A.R. Leakey*)

Although the Germans could be said to have won the battle, the eventual outcome of 'Crusader' was a territorial advantage to the British. In addition, Rommel was running short of everything. The 'elastic' had stretched just that little bit too far and he was forced to order a general withdrawal, so that by the end of 1941, he was right back at El Agheila where he had started some nine months previously.

Rommel attacks. Just three short weeks after he had withdrawn into Tripolitania, Rommel and his DAK were on their way forward once again, bolstered by the arrival of more reinforcements. This time it was the British who were over-extended and vulnerable. After some moments of chaos, the front was at last stabilized along the Gazala–Bir Hacheim line, where it remained for the next three months while both sides again built up their strength. It was here, on the 'Gazala Line' that Rea Leakey returned to the desert war, still refusing to be a staff officer and destined, as we shall see, to have a personal encounter with the 'Desert Fox'.

Rea Leakey The journey from Tobruk to Alexandria was not uneventful; the destroyer was attacked by aircraft on three occasions, but suffered only slight damage from 'near misses'. At least this is what I was told when they finally woke me up, and we were then in Alexandria harbour. I wasted no time in getting to Cairo and still clad in my filthy clothes I reported to Lt Col George Webb, who was one of the Royal Armoured Corps staff officers in GHQ. He was an old friend of mine, and he hardly recognized me. I asked why, and he said I was so thin. Tobruk had left its mark; when I went there in April 1940 I must have weighed just under 12 stone, and when George weighed me in his office five months later, I was 8 stone 2 pounds. He told me I had been selected to attend a course at the Staff College at Haifa in Palestine. I thought he was pulling my leg, as I was still very young to attend such a course, and I thought he knew of my dislike for Staff Officers.

When I realized he was serious I started to protest and asked to be sent back to Tobruk, but he would listen to none of my arguments. I had to go and be taught to be a staff officer, and that was that. He then told me that, as I had virtually no staff experience, he had got me back to Cairo a week before the course started, so that I could spend this time sitting in with one of the staff officers in GHQ, and thus glean a little knowledge. I realized that there was no point in trying to argue with him, so I set off down the corridors to find this officer. When he saw me, he told me to go away and get some clean clothes and a bath before daring to set foot in his office again. I did not relish the thought of working with him, even for only a week.

I headed for Shepherds Hotel in the hope of finding somebody who would buy me a drink. As I walked up the steps to the entrance, the Provost Marshal (a Brigadier, I believe) was coming down. He stopped me and told me the hotel was for officers only – I had not yet bought badges of rank. I explained my position, but he would not believe me and started to complain about my dirty clothes. He was very unpleasant to me and started to hit me with his 'swagger stick'. I used to box for my Regiment, and I 'tapped' him on the chin. He sank to his knees, and I continued on my way to the bar.

Four South African Air Force officers witnessed the scene and followed me. They said I had their sympathy and bought me a beer. One of them went to the hall and soon returned. 'Man,' he said, 'your friend has come to and has sent for reinforcements – I suggest you follow us to the back door before you are arrested for striking a superior officer.' They had a staff car waiting for them and the five of us drove off before the Military Police caught up with us.

'Where are you going?' I asked.

'To Heliopolis Airport – we fly a shuttle service from Cape Town to Cairo.'

'Would you by any chance be going via Kenya?' Yes, they were, and they agreed to take me with them. I explained that I had been born in Kenya, and that my father still farmed there. I had left to go to school in England when I was 12 years old, and I had not seen him since.

Fortunately nobody at the airport asked to see my papers – I had none – and an hour after leaving Shepherds Hotel I was sitting in a comfortable passenger plane heading for Nairobi. That night we stopped at Wadi Halfa and the crew could not have been more helpful. We stayed at an RAF station and they bought me the necessities of life – I had no money.

Next day we flew to Khartoum airport to refuel. Soon after we landed, the plane coming north from Cape Town joined us. One of the passengers was a tall thin Brigadier, and he recognized me as a fellow British Officer. 'You have obviously just come from the Western Desert. What is happening there?' I told him I had been in Tobruk, so had little knowledge of the position on the Frontier.

'Where are you going?'

'To Kenya, sir.'

'How nice, have you been given a job there?'

'No, I am going to visit my parents.'

'So you are on leave?'

'Well, no, not quite. I am supposed to be doing a week's staff work in GHQ, Cairo, before going to the Haifa Staff College. However, the officer under whom I was to work was so rude to me that I decided I would learn little from him.'

'So you decided on a few days leave instead. Good for you. Are you pleased with the idea of going to the Staff College?'

'Not really – I have no wish to be a member of the "Short Range Shepherds Group" and anyhow I have no idea when I will return to Cairo.'

'Don't say any more. I happen to be the Commandant of the Staff College, and I look forward to seeing you in six days' time. Enjoy yourself.'

We landed at Nairobi airport at about 11 a.m. the next day and I had no difficulty in getting a lift into town. Now came the problem of making contact with my father, whose farm was at Kiganjo, 100 miles from Nairobi, and I had no money. I remembered that my father was a great friend of Dr Anderson, who lived in Nairobi. I borrowed 10 cents from the girl at the desk of the New Stanley Hotel, and got his secretary. I gave my name and tried to explain my problem, but she cut me short. 'This is the surgery, and we are very busy. Be at the entrance of the New Stanley Hotel at 2 p.m. and I will arrange for a car to pick you up.'

At 2 p.m. I took my stand outside the hotel, and I did not have long to wait. A maroon-coloured Chevrolet car drove up and stopped. My father was the driver. He very seldom visited Nairobi, especially during the war years, but when he did he usually stayed with the Andersons. He was not a little surprised to see me. His last information of me was that I was reported missing in the Western Desert. Not three months before he had been told that my eldest brother, Nigel, was 'missing, believed killed' fighting in Abyssinia. Unfortunately, in this case the information proved to be correct. My brother was killed in a battle with some Italian tanks. He was serving as an infantryman in the King's African Rifles, and when his position was overrun by these tanks he managed to destroy at least two of them by jumping on to them, prising open the lids and shooting the crews. He was awarded the Victoria Cross. His body was never found.

When he had got over the shock of seeing me, I told my father that I was on 'French leave', and before we disappeared upcountry I had better try and fix my return passage to Cairo. So next morning we visited Army Headquarters in Nairobi; I tried my luck with the staff officer who dealt with Air Movements. He was unusually rude, even for a harassed Staff Officer, and I got no change out of him. He told me I had not a chance of getting a seat on a plane without the GOC in C's personal approval, and even the sea passages were all booked up for the next three months. I explained that the Staff College course only lasted four months, and if I went by boat I would miss the whole course, but he could not care less.

I left him in disgust, and wandered down the various corridors looking at the names on the doors. At last I found one that I thought knew, 'Major Lyons. GSO 2 (Plans)'. There was a Maj 'Tiger' Lyons in the Royal Tank Regiment, and I remembered him telling me that he had a brother who was a farmer in Kenya. It was a fair bet that this was the brother, now serving in the Army. I walked into the office and asked one of the two occupants if he was Maj Lyons. Yes, he was Maj Lyons. 'I thought I recognized you. I know your brother, Tiger. I suppose you know he was taken prisoner at Calais?'

And so we got talking, and at last he asked if he could do anything for me. 'Well, perhaps you could do me a small favour. Would you get the C in C to sign a paper authorizing me to have a priority air passage back to Cairo. Most important I get back there in the next day or so.'

Ten minutes later I walked out of his office armed with the necessary certificate, and I had much pleasure in waving it in the face of the Air Movements Officer. But he won the day! Yes, he would now put me on the next plane to Cairo, but I would have to pay my own passage, £75. I then realized that this, the next plane, would land me in Cairo on the day I was to report to the Staff College. A pity that I should be late, but it could not be helped. I would take my punishment. In the meantime I intended to enjoy myself.

What a joy it was to be back on the farm, fish for trout in the cool forest streams and to meet friends who knew me when I was a boy. One of these was a Kikuyu who had once been my male nurse when I was a baby. I was spoilt by everybody, and I loved it! Then all too soon came the time to part, and I found it very hard to say farewell to my father and to Kenya.

I landed in Cairo at about 6 p.m. on a Sunday evening, and I should have reported to the Staff College that morning at the latest. However, I was determined to get there in time for work, which I knew would probably start at 9 a.m. on the Monday morning. Fortunately I still owned a small car which I had left with friends in Cairo. They also kept my clothes, and would always give me a bed in their house. I soon had them busy packing up my belongings and getting the car ready for the long journey to Haifa.

I fell asleep at the wheel twice while driving across the Sinai Desert, but somehow managed to keep going throughout the night, and as dawn was breaking I passed through the deserted streets of Jerusalem. In Haifa I had a certain amount of trouble finding the Staff College, but in the end one of the Jewish inhabitants directed me to the top of Mount Carmel, and there I found it.

'Ah, the missing student!' said the hall porter as I walked into the hall. 'But hurry, sir, down the passage and first door on the left. They are all in there waiting for the Commandant who is to give the opening address.' As I walked in one door leading to the main lecture hall, he came in through another, and he recognized me at once. 'Well done, you have fifteen seconds to spare. Go and sit down.'

Looking back on it now, I realize that my superiors knew that it was time I should come out of the desert and away from the fighting. I enjoyed the four months we spent in Palestine, and after forty-four years I still keep in touch with fellow students in Australia, New Zealand, South Africa, and, of course, Britain.

In November 1941, Operation 'Crusader' was launched with the object of driving Rommel and his men out of Cyrenaica. Gen Wavell had been replaced by Gen Auchinleck as C in C. Naturally we followed every move of the battle with interest, and many wished they were back with their regiments. We had not long to wait. On 2 January 1942, the course ended. The Commandant, Brig Dorman Smith, sent for me. 'Leakey, I cannot fail you, so you have got to accept a staff appointment. There are ninety-eight of you, and this is the list of appointments to be filled. Take your pick.' He was an able Officer, and rose to the rank of major general on the staff, but, like a number of others of his rank, he fell foul of Gen Montgomery and left the Army an embittered man, and highly critical of 'Monty'.

I was given the job of my choice, GSO 2 Air Intelligence Liaison Officer with 451 Royal Australian Air Force Squadron, and a few days later I joined them at Sidi Azeiz airfield, not many miles from Fort Capuzzo. They were a reconnaissance squadron equipped with Hurricanes, and my task was to brief the pilots on what the Army wanted them to look for. It was an interesting appointment, and it was good to be back with the Aussies. In February the squadron was withdrawn from the Western Desert, and we found ourselves at Rayak in Syria. At this time there was no enemy activity in this part of the world, so we spent our time exploring the country and training. There was plenty of desert stretching as far as Baghdad, Amman and Kuwait, and we would send out teams of ground-crewmen to establish forward landing areas many hundreds of miles from our base. The squadron commander, Wg Cdr 'Dixie' Chapman taught me to fly a two-seater plane which had been 'acquired'. He enjoyed his pint or two of beer and on one occasion after an alcoholic lunch, he turned to me and recommended a breath of fresh air. We took off and set course to fly to a small base that had been established in the desert some 200 miles away in the general direction of Baghdad.

After being airborne for some ten minutes, Dixie waved his joy stick in the air with the comment, 'All yours, I am going to sleep'. He removed his headphones and did just that. Two hours later I noticed that we were getting short of fuel, and there was no sign of the three or four vehicles that formed the so-called base. I was sitting in the rear seat and there was no way I could contact Dixie, unless I discovered how to extract my joy stick and hit him on the head with it. So I circled round until I found a reasonably flat area. We spent a cold night sitting in the plane with no food or drink. Next morning the squadron was sent out to find us, which they did at about midday. They were a happy-go-lucky lot, those Aussies.

On 26 May 1942 I received a signal from GHQ Cairo ordering me to report there as soon as possible. On the same day Rommel launched a major attack against the British so-called 'Gazala Line', consisting of fortified localities, known as 'Boxes', which stretched from the sea at Gazala to Bir Hacheim 40 miles to the south-east.

At this time I owned my own Jeep – that versatile small American vehicle which seldom failed – so it was not long before I was on my way to Cairo. I reported to Lt Col George Webb, who congratulated me on my rapid move from Syria, and then told me the bad news. No, I was not returning to 1 RTR, who were now heavily engaged in battle; I was to proceed to Baghdad to become a Staff Officer of HQ 10th Army.

I thought he was pulling my leg but soon realized that he meant it. I got angry and told him that I would not obey the order. He had no alternative but to bring me before his superior – Maj Gen Richard McCreery. 'So you refuse to go to Iraq. You deserve a Court Martial, but I feel you are tired after your long journey. Go away, have a bath and a sleep, and report back here at 5 p.m.' When I returned, he told me I must go to Baghdad, but I could take ten days' leave. I could spend this time in the Western Desert, but I was not to get involved in the fighting, and under no circumstances was I to overstay my leave. I felt that much could happen in ten days, and it did.

Later that same night I set out for the front alone in my Jeep, and I drove all night. At about 10 a.m. next morning, I passed through the ruins of Fort Capuzzo, and here I met an old friend of mine, Maj Dennis Coulson. He was one of the twelve young officers in 1 RTR at the beginning of the war, but was now a squadron commander in 6 RTR. They were preparing to move forward to the area south of Tobruk, where by now the battle was raging. He offered me a job in his squadron, but I declined as I wanted to find Walter Benzie and my old crew.

Things had not gone well for us. Rommel sent his armour south, deep into the desert and round Bir Hacheim, which was our most southerly defended position of the Gazala Line. He then moved north-east in an endeavour to cut off the British forces. This move of his was not unexpected by the British Commander, Gen Ritchie, but things went wrong with his plans, and Rommel was able to take on each of our two armoured Divisions in turn. But, just as bad, was 7th Armoured Division's encounter with the enemy on the morning of 27 May. Armoured cars had been reporting the movements of the German armour throughout the night, and certainly HQ 30 Corps, commanded by Gen Norrie, were well aware of the enemy force moving round Bir Hacheim. The GSO 2 Operations was Maj (now FM) Mike Carver. He also was one of the twelve 1 RTR young Officers. The information from the armoured cars was passed on to HQ 7th Armoured Division by him, and he stated that he was up all night doing just this, but the GSO 1 of the Division – Lt Col Peter Pyman (RTR) does not seem to have passed it on to HQ 4th Armoured Brigade commanded by Brig Richards (RTR), because at 8 a.m. Rommel's tanks caught the 8th Hussars with their trousers down and 3 RTR in the process of pulling theirs up.

And that was not the end of the Division's troubles. Rommel's armoured cars over-ran a number of the HQ vehicles, including No.1 Armoured Command Vehicle (ACV). The 'bag' in this vehicle included the Divisional Commander, Maj Gen Messervy, the GSO 1, the GSO 2 – Maj Jim Richardson (RTR), and Capt Reid. They had time to remove their badges of rank, and a German Officer commented to Messervy that he was surely too old to be fighting in the desert. 'I am the Officers' Mess Cook', he replied. However, that night they escaped, and it was not long before HQ 7th Armoured Division was back to normal.

It was at this stage in the battle that I reached the forward area, and there was much confusion – not unusual in these desert battles. As darkness closed in, I was directed to an armoured divisional HQ It was the 1st and not the 7th which I was seeking. They suggested that I should stay the night with them and resume my search in the morning because they had no idea where the 7th were, but they confirmed that 1 RTR were under their command.

I drove my Jeep to the outskirts of the leaguer, climbed into my bedroll, and fell into a deep sleep. It was the noise of vehicles that awakened me and, although it was misty and the sun had not yet risen, I had no trouble in identifying the man who was staring down at me. He was in the turret of a British armoured vehicle which was adorned with the black Iron Cross.[2] Yes, it was Rommel with his escort of eight-wheeled armoured cars.

A few hours after I had fallen asleep, HQ 1st Armoured Division were warned that a large enemy column of enemy vehicles was heading their way, so they moved. They failed to wake me, and I was unaware of their departure.

Never have I acted so fast. Within seconds I was in the driving seat and off into the misty morning. But to this day I still recall the sound of guns being cocked and Rommel's voice shouting at his men. 'Nein, nein' were the words that I recall, and clearly he was saying, 'No, no, hold your fire, give the poor bastard a chance.' Then a hail of bullets whistled round my head, and once again my guardian angel looked after me.

By this time Rommel's situation was not too healthy. He had lost quite a proportion of his tanks, and he had failed to reach the sea and so cut off the British forces. His supply situation was desperate; despite very heavy attacks, the Free French Forces still held out at Bir Hacheim, which meant that Rommel's supply vehicles had to make a long detour round to the south, and they were constantly attacked by British armoured cars and aircraft. He realized that without a secure supply route it would be madness for him to continue advancing east or north, and so he turned west. Our line from the coast to Bir Hacheim was not a continuous line of defences; it consisted of a series of defended boxes which were connected by minefields. Rommel launched his full armoured force against one of these boxes and it fell. He now had a clear way through our line and back towards his own starting point. He pulled back most of his remaining tanks and held the entrance to the hole he had punched with a mass of anti-tank guns and infantry. This area became known as the Cauldron.

Throughout this period there was intensive and confused fighting in which neither side really knew exactly what was happening. We, too, had suffered heavy tank casualties, but there were still replacements available, and as fast as they reached the front so they were thrown into the battle. It was not until the afternoon of the day I met Rommel that I found 7th Armoured Division. By lunch I had found HQ 4th Armoured Brigade, and at last I was among old friends. I had a long talk with Brig Richards, who commanded the Brigade, and even he was not too certain of the exact location of all the enemy positions on his part of the front. I asked him where my old Regiment was, and he pointed across the desert. In the dim distance I thought I could make out some tanks, so I climbed into my Jeep and headed towards them.

I had travelled about 2 miles when I had a feeling that all was not well; I was moving along in low ground and the place seemed unusually quiet.

I was not more than 100 yards from it when I noticed the long barrel of an 88 mm anti-tank gun slowly swinging round in my direction, and I could clearly see the grim German faces watching my every movement. I swung the Jeep round and put my foot hard on the accelerator, and for the second time that day I became the lone target for German soldiers. The anti-tank gun only fired one shell at me, and it missed me by inches; but a machine-gun gave me several most anxious moments and punctured both rear tyres. It was an exciting few minutes and I was lucky to escape untouched. There were at least a dozen bullet holes in the Jeep.

I had been in dead ground to the Brigadier and his staff, and at first they would not believe me when I told them I had been soundly shot up, and then all they did was to laugh at me, and told me it served me right for spending my leave in the desert. It was almost dark before I finally joined Walter Benzie and his squadron, and it was good to see his cheerful face again. Since I had left them in Tobruk the squadron had fought many battles, especially during the breakout from Tobruk. Only one member of my old crew remained, and this was Adams, my wireless operator; he was now a sergeant and a tank commander.

The squadron was equipped with American tanks, and for the first time in the desert war against the Germans we were meeting them on more or less even terms. These 'General Grant' tanks mounted a 75 mm gun which was about as good as the best German tank gun. But it was not mounted in the main turret; instead it was built into the front of the tank beside the driver. It had a very limited traverse, so that if the tank was not facing almost directly towards the target the chances were that the gun could not engage that target. Also, it was comparatively low down, so that when engaging a target the main bulk of the tank was exposed to the enemy, and these Grants were big tanks. They had a crew of six: a driver, a gunner and loader for the 75 mm gun; then in the main turret there was the commander, the wireless operator, and another gunner who fired the turret guns. These consisted of a 37 mm gun, which was the equivalent of our 2-pounder, and a machine-gun.

While I was talking to Benzie, one of his subalterns reported that the turret gunner in his tank had hurt his hand, and in consequence was not capable of firing the guns. There were no spare crews available. I told Walter I was quite prepared to act as gunner in this tank, and my offer was gladly accepted. Fortunately the man whose place I was taking could drive a vehicle, so I gave him my Jeep to look after, and he was delighted – so was I! And so started my short career as gunner in a Grant tank.

At dawn the next morning the Regiment was ordered to move south and attack a column of enemy vehicles, including tanks that were stuck in a minefield in the Cauldron area. By the time we found them, they had extricated themselves, and only a few remained. They soon withdrew when we opened fire, and we had orders not to follow them. At least I had the satisfaction of firing my first shot from an American tank.[3]

Now came a lull in the battle; each side was busy building up its strength for the next round which was bound to come in the next few days. During this period we were kept busy in the Cauldron area probing forward and inflicting casualties on the enemy wherever we got the chance. But we made little progress as the Germans seemed to have an unlimited number of anti-tank guns and, without strong artillery support it was madness to attack them. Every evening as the sun was setting, the German tanks would move forward and give battle. They had the sun behind them, and we were forced to look straight into it. But even so, they did not venture too close to us, and a long-range shooting match would only end when darkness closed in. Then only the burning tanks remained to mark the scene of battle.

To the south of us Bir Hacheim was being subjected to a series of attacks which mounted in fury as the days went on. We were sent down to try and help the gallant Free French, and we did manage to destroy several enemy tanks. But then we were recalled to the Cauldron area. A major tank thrust was to be launched against the enemy in this area, and never before or since have I known armour to be handled so badly. It shook my faith in the Senior Armoured Corps Commanders. Those responsible had been trained to handle horses, and in a few cases it required a year of war to convince these gentlemen that the day of the horse in battle was over. But, of course, I was only a gunner in a tank in this battle, and my knowledge of the larger picture was very limited. However, on this fateful day there were few who did not realize that we were being launched into an attack that was doomed to failure from the start. But ours was not to reason why.

Regiment after regiment of tanks moved up on either side of us and halted. Almost as far as the eye could see stretched this long line of tanks. We had artillery support but very little; as far as I can remember, our allotment was four guns and there was certainly no preliminary bombardment. Some 2 miles ahead of us the ground rose slightly, and then it fell away. It was here the enemy waited for us, not tanks but many carefully concealed anti-tank guns. At least the plan was simple; this great line of tanks that stretched across the desert was to roll forward, crash through the enemy and on to the undefended spaces beyond. I remember my CO protesting bitterly at the madness of this attack. He knew so well what lay beyond that ridge, but all he got for an answer was the sack.

At 10 o'clock the long line of tanks moved forward and the roar of hundreds of powerful engines filled the air and warned the waiting Germans that we were coming. As I sat with my eye glued to the gunner's periscope I thought of my old gunner, Milligan, and silently prayed that I might shoot as accurately as he. Sgt Adams was commanding the tank immediately on my right, and I wondered what jokes he was telling to keep his crew amused. The subaltern in command of my tank was nervous, and tried to conceal it by singing lustily. I checked the firing gear for the last time, and all was in order. The guns were loaded.

As we approached the crest of the rise, the order was given to speed up and the tanks on either side of us followed suit. But we were the first to reach the skyline, at least of those in our immediate vicinity, and as we came into full view of the enemy so the shells arrived. Clouds of smoke and dust soon blinded my vision and I never saw one of the many anti-tank guns that now started to take their toll. In the first second we must have received at least four direct hits from armour piercing shells. The engine was knocked out, a track was broken and one shell hit the barrel of the 75 mm gun and broke it. Then quite a heavy high explosive shell dropped on the mantlet of my 37 mm gun and pushed it back against the recoil springs. That shell landed inches above my head but the armour plating held firm, and I suffered nothing more than a 'singing in the ears'. But a splinter hit the subaltern in the head, and he fell to the floor of the turret dead. I found that my gun would not fire.

Almost every tank in that battle met with the same treatment, and the whole line was halted on the crest of that small ridge. I half climbed out of the gunner's seat so that I could see over the top of the turret, and the sight that met my eyes was terrifying. These Grant tanks carried a large supply of ammunition for the 75 mm gun stowed underneath the main turret. If an armour piercing shell happened to penetrate the armour and hit the ammunition, the result had to be seen to be believed.

Sgt Adams' tank was halted less than 10 yards from me, and as I looked across I saw him and his crew start to bale out. He had one leg out of the cupola when suddenly his tank just disintegrated; the turret, which weighed about 8 tons, went sailing into the air and landed with a dull thud in front of my tank; the sides of the tank split open with the force of the explosion and exposed what remained of the inside – a blazing jumble of twisted metal. Not a member of the crew had a chance of survival.

Benzie's squadron went into this action with a strength of twelve tanks. In under a minute all but one were in flames, and all along the line it was more or less the same story. Why my tank was not on fire was a mystery to me, we had been hit often enough. But we were now manning a useless lump of metal, we could not move, and our guns were out of action. Our orders were clear, 'No baling out unless the tank is on fire.' Anyhow, by now it was almost safer to stay where we were, because the whole area was still under heavy shell fire, although the anti-tank gunners were blinded by the pillars of black smoke that swirled up from each burning tank.

I bent down and removed the wireless headphones from our dead tank commander, and put them on. At least the wireless was still working, and I called up Regimental Headquarters. 'Why, are you still alive? Thank God somebody is.' I explained our position, and the Adjutant said he would send up a tank to try and tow us back when things had quietened down. I lit a cigarette and gave the wireless operator one, and so we sat and smoked in silence. There seemed to be little to talk about. After a while the shelling stopped and the dust and smoke began to clear. Then I looked at my gun and saw that the recoil springs had reasserted themselves so that now the gun would fire. I started to take an interest in life.

I looked through the periscope and now there was no need to search the ground with care to try and spot the enemy and his murderous guns. The battle for them was over for the time being and they stood around in the open beside their guns, admiring the line of burning tanks. They had every right to be pleased with themselves. There was one 88 mm gun not more than two hundred yards away, and the crew were literally dancing around with joy. Then three German tanks drove up and stopped broadside on to me not more than 500 yards away. My blood boiled.

I spoke to the Adjutant on the wireless and asked him to warn the Artillery to be prepared to fire smoke shells around my tank when I gave the word, and to have a tank ready to move up and tow mine out of action. When all was ready I slowly traversed the gun and got the dancing crew lined up in my sights. I pressed the trigger, and the fight was on. In a few seconds I had disposed of that crew and their gun, and I then switched my attention to the three tanks and had the satisfaction of seeing them go up in flames.

But that was not all. There were too many anti-tank guns around and this time my tank was the only target. A solid shell tore through the armour plating just above my head and buried itself in the wireless set at the top of the turret. Then several more penetrated and set the tank on fire. As soon as I had started firing I had told the driver and the 75 millimetre gun crew to get out and, thank goodness, they had done so. These tanks burned high grade aero petrol and in a matter of seconds the inside of the tank was a mass of roaring flames. The operator was out of the turret in a flash; he, too, had seen what happened when the ammunition exploded in one of these tanks. It was not an easy climb from the gunner's seat, but I was out of that turret faster than a champagne cork leaving the neck of a bottle. I had less than a second to spare, for as my feet touched the ground the tank exploded, and I saw the turret sail over my head. To say that I was frightened is to put it mildly.

The Germans had obviously seen us bale out, and poured machine-gun bullets at us. I dropped down and crawled back through the sand as fast as I could. When at last I was out of danger I stopped and looked around me. My crew was safe, and I told them to walk on back while I had a look round to make sure there were no wounded still lying out in this area. Yes, there was somebody else not far off, but he was obviously all right because he was calmly lighting a pipe. I walked over to him and wiped the filth off his face to see who it was. It was Dennis Coulson from the 6th Royal Tank Regiment, and he, too, had been brewed up. 'And what the hell are you doing?' I asked.

'Well,' he said in his broad Irish accent, 'I have just been brewed out of my twelfth tank, and it is away I am to find my thirteenth.' There are few men alive today who have been brewed up so often and are still sane. We walked back together to find new tanks.

Walter Benzie had escaped uninjured, and, in fact, I was surprised at the number of people who did come out of that massacre. But it was a useless slaughter and we could not afford to lose those tanks. In fact, Adams survived, but that is another story. That night some replacement tanks did come up, but only very few, and we were told these would be the last we should get for some time. Walter again gave me a place in one of the crews.

On 11 June Bir Hacheim fell, and that was the beginning of the end of the battle. This, combined with our heavy tank losses, gave Rommel his chance and he took it. Once again, his two Armoured Divisions swung round from the south and from the Cauldron area, and this time there was little to oppose him. Slowly but surely he started to push us back towards the Tobruk perimeter, and soon there was the danger that our two infantry divisions which were holding positions in the Gazala area would be cut off. We were told to prevent the German forces cutting the Tobruk–Gazala road, but it was an impossible task, and almost too late the order was given for the two Infantry Divisions to withdraw back through Tobruk.

Two days later I was told to report to Brig Richards. 'Jim Richardson has just been killed, and I have been asked to find a replacement as GSO 2 of 7th Armoured Division. Off you go.' I said farewell to Walter, and that was the last time I saw him.

Notes

1.   The gallant Capt Bach did not surrender until starvation forced him to do so on 17 January 1942, long after the rest of the DAK had been withdrawn.

2.   Rommel had captured three British Armoured Command vehicles – AEC Mk I – earlier in the campaign and had kept two for his own use. They were called 'Mammoths' (Mammuten) by the Germans and nicknamed 'Max' and 'Moritz' after two characters in a children's story by Wilhelm Busch. Rommel used them as part of his 'Gefechtsstaffel' (lit: 'Action Staff' or 'Fighting Echelon') which also contained armoured cars and staff cars. Rommel often used to drive one of the 'Mammuts' – one night driving by the stars across the desert to a new location, until it clouded over, so they had to wait until morning to complete their journey.

3.   The very generous American gesture of giving the British numerous modern tanks quite early on in the desert war, began with a batch of M3 lights (Stuarts) and M3 mediums (Grants and Lees). These latter were the first tank in British Army service with a decent-sized dual-purpose main gun (75 mm), since the Heavy Mk Vs of the First World War! Rommel was very shaken by the success of the Grant, writing in his diary: 'The advent of the new American tank has torn great holes in our ranks. Our entire force now stands in heavy and destructive combat with a superior enemy.' This new firepower was, however, completely lost in this particular engagement, as Rea Leakey explains, by the incompetence of some senior armoured corps commanders of the time.

CHAPTER NINE

Backs to the Wall

Editor As Rea Leakey mentioned at the end of the last chapter, the gallant Free French defenders of Bir Hacheim were forced to withdraw on the night 10/11 June, however, they had made Rommel expend a great amount of time and effort on them. Next day the panzers burst out of the 'Cauldron' ('Das Hexenkessel' as the Germans called it) striking out to both south and east. They forced the Eighth Army to completely evacuate the Gazala Line and fall back on Tobruk and further to the east. By 18 June, the Germans had once again besieged Tobruk and began a blistering attack on the garrison on 20 June. This time the South African defenders were unable to withstand the pressure, especially after a series of heavy air attacks. By 1600 hrs most of the main defences had been overrun and the airfield taken. At 0800 hrs the following day, Maj Gen Klopper, the garrison commander, formally surrendered. This was undoubtedly the high spot of Rommel's career. Hitler was delighted and promoted him to FM – at fifty, the youngest in the German Army. However, it had not been achieved without considerable sacrifice both to Rommel's health and to his precious panzers, although physical casualties had been less than 3,500.

And this was not the end of the German–Italian advance: Panzergruppe Afrika, as it was now called, pressed on, the Eighth Army still being in considerable disarray. The Eighth Army was given permission to withdraw to Mersa Matruh, having lost over 50,000 men and much of its armour. Auchinleck then relieved Ritchie and took personal command. He swiftly appreciated that his forces were far too scattered to provide a cohesive defence, so he decided that, if the enemy continued to attack, he would withdraw to the more easily defended El Alamein position. Despite being down to under sixty tanks, the Panzergruppe, with 'Rommel an der Spitze!' (i.e. Rommel Leading!) swiftly surrounded Matruh and the British were forced back. With the Delta beckoning, Rommel hardly paused to draw breath before continuing his advance and during 2–4 July, he made a number of attacks but all were repulsed with considerable loss. Rommel quickly realized that a stalemate had been reached and that there would have to be a pause to allow his forces to regroup, before making one more determined effort. In the British camp it was 'all change' once again. Auchinleck stubbornly (and with good reason), had refused to consider any further attacks until he had built up his forces and this led to Churchill replacing him with Gen Harold Alexander, while a new GOC in C appeared to take over the Eighth Army, namely Lt Gen Bernard Montgomery.[1]

Rea Leakey I found HQ 7th Armoured Division and reported to the GSO 1, Lt Col Pete Pyman. He was in the ACV directing operations on the wireless, and the battle was moving fast. He was very tired and only too glad to hand over control to me, so that at least he could get out and stretch his legs.

I had only been in the 'hot seat' for some 15 minutes when our armoured cars reported enemy tanks moving in our direction. The order was given to move east. I nearly lost my Jeep, which contained my few possessions, because there was no driver. Fortunately, I saw one of our Liaison Officers walking past and hailed him. It was Capt Roy Farran, and he took it over. He was a remarkable soldier, and his book *Winged Dagger* is worth reading.[2]

Gen Messervy had been away visiting the forward units, and joined us in the ACV as we moved off. This vehicle was the nerve centre from which all orders went out and to which all reports of enemy movements came in, as did orders to the Division from Corps Headquarters. Conditions on the move with the full operational staff inside were, I suspect, worse than those in a submarine. Marking up the map or writing messages as this thinly armoured vehicle bounced across the desert needed much practice, and it was essential to have a well trained crew down to the most junior wireless operator. Space was at a premium, as I was to discover not many days after joining the team.

As we moved east we came under shellfire, and we could clearly see a few enemy tanks on a ridge not more than 2 miles to the south of us. We hastened back towards Sidi Rezegh where 4th Armoured Brigade were busily reorganizing after their recent battles. The Germans were already beginning to close up on the Tobruk perimeter. Two boxes, each held by an Indian Brigade, were all that remained of our defended positions. The El Adem airfield box lay some 7 miles south of Tobruk perimeter, and the other, Bel Hamed, was situated about 10 miles to the south-east of the perimeter, not far from Sidi Rezegh.

At this stage Tobruk perimeter was not fully manned nor had the old defensive line been maintained; in fact, many of the anti-tank mines had been removed and used in the Gazala line. Now, with the collapse of the Gazala line, there was no coordinated firm defensive line between Rommel's troops and Cairo. There were only two ways in which he could be halted. One was by defeating him in battle in the open desert, and this was now out of the question, as we had lost the majority of our tanks; the other was by denying him the use of Tobruk harbour and so forcing him to halt until he had built up sufficient stocks of supplies to carry him on to the Delta.

However, as early as 1939 Gen Wavell's staff had foreseen the possibility of an enemy advance such as was now about to occur, and had at least planned a possible defensive line. This line lay some 60 miles west of Alexandria, and stretched from the coast of El Alamein to the Qattara Depression, some 40 miles to the south. But at this stage of the battle there were few, if any, who even thought about a defensive position so far to the east. As a very new member of the Divisional staff, I did not fully appreciate the seriousness of the situation, although it was painfully obvious that we had lost the tank battle and therefore command of the open desert.

I felt sure that Tobruk was as strong a fortress as ever, and would once again save the day. So it was a considerable shock to me when a message was handed to me, which read something like this: 'Tobruk will NOT, repeat NOT, be held. All troops in Tobruk will be evacuated. All supplies will be destroyed.' I have no access to documents, but, as far as I remember, we received that message on 16 June 1942. There were large dumps of petrol, ammunition, and other supplies in Tobruk, and on this date thousands of troops were pouring through from the Gazala line. The western sector of the perimeter was held by units of the 2nd South African Infantry Division.

On that same day, Rommel's forces closed in on the El Adem box, and it was attacked, but the Indians held firm. In the open desert to the south of Tobruk 7th Armoured Division was the only formation that still remained fully operational, but we had very few tanks left and therefore could not take the initiative. We were a threat to Rommel's open flank and, before he could surround Tobruk, he had to push us out of the way. Also he had to eliminate the El Adem and Bel Hamed boxes. They were now put under the command of 7th Armoured Division.

Next day, almost exactly 24 hours after receiving that first signal about Tobruk, we received another which read: 'Tobruk will, repeat will, be held, 7th Armoured Division will ensure the road Tobruk–Bardia is kept open for at least three days.' The 2nd South African Infantry Division was given the task of holding Tobruk. To assist them in this important task, a number of other formations and units were put under their command, including a Guards Brigade, and the 4th and 7th Royal Tank Regiments. I felt it was a pity 9th Australian Division were not readily available at they knew Tobruk better than any.

All that day German forces continued to move east, and it was obvious that the El Adem box, which was now surrounded, could not hold out much longer. Gen Messervy gave orders for the garrison to break out at night and withdraw to the east. This they did, and a surprisingly large number of the men escaped, but very little equipment could be saved.

Now only the Bel Hamed box and 7th Armoured Division stood between Rommel and the sea to the east of Tobruk perimeter. The rest of the perimeter was already under siege.

Next day, 18 June, the three armoured-car regiments who were also under command of 7th Armoured Division, sent in report after report of German tanks moving east towards Bel Hamed and Sidi Rezegh. We knew only too well that Rommel's next target was Bel Hamed. The 4th Armoured Brigade, who now had at the most some fifty tanks, were positioned on high ground to the south of Bel Hamed box.

At about 3 o'clock that afternoon Gen Messervy ordered 4th Armoured Brigade to move north and position themselves in an area immediately adjacent to the box. Brigadier Richards, commanding the Brigade, spoke on the wireless and tried to explain to the General that such a move would jeopardize his position and allow the German tanks to move on to the dominating high ground which he was holding.

Gen Messervy answered back that it was essential for the armour to move north. The Brigadier was far from happy about this order and requested a meeting with the General and the Corps Commander. This was agreed to by Messervy, but he ordered the Brigadier to start moving his Brigade. A rendezvous was arranged, and the three commanders went off from their respective headquarters to meet at this central point. Gen Messervy took the GSO 1, Lt Col Pyman, with him and, before he left, told me that under no circumstances was I to move the Headquarters while he was away.

About 15 minutes after they had left me, the forward control wireless set began to hum with reports:

'Information. Twenty enemy tanks at map reference 621305 moving East.'

'Information. Thirty-five enemy tanks and other vehicles at map reference 610315 moving East.'

'Information. Large column of tanks, guns and lorries in area 6331 moving East.'

One after another the reports came pouring in from the armoured cars; very soon the map was covered with arrows showing the location and direction of movement of the numerous enemy columns.

The 4th Armoured Brigade reported that they were being heavily attacked by enemy tanks and their position was precarious as half of their available force had already moved north off the high ground. They requested orders. But I had no chance to reply, because the second their Staff Officer stopped talking, the armoured cars butted in with urgent reports of further enemy columns moving east.

The General and the GSO 1, who were in an armoured car, should have heard all these reports, but, as luck would have it, their wireless set was not working properly and they continued on their way to the rendezvous. Little did they realize that the two German armoured divisions were hard on their heels.

Bel Hamed Box now came on the air, and reported that they were being heavily attacked. Could help be sent? At this time Divisional Headquarters was located astride one of the very few clearly marked tracks in this part of the desert. It ran from El Adem to the Frontier and it was frequently used as an axis of advance by both sides.

As the numerous reports came through from the armoured cars, I could not help noticing that one column of tanks was moving along the track towards our position, but I was much too busy to give the matter serious thought. I became a little concerned when I noticed an ever increasing stream of vehicles, including armoured cars, driving past the ACV as fast as they could go. I became even more concerned when I saw our own HQ Officers' mess lorry drive past, and then highly alarmed when a shell dropped only a few yards away. At that moment Roy Farran appeared at the door of the ACV, and I told him to get in an armoured car and drive half a mile west along the track. As soon as the enemy tanks were within a mile of him, he was to let me know on the wireless. Although the General's last order was no move until he returned, I was not going to be put 'in the bag' for him or anybody else. Roy covered the half-mile, but he never reported to me on the wireless, because the German tanks knocked out his armoured car before he had a chance. He escaped in my Jeep. By this time armour-piercing shells started to come over, and I waited no longer. There was no need to tell the driver to 'step on it', the enemy shells were quite sufficient, and those tanks were hard on our heels.

Still the reports came pouring in, but I did manage to tell 4th Armoured Brigade to withdraw, and I gave them a bearing which would lead them towards the frontier. I hoped the General would approve. By this time he had met the Corps Commander, and then Brig Richards raced up, told them what was happening, and returned to his headquarters. The Corps Commander decided to accompany Gen Messervy, and climbed on to his armoured car.

They were very nearly captured by the tanks that were chasing us, but eventually caught us up. Yet we did not dare stop to let them aboard the ACV, so one after another they had to make a most daring jump from vehicle to vehicle on the move. What a prize it would have been for the Germans if they could have captured this overloaded ACV. The passenger list on this groaning vehicle was as follows:

The Corps Commander, Lt Gen Sir Willoughby Norrie
The Divisional Commander, Maj Gen Frank Messervy
Lt Col Pete Pyman (GSO 1)
Myself
Two GSO 3 Staff Officers
Two Wireless Operators
The Driver

Mile after mile the chase went on, and we, the staff, continued to exercise control of the few remaining units between the enemy and Egypt. I remember General Messervy giving orders to the Commander of the Bel Hamed Box in Urdu. This saved the effort of using code words, as it was highly unlikely that the Germans had interpreters in that language. But there was little the two Generals could do to influence the flow of battle.

I had been sitting in this bounding monster with the wireless headsets on for a long time, and at last Pete Pyman took pity on me, took over, and sent me on to the roof of the vehicle. What a relief it was to get a breath of fresh air, and of interest to witness the flood of armoured cars, command vehicles and lorries bounding across the desert. A column of strange looking vehicles caught my attention. They were dummy tanks – lorries fitted out with a wooden gun, turret and skirting boards painted to resemble tracks. Stupidly

I tried to inject a little humour into this grim spectacle. I put my head down into the vehicle and shouted 'Tanks on the starboard side, closing fast.' Pete's reaction was startling; he was out of his seat in a flash, and looked across the desert. 'Yes, tanks,' he shouted, and ordered the driver to go even faster. 'Don't worry,' I said, 'They are dummies.' He was not amused.

And so back to the ignominious retreat, and nothing can be more degrading. Those inside the vehicle seemed to have fallen into a state of numbness. It was only when, for the second time, I poked my head down and told them that the sun was set and soon our vehicles would be short of fuel, that a plan was agreed. We turned south off the Trigh Capuzzo track which we and the enemy had been following and stopped 3 miles from it. The Germans kept going, and we spent the night peacefully only a few miles from each other.

Behind us was chaos. Bel Hamed box was overrun, and, soon after, Rommel cut the Tobruk–Bardia road, thus encircling Tobruk. The 2nd South African Division was alone and charged with the task of keeping Tobruk intact. The 4th Armoured Brigade, or what remained of it, had withdrawn to the frontier; the remainder of the Division was split into 'Jock Columns'[3], and for the next few days these mixed columns of gunners and infantry harassed the enemy flanks from the south.

The next day, before dawn. Divisional Headquarters moved east, and by midday we were halted a few miles east of the Egyptian frontier. With what was left of our force we tried to strike back at the enemy, but, in the desert, fighting tanks were the weapons that counted, and we had very few. Rommel was now in a position to attack Tobruk with almost all his available forces, and there was little we could do to help the beleaguered garrison. On 20 June he launched his attack; the South Africans failed to hold him, and in two days it was all over. Tobruk harbour was in enemy hands and now Rommel was free to continue his advance to the east.

One of my duties as GSO 2 was to deal with signals and correspondence that came in from higher headquarters. During these hectic days the Chief Clerk never bothered me with any but those of significance. Soon after my arrival, he showed me one which read: 'If Maj Leakey is located, he is to be ordered to report immediately to GHQ Cairo.' I told him to burn it. A few days later when the third such signal was handed to me, I felt it was time to 'come clean'. By this time I had got to know the General well, and I am sure he knew that I held him in high regard. I think he found it difficult to confide in Pete Pyman, and that is not surprising. So it was that at the end of a hard day, he would talk to me. He told me he was very tired (that was obvious), that he had lost self-confidence, and felt it was time he was relieved of command. I feel in retrospect I was right in passing this on to a senior officer on the staff of our masters – HQ 30 Corps.

I told him of my little problem with Gen McCreery and of the signals he was sending out. It was madness to replace me at this difficult phase of the battle, and he told me to stay on until the situation eased up. The day after

Tobruk fell my situation was not eased when Gen Messervy was relieved of his command. We were all very sorry to see him go. It was a right decision, and he went on to promotion in command of a Corps in Burma.

His relief was Brig Callam Renton – known as 'Wingie' because he only had one arm. He had been in command of the Motor Brigade,[4] part of the Division, so he was well known by the staff, but I had never met him. He arrived at about 8 p.m. and was greeted by friends outside ACV I, where I was on duty. He had a high-pitched voice and I had no difficulty in hearing his comments. 'I must say how delighted I am in getting command of the Division, but I confess I have little idea of how to handle armour. I have never been in a tank, and hate the beastly things. As for Officers who wear a black beret (RTR), I have little time for them.'

And so with a new Divisional Commander with few troops left to fight back, we continued the painful withdrawal. The New Zealand Division had been brought forward, and with a few other troops established a defensive line based on Mersa Matruh and stretching some 20 miles south into the desert. The 7th Armoured Division did what it could to delay the enemy, and endeavoured to stop them passing south of our defences, but with little success. The New Zealanders were forced to withdraw and the next step was the El Alamein line of defences.

It was the morning after the Matruh line collapsed that I got the sack, and it was not unexpected as far as I was concerned. Gen Renton did not even understand wireless procedure, and I well remember him grabbing the microphone from me and shouting into it. 'Rickie, Rickie, Callam speaking, where are you?' I tried to explain to him why Brig Richards did not immediately reply, but with no success. I had been on duty all night, and, in fact, had had little sleep since joining the Headquarters, Renton called me aside and said, 'Leakey, I feel you do not like me. Why?'

'Do you want an honest answer?', 'Yes,' he said, and I gave it to him. I told him about the conversation I could not fail to hear which he had his friends the night he took over command, and went on to say that, in my opinion, he was quite right in saying that he had little idea of how to command an Armoured Division. At least his reaction was honest. 'Thank God I am senior to you. One of us must go, and the sooner we part the better.' So it was that I collected my jeep from Roy Farran, joined the mass of vehicles moving back to the El Alamein line, and then on to Cairo. Renton did not last long as GOC of the Desert Rats. Soon after he took over command of Eighth Army, Montgomery sacked him.

That evening I reported to Lt Col George Webb, Gen McCreery's Senior Staff Officer. I will never forget the expression on his face as I walked into his office. He ducked under his desk, then peeped up, stared at me again, and said, 'As we got no reaction to all the signals we sent, we presumed you were dead, until General Messervy told us of your new appointment. And now here you are ready go to to Baghdad at long last.' I was marched into the General's office and he told me what he thought of me and my ancestors, and went on to say that had it not been for the report Gen Messervy gave, he would have had me court-martialled for disobeying rules. No more leave; I was to depart for Baghdad immediately handcuffed to a Military Police Officer.

But that was not to be. As there were no means of transporting me to Baghdad that night, George agreed that I could stay the night with friends and at least enjoy the comfort of a bath. And that was a night I shall never forget. Among several friends I met at Gezira Club I dined with a girl who was going to marry Peter Page (1 RTR). He was killed at Sidi Rezegh in 1941. She told me that, with many other British women, she was to be evacuated to South Africa and she did not want to go. If she got married to a Service person based in Egypt, she would be allowed to stay because she was employed in GHQ Cairo working for a Senior RAF Staff Officer. Would I marry her? Certainly, I said, but not the next day, because my presence was demanded in Baghdad. So it was agreed that the engagement should be announced immediately, and so she could stay in Cairo.

But that was not the end of the evening's happenings. George Webb appeared, having traced me to the Club. He told me that Gen Auchinleck – the C in C – had sacked Gen Ritchie, Commander Eighth Army and was moving out into the desert to take command at El Alamein. He had asked for a Senior RTR Officer to act as his 'spokesman' on the wireless, and my name had been given to him. I was to leave at dawn. Once again I set off in my jeep and this time had no trouble in locating HQ Eighth Army. That evening the 'Auk' appeared, greeted me, thanked me for coming, but said he had changed his mind. He wanted a Signals Officer. I suspect he had been tipped off that by no way was I a Senior RTR Officer!

By this time Rommel's tanks had reached the El Alamein line, and here they were stopped. 1 RTR were back in the battle, and I found them in action the next day. It was the late evening, and the usual tank battle was in full swing. I climbed on to one of the tanks to watch the climax. One lone Grant tank was well forward fighting it out to the end. It was Walter Benzie. He told us that he and the gunner were the only two alive, and they were both wounded but they still had some ammunition. The end was inevitable. A blinding flash and Benzie and his tank were no more. And that was the way he wanted to sell his life – for his country, and, as I thought, because he had lost his Joan.

Not so long ago, as Director General of Fighting Vehicles in Whitehall, I was the Guest of Honour at one of the major motor manufacturers' Annual Dinner. Towards the end of the evening, a man approached me and said, 'You were a great friend of Walter Benzie, and I am told you explain his gallant exploits in the war were because he no longer wanted to live, having lost Joan, who died of TB.'

'Yes,' I said, 'that is so.'

'She is still alive, happily married, living in Edinburgh – nice to have met you.'

What we men do for women! And so on to my own saga so far as women are concerned. Back to Cairo I went, and told George Webb he had better arrange for me to be sent to Baghdad immediately before somebody else decided my future lay in the Western Desert. 'No,' he said, 'all has been fixed; we have found a Naval parson whose ship was sunk a few days ago, and he has agreed to marry you in Cairo Anglican Cathedral tomorrow morning. The reception will be held at Shepherds Hotel and Tony Lascelles and I hope to be present to drink your health.'

When the war ended and 'Leakey's Luck' had held out and I had survived, we were divorced, and she married her RAF Officer.

Notes

1. The officer originally chosen to command the Eighth Army had been Lt Gen William 'Strafer' Gott, who had commanded both 7th Armd Div and then XIII Corps. On his way back to Cairo from the desert on 7 August 1942, his aircraft was shot down. He survived the crash but was killed by machine-gun fire while trying to rescue others from the wreckage.

2. *Winged Dagger* by Roy Farran was first published by Collins in 1948, then by Arms & Armour Press in 1986, and was recently republished in The Cassell Military Classics series in 1998.

3. Jock Columns were named after another remarkable soldier, Maj Gen 'Jock' Campbell, VC, DSO, MC, who conceived these mobile, harassing columns. Each column usually comprised two troops of 25-pdr artillery guns (the main hitting power), one or two motor companies of infantry, anti-tank and AA artillery, a sapper detachment and, for protection, armoured cars and tanks. The Column Commander had his own Adjutant, Signals and Intelligence Officers and the Column was supported by a specially designed 'B' Echelon. Campbell had commanded 7th Armd Div and was killed when his staff car skidded and overturned near Halfaya Pass in February 1942. He won his Victoria Cross at the battle of Sidi Rezegh on 21 November 1941, leading columns of tanks into action, standing in an open, unprotected staff car, with a large blue flag!

4. The 7th Motor Brigade was the infantry element of the Division and was termed 'mounted infantry' as the infantrymen were carried in lorries. Within Armoured Brigades there was also a Motor Battalion, which contained a high proportion of armoured scout carriers, scout cars and anti-tank guns, so that they could provide the tanks with immediate infantry support.

CHAPTER TEN

Persia and Iraq

Editor **Tenth Army**. Before dealing with the doings of Rea Leakey during this chapter or keeping pace with the continued progress of the war in North Africa, it would be valuable to explain exactly the role of Tenth Army and how it came into existence. When Wavell's new HQ had been established in Cairo in 1939, the separate army commands of Egypt, Sudan and Palestine–Jordan, now came together with Cyprus, under his all-embracing Middle East Command (MEC). In early 1940 this was extended to cover East Africa and British Somaliland, plus any British land forces sent to operate in Turkey, the Balkans, Iraq, Aden or the shores of the Persian Gulf – truly a massive command! In the autumn of 1941, however, MEC was reorganized under Auchinleck, the troops in Syria and Palestine becoming the Ninth Army and those in the Western Desert, the Eighth Army. Then, in January 1942, Persia and Iraq were detached from under command of the C in C India and put under MEC, while the troops there were designated as the Tenth Army, their formation sign being a yellow Assyrian lion. Commander-in-Chief of the Tenth Army was Lt Gen Sir Edward Quinan, KCIE, CB, DSO, OBE, ex-Indian Army, who had been the British commander in Persia. In August 1942, after Rea had joined HQ Tenth Army, Persia and Iraq were formed into a separate Command known as 'Paiforce'. It then contained British, Indian and Polish troops – the last of these being Gen Wladyslaw Anders' 2nd Polish Corps which later fought in Italy. The main tasks of 'Paiforce' were to defend the vast oilfields in Persia and Iraq, and to safeguard the flow of 'Lend-Lease' supplies to the USSR from Persia, some five million tons in total. In 1943, Gen Quinan went to India as C in C Northwestern Army and retired that same year.

North Africa. During the period that Rea was in Persia and Iraq (July 1942–April 1943), the continual 'see-saw' from one end of the Western Desert to the other, which had been the main feature of the desert war, had at long last been resolved. When he had left Egypt, the British and Commonwealth forces had their 'backs to the wall' at Alam Halfa. However, two new 'players' – Alexander and Montgomery – were arriving on the scene. The former, a suave, debonair Guardsman, was the perfect diplomat, well able to cope with the political and military intrigues of Cairo – and no mean soldier to boot; with a DSO and MC from the First World War. He had been promoted to Major General in 1937 – the youngest in the British Army at that time – and had earned an excellent reputation for guts and determination in France, then in Burma. He reached Cairo on 9 August 1942, just a few days after the arrival of the equally brilliant, somewhat eccentric and idiosyncratic, Bernard Law Montgomery with whom he was to have an ideal relationship. Montgomery had also won a DSO in the First World War and then had commanded 3rd Infantry Division in France with the BEF in 1940. He was picked to command the Eighth Army by the CIGS, but the assignment went to Gen 'Strafer' Gott, who was killed, as I have already explained, on his way to take command. Thus fate determined that Montgomery would be thrust into the limelight. The austere General, who neither smoked nor drank, almost mirrored Rommel in his spartan living and instinctive 'feel' for the battlefield. Montgomery quickly realized that he must inject some pride and a sense of purpose into the demoralized Eighth Army and give them a simple plan which everyone could understand and follow. What better than to formulate a plan based upon the two things which the British soldier could do superlatively well – namely, fight doggedly and hold ground. 'Monty', as he quickly became called by everyone, was as a great showman and knew the value of projecting his personal charisma, so, having formulated his plan, he rapidly toured all his units talking informally to his soldiers and getting his message across. There would be no more withdrawals and no more talk of defeat. Monty moved everything up into the frontline, removing 'Evacuation transport' and bringing forward as much ammunition, fuel and supplies as possible. His lines of supply were short, while those of the 'Desert Fox' stretched back for miles (Tobruk was not yet functioning as a port).

The Battle of Alam Halfa which began on the night of 30/31 August was a near-run thing, but the British and their Commonwealth Allies held firm, so that by dawn on 2 September it was clear that the Panzerarmee Afrika had shot its bolt. This was undoubtedly a major turning point in the desert war and marked the furthest east that Rommel would ever reach. Now it was time for Monty to 'knock the enemy for six'. However, before doing so, he was determined to build up the wherewithal to achieve success. He was also a strong enough character – as was Alexander – not to be bullied by Churchill who was constantly demanding action. So, from early September until mid October, both sides prepared for the major battle that would seal the fate of the desert war. It was to take place at El Alamein and Rea would miss this historic battle, which is well-enough documented elswhere for me not to have to cover it here in any detail. Suffice it to say that it was no 'pushover'. Despite all their supply and reinforcement problems, Rommel and his Panzerarmee Afrika had constructed a formidable defensive line, from the coast down to the Qattara Depression, the main static positions being based upon Rommel's 'Devil's Gardens', namely extensive minefields adjoining no man's land, containing thousands of captured enemy bombs and shells (suitably wired) and all the available anti-tank and anti-personnel mines. Behind these main defensive positions were the mobile forces, but it has to be said that British armour was available in far greater quantity – there being 1,029 Grants, Shermans, Crusaders, Stuarts and Valentines, compared with just 211 PzKpfw IIIs and IVs.[1] Rommel was away in Germany on sick leave when the battle began on 23 October 1942, but swiftly returned to take personal command. On 3 November Hitler intervened with one of his disastrous 'No Retreat' orders. It was rescinded two days later, but the delay proved fatal. Rommel extricated what he could of his forces, leaving behind most of the Italian infantry. By 9 November, it was all over and the great withdrawal had begun. Nevertheless, this retreat never became a rout, as Montgomery's Eighth Army always advanced with caution and showed respect for the continuing fighting ability of the DAK. The Panzerarmee withdrew in good order, fighting every inch of the way back to the Mareth Line in Tunisia, which they reached on 15 February 1943, after making notable stands at Mersa Matruh, El Agheila and the Wadi Zem Zem. Early on in their 900 mile withdrawal they also had the disquieting news of the Allied 'Torch' landings on 8 November in north-west Africa, so there were now enemy troops both in front and behind Rommel and his battling 'Afrikaners'.

Rea Leakey So it was that at the beginning of July 1942 I found myself in Baghdad as a Staff Officer (GSO 2) at HQ 10th Army. I lived in the Zia Hotel in reasonable comfort, but the Western Desert was cool compared to Baghdad. There was no air conditioning, and even the nights were unbearable. One had a hot shower (there was no cold water), wrapped a towel round one's waist and repaired to the flat roof, where there were rows of beds and you took your pick. At dawn you stumbled downstairs to have another hot shower, and so to work in a stuffy office doing a mundane staff job, which seemed to me of little importance.

The General, Quinan, and almost all the officers were Indian Army, so naturally I knew none of them. I did not ask for a batman because the hotel staff did all that I required, but I discovered that it was the 'correct thing' to have one when one was on the staff of an Indian Army HQ. One morning, as I was leaving the hotel, an Indian soldier thrust a piece of paper into my hand. It was a note from the Camp Commandant saying that the bearer was my batman and would I 'please sign the attached receipt'. On many occasions I had signed a receipt for Army property, but never before for a human being.

I examined my new acquisition, and it was not a promising sight except that he possessed a cheerful grin. He was small and badly turned out, his boots were unlaced, and he wore a dilapidated boy-scout type hat, which looked as if it had been retrieved from the dustbin. He did not speak Urdu, English or any other known language, as far as I could make out. Eventually I did find an Indian Officer who knew his dialect, and I discovered that he had only been in the Army a short time, so his knowledge of soldiering was next to nil. I had a good mind to send him back to his unit and ask for somebody more reasonable, if it was intended that I should have a batman. But he looked so pathetic and so terrified of the impact of civilization, that I had not the heart to turn him away. I had it explained to him that he and I would learn Urdu and use that as our common language. I then took him to my room and tried to explain his duties. Boot polish fascinated him, and he tried to eat it. I very nearly gave up the unequal struggle, but somehow the idea of sacking him seemed so cruel. I christened him The Dustman, because of his hat. Within a month he had become the best batman I had ever known, and he continued to improve every day.

Not long after my arrival Gen Quinan held a study period for all the officers under his immediate command, and there must have been at least 350 present. The subject was lessons from the battles in the Western Desert. And who was the principal speaker? – the most recently arrived member of the Staff and the youngest Major by a long way. Among those present was Maj Gen Gairdner, who knew me well, if only because I got him involved with fifteen virgins (see Chapter 3).

The next day I was told to report to Gen Quinan. I thought I was in for a 'hiding' for being so outspoken about the qualities of leadership of some of the senior officers involved in the fighting. Not so. He said I was to amend my words and tour Persia and Iraq, lecturing the British civilians working in the oilfields and other industries, on the war in the Western Desert. An aeroplane was 'put at my disposal.'

My first talk was to the British civilians in Baghdad, and the cinema was packed. I enjoyed it, if only because I was kept on the platform for 2½ hours on a very hot night. One of the outcomes of this venture was slightly tragic. The night after I gave this talk, one of the hotel staff said a Baghdad chauffeur wanted to see me. He told me that Mrs 'Blank' had been present at the talk and wanted me to dine with her, and named an evening. He told me she was a wealthy widow who lived in a beautiful house on the outskirts of the town. I accepted, and he said he would pick me up at 7 p.m. in the Rolls-Royce.

And so it was that I found myself being shown into the drawing-room by the butler, and it certainly was a sumptuous house. I expected to see other guests, but the beautiful room seemed deserted. Where was my hostess? – the widow who I imagined was an octogenarian and possibly in a wheelchair. Then I noticed a settee occupied by a beautiful blonde aged about thirty, I thought.

'Mrs. Blank,' I said.

'Yes, nice to see you again. I enjoyed your talk. Help yourself, the whisky is on the side-table, and please refurbish my glass.'

No other guests arrived, and the two of us sat drinking whiskies. At about 9 p.m. she suggested food, and, to put it mildly, I was starving. She got off the couch, rang the bell, and the butler brought her fur coat. We went out and into the Rolls-Royce to be driven to the banks of the River Tigris. A long rowing-boat was waiting for us, and she and I were settled comfortably with a bottle of champagne. The six oarsmen rowed us upstream to an island where servants had a barbecue cooking fish, and the smell was superb.

By this time my hostess was high, and when we settled down on the rugs not far from the food, the one thing she wanted was sex, but she had taken several glasses too many and proceeded to be violently sick. Her staff knew the form – she was carried back to the boat, and I had trouble in delaying our return so as to have something to eat.

I discovered that she was a very wealthy lady and had married an elderly businessman who had left her a fortune, much of which she spent on alcohol. So much for Baghdad. I saw little more of the town, because on returning from my lecture tours of the oilfields I was asked if I would volunteer for a dangerous mission in Persia. Of course, I accepted, because anything was better than working in an office in that unpleasant town.

In 1941 the Germans had tried to seize control of Persia, and started to fly troops into Teheran. Russian and British forces moved in from the north and south respectively. When the Germans were thrown out and peace was restored, the occupying forces agreed on a line of demarcation, and the Russians soon erected their normal 'iron curtain'. At this time there was a danger that the Germans might break through the Caucasus mountains, move south through Persia and capture the oilfields in that country and those in Iraq. Tenth Army HQ was moved into Persia and a defensive line was being prepared in the British Zone. However, the obvious place to stop an attack was between the Caspian Sea and Turkey. This was in the Russian zone of occupation.

Four of us 'volunteers' were selected to reconnoitre this area, and we were told of all but one of the dangers involved. We were to be unarmed, dressed in civilian clothes, and travel in two old Persian trucks. Our first trip lasted a fortnight, and all went well. Our route led us into some of the wildest country in Persia inhabited by a people who were equally wild. They were friendly, and one of the officers had been selected because he spoke Persian. We made it clear to them that we were not anxious to meet Russians, and they warned us that a Cavalry Regiment patrolled that area.

In this country the horse had the advantage of speed. Often the only way we could travel was along the bed of a stream, and on several occasions we had to summon help to push the vehicles through pools or up steep slopes. Most nights we stopped near a village, and we were always well entertained. They fed us and plied us with their local brew of alcohol, and offered us opium pipes. Before dawn they sent their horsemen along our proposed route to make sure there were no Russians in the neighbourhood.

One morning our 'braves' overslept, having dined and wined too well, and we met a patrol on horseback. Fortunately, we were travelling across 'good-going' for the truck, and after a 3-mile chase the Russians turned back. They fired at us throughout the chase, but did not damage us or the vehicles. On arrival back at the village, the headman was full of apologies, and admitted that his men had overslept. He said he had punished them, and it would not happen again; he showed us the corpses. We decided to return to base and write up our report.

This was the first time I had left the Dustman behind since I had signed for him, and what a welcome he gave me when I returned. My tent was full of wild flowers, and he presented me with a bowl of fruit which he had bought in one of the local villages at great expense to himself, but he was very annoyed at having been left behind.

After a week in camp we again set out for the Russian sector, and I had great difficulty in making the Dustman understand that he could not come with me. This time we found ourselves in an area where many of the inhabitants had obviously never before seen a white man, let alone a vehicle. At first they were terrified, but at last, when they realized we meant no harm, they would cluster round and stare at us, and finally pluck up sufficient courage to touch one of the vehicles. There were no Russians in this area, and it was just as well, as the going was so difficult that we were forced to carry out many reconnaissances on foot, or on borrowed horses. At night we were attacked by swarms of mosquitoes and we were glad that we had brought mosquito nets with us. But even so, we were bitten and infected with malaria. Soon all four of us were shivering even in the bright sunshine, and our temperatures were high. Unfortunately, we had no medicine with us and, on the second day of this, we decided we had better get back to base. We made good progress that day, but next morning two of my party were so ill that they were incapable of walking more than a few paces, and obviously could not take their turn at driving. The two of us drove on as fast as we dared.

In the afternoon I discovered that the second vehicle was not following me, and I turned back to find out what had happened. It was by sheer luck that I spotted the vehicle some distance off the track halted in front of a steep bank. The driver had passed out, and it was fortunate that the bank had stopped the vehicle, as otherwise it might well have dropped down one of the numerous deep ravines. After a struggle I managed to get these two officers into my truck, and the rest of that drive was a nightmare.

My head was going round and round, my eyes would not focus properly, and most of the time I was crying like a child. Somehow I managed to keep going and keep direction; although all I could do was to make sure that the track I followed went south. I drove on through the night, and at last I hit a road which was obviously in use. I could go no further, so stopped the vehicle in the middle of the road and left my headlights burning, simply because I had not the energy to turn them off.

When next I regained consciousness I was in a bunk in a train which seemed to be travelling through one tunnel after another. It was only months later that I discovered what had happened to us. An army convoy had been stopped by our vehicle which blocked the road. The leading driver got out and tried to wake us, thinking we were drunk. As luck would have it, the next vehicle in the column was an ambulance which carried a doctor, and he soon realized that our condition was not due to excess of alcohol.

There was no hospital within many miles, but the railway train from the Persian Gulf to Teheran was not far off, and he decided to put us on the first train to pass, no matter which direction it was going. And thus it was that we found ourselves heading for the town of Ahwaz, probably one of the hottest places in this part of the world, but at least it boasted a military hospital.

The four of us were put in a ward on our own, and on the evening of the second day in walked the Dustman. 'How did you know I was in hospital, and where is my kit?' His reply was vague, but not one item of my personal belongings was missing. He was a remarkable little man.

The next night we had another surprise, but this was not so pleasant. The night sister came into our ward and was talking to one of 'the four' who had been moody and irritable all day. Suddenly he jumped on her, got her by the throat and started to strangle her. For a second or two we thought he was playing the fool, but one look at the girl's face was enough to convince us that this was no joking matter. The three of us fought him and managed to free her, but not before she was badly bruised, and she dashed from the ward screaming her head off.

Meanwhile, we were left trying to subdue our fellow patient who had gone 'off his head'. Our ward was at the end of a long corridor, and was, as it were, an 'isolated ward'. So it was that we had to fight this fellow for several minutes before help arrived. This consisted of a straitjacket thrown to us by one of the other night nurses. That night we got little sleep, as our friend was either yelling, moaning or mumbling to himself. Nobody visited us. In the morning my faithful Dustman appeared, and from then on for the next two days he and some of his friends fed us, emptied our 'jerries', and gave us our pills.

Then Number Two went mad, but this time there was a spare straitjacket in the ward, and with the help of the Dustman he was soon strapped to his bed. The hospital staff did what they could for us, but they were hard pressed, and later I was told that nursing sisters were not allowed near us. Indeed, so dangerous were we considered to be, that a platoon of the Black Watch was flown from Egypt to Ahwaz to mount guard over us. When we 'volunteered', we had not been told about the Persian mosquito – it carried cerebral malaria. It was no joke living in a ward with two madmen and wondering who was next to be strapped to his bed.

I suppose it was a fortnight later that we two 'sane inmates' were allowed out under escort, and well I remember attending an ENSA concert consisting of servicemen who had artistic talents. At this time and in this particular theatre of the war there were no professional actors as members of the ENSA casts. I thought I recognized one of the actors, and during the interval confirmed that he was Trooper (Private) Tyler (1 RTR). In 1938 he had been my batman for a short spell, and I knew he was talented, but I did not know then that he was a singer.

I suppose it was six weeks before the two of us were cleared as allegedly sane, and we returned to HQ Tenth Army to complete our report. Well do I recall the morning the Dustman arrived with our cup of tea. My companion lay, as I did, on the floor of the tent, unable to move. He was paralysed down one side of his body. He was taken back to hospital and later I was told that I was the only survivor.

I was not asked to take out further reconnaissance parties into Northern Persia. Instead I was posted as Brigade Major to HQ 252 Indian Armoured Brigade under the command of HQ 31st Indian Armoured Division under canvas in Southern Persia. It was an interesting assignment; I was one of the very few who had seen active operations. Indeed one of the Cavalry Regiments in the Brigade was the 14/20 Hussars. I think I am correct in saying that after the Indian Mutiny it was the policy to have a proportion of British units with an Indian formation.

In the First World War the 14/20 Hussars never fired a shot in anger – they were in India. And here they were – one of the three armoured regiments in the Brigade. My Brigadier, Gus Carr-White, was a most likeable man – short, stout and cheerful. In his day he had been a good polo player. His knowledge of armoured warfare was not great, and he was not alone in this respect. Perhaps it was just as well that this Division never went to war. I was the youngest Major in the Division by many years; there was one other RTR officer, and he was GSO 2 of the HQ – he must have been the second youngest, five years older than me.

Not long after joining the Brigade, we were moved to Shaiba, a military base in the desert some 30 miles from Basra, and in this unpleasant place I remained until 1 April 1943. But even before this move, I was asked by the CO of 46 RTR, Lt Col Eric Offord, to join him as his second in command, and they were in the Western Desert. My Brigadier flatly refused to allow me to go. I told Maj Gerry Hopkinson, the other RTR Officer, of this correspondence, and suggested that he should go instead, and I pointed out that, were he in the Western Desert, at his age he would either be dead or in command of an RTR Regiment. Eric Offord accepted him in my stead, and that is not the end of the story.

I need hardly say that neither the Dustman nor I were welcomed with open arms into this élite Cavalry Brigade. I think he belonged to the Indian Pioneer Corps, and his dress and bearing had little in common with his new fellow soldiers – neither had mine. This did not disturb me, but he felt the pressure. He told me that he was losing face with his fellow batmen or bearers, because I was the only officer who did not have a tin bath. This was indeed true, and I suggested that as he was such a 'versatile bearer' perhaps he could buy me one. As usual, he grinned, and promised he would do his best.

Much to my amazement, when I went to my tent the next evening, there was a tin bath filled with warm water. I had learnt not to ask the Dustman where or how he had got it, but it was not long before I discovered. In fact, I was in the bath when the fight started, not far from where I was. When I arrived on the scene, my little batman was bleeding and being held back by the Sergeant Major, who told me that indirectly I was the cause of the fight. The Brigadier's bath was missing. Sergeant Majors the world over are wise to these events. The two contestants were removed to the guardroom for some 10 minutes, which gave me time to replace the offending article in the Brigadier's tent. Face was saved, but the next day I journeyed to Basra and bought the best tin bath that money could buy.

I suppose, in retrospect, the 'powers that be' were right in posting such a young officer to fill the senior appointment on the staff of this HQ, and had we been committed to battle my experience would have been of value. Yet I felt that it would be many a day before this happened, and it was not long before I asked the Brigadier if he would agree to my going back to the Western Desert. He refused.

By this time the battle of El Alamein had been won, and I was determined to be in at the kill, so I tried again. The Brigadier showed me a letter from HQ Baghdad confirming that my appointment as Brigade Major was for two years. With his permission I went to Baghdad and had an interview with the Military Secretary, the man responsible for staff appointments. He was sympathetic, but said I could go on condition that I carried an adverse confidential report which I should deliver to GHQ Cairo on arrival. This I accepted, but asked that he should give me a 24-hour start of the report; he must have given me a 24-day start – bless him!

It was with a heavy heart that I left 252 Indian Armoured Brigade; from the Brigadier downwards they had accepted me, and the Indian soldiers of the HQ, in particular, gave me a wonderful send-off. Yet quite the most difficult parting was with the Dustman. I had signed for him, and so I was his until the day the war ended – that was his outlook on the matter, and he would follow me wherever I went, as he had done in the past months.

So well I remember the night I left Shaiba on 1 April 1943, to catch the train from Basra to Baghdad. My little friend had to be forced off the truck and locked in the guardroom. The next morning when I arrived at Baghdad station, I looked round for a porter to help me with my baggage, but I need not have bothered. The Dustman had the matter under control. Even the tin bath, which I had deliberately left behind, was being cared for like a child in arms. It was with tears in my eyes that I handed him over to the Military Police with orders not to release him until long after I left for Cairo. As the years roll by, I continue to meet old soldiers with whom I served, but the one I would wish to meet again more than any, is the Dustman.

Notes

1.   A full summary of the opposing tank forces was as follows:

British	German
170 Grants	85 PzKpfw III L/42
252 Shermans	88 PzKpfw III L/60
216 Crusaders Mk I & II	8 PzKpfw IV L/24
119 Stuarts	30 PzKpfw IV L/43
194 Valentines	
Total 1,029	Total 211

(NB: Not included are the by now obsolete Vickers Lt Mk VIs or PzKpfw Is and IIs)

CHAPTER ELEVEN

Finale in the Desert

Editor When Rea returned to North Africa much had happened and the action was now in Tunisia, where Rommel's Army Group 'Afrika' was being squeezed into a tight perimeter around Tunis and Bizerta, based on the last ring of hills before the coastal plain. They held First Army, but the Eighth Army managed to advance just south of Enfidaville. The Axis forces were now heavily outnumbered, especially in tanks and guns – the 19 Allied divisions, for example, had 1,200 tanks and 1,500 guns as compared with the 12 Axis divisions which could only field 130 tanks and 500 guns. Rea joined 3 RTR as a squadron commander and took part in these final actions. The end was inevitable and at 1200 hours of the 12 May 1943, Col Gen von Arnim, then Heeresgruppe commander, capitulated on behalf of both his Heeresgruppe Afrika staff and the DAK. Rommel, sick in mind and body, had already left – on 9 March – to beg Hitler to rescue his beloved Afrikaners. But it was not to be. And Rommel would not be allowed to return to Africa.

Instead, once his health was partly restored, the 'Desert Fox' was sent to Italy, which is also where Rea Leakey would next find himself, after being selected to become Second in Command of the 44 RTR[1], in early December 1943. The 44th were then located on the Adriatic coast, part of 4th Armoured Brigade in support of 1st Canadian Division on the River Morro. After taking part in some successful actions, such as at Roalti and Ortona, the fighting became more static. By the middle of December the 44th had been withdrawn from the frontline and rumours were rife that they were about to return to England. For once the rumours proved to be correct and they were selected as one of the more battle-experienced regiments to be sent home to England to take part in the forthcoming invasion of Normandy. They handed over their tanks, moved south to Taranto and two weeks later embarked upon the *Ranchi*. After an uneventful voyage they disembarked on 10 February in Scotland.

The 44 RTR, still part of 4th Armd Bde, was re-equipped with Sherman medium tanks, including a number – roughly one per troop – of Sherman Fireflies, which mounted the British 17-pdr gun as its main armament. At last they had a tank that could deal with the heavier German armour, although with only one per troop they were still at a disadvantage. Another battle-experienced formation to return from Italy at this time, was the 7th Armd Div, in which Rea had served for so long at the start of the desert war. Their units had to exchange their Shermans for lighter, faster Cromwell cruiser tanks, which many crews considered to be inferior. It was a busy period getting the tanks ready and, as he explains, the waterproofing of vehicles for landing across the Normandy beaches was a tricky and time-consuming task.

Rea Leakey I had left my Jeep in Baghdad, so once again on my own, I drove to Cairo. George Webb was not surprised to see me back in his office. He had been asked to find an RTR officer to replace me, but he did not, at this time, tell Gen McGreery, how I had escaped from Iraq. Yes, he agreed, I could return to Eighth Army, who were now in Tripolitania – west of Tripoli. Conscious of the fact that my adverse confidential report was 'on my heels', I did not linger long in Cairo. In Alexandria harbour a convoy of ships was about to sail for Tripoli, and I 'talked my way' on to a troopship just before she sailed. I sometimes wonder what became of my Jeep which had served me so well – I abandoned it at the quayside.

The journey to Tripoli was not uneventful. The ship was one of a large convoy which attracted considerable attention from the enemy. Not long after we left Alexandria, the thump of depth charges indicated that submarines were around, and indeed two ships were sunk. But the worst was still to come. On the evening before we reached Tripoli harbour, the convoy was attacked by a large formation of enemy bombers. They timed their arrival with typical Teutonic precision – minutes after the RAF fighter cover had left.

The next thirty minutes were not pleasant. The drill on a troopship was for all ranks to go below decks. I happened to be in charge of 'F' deck, which was located at the bottom of the ship. If the ship was hit, 'A' deck came up first, 'B' second, and so on. We had, of course, practised the drill, and I recall it took 20 minutes to clear the decks above mine.

Being a 'rebel', it was not surprising to find myself in command of a bunch of similar characters. A number were members of 51st Highland Division who suffered heavily at the battle of Alamein. They were being shipped back to their units to face various charges, including desertion, and that is why they were in 'F' deck.

Because we were below the waterline, each bomb that exploded near the ship sent out sound waves that cracked against the hull. Never in my life have I felt so helpless, and all of us in 'F' deck knew that if we received a direct hit, our chances of survival were slender. It was an experience I can never forget. The explosion of a bomb close to the ship would knock those soldiers sitting on benches next to the hull across their tightly packed fellows. Looking back on this particular episode, I feel pride in the discipline of these men. They knew they were 'rats in a trap', yet there was no panic, no move from any man to go up the gangway. Indeed they suggested that I should go up and tell them what was happening. This I did, and I witnessed a troopship receive a direct hit, and then a tanker carrying high octane fuel explode in a ball of fire. Then a 'near miss' exploded yards in front of the bows of the ship, and I returned below soaked to the skin. If nothing else, this caused a good laugh.

At HQ Eighth Army I was greeted by Maj Tony Lascelles, who was on the staff and responsible for Officer postings, among other duties. 1 RTR, now commanded by Lt Col Mike Carver, were up to strength in Officers, but 3 RTR had a vacancy. A few days later I took over command of B Squadron 3 RTR. I found that I was the only prewar regular officer in the Regiment, and indeed the CO, Lt Col Ian Spence, was a Staffordshire Yeoman. I was to learn that this was not unusual; the RTR had expanded, and it appeared we had run out of officers senior enough to command our regiments.

The 3rd were part of 8th Armoured Brigade and fighting in the final battles in North Africa. We fought our way through to Tunis, and were present at the Victory Parade in that town when the Prime Minister, Winston Churchill, took the salute. That was on 8 May 1943. Not long after the fighting ended, the CO decided to take us round the battlefield at Enfidaville, where the Regiment had fought its last encounter with Rommel's 'Panzers'. Driving through the enemy defensive positions, we found ourselves in a minefield; this we did not know until the vehicle behind the one Ian and I were in triggered off a 'jumping jack'. This was a vicious anti-personnel mine which first jumped up four feet, then exploded, scattering lead pellets in all directions. Fortunately, only two officers in the following vehicle were hit. One was Maj Bill Close. He was a typical RTR prewar soldier who came through the ranks from Trooper – or, as I am sure he would say, from Private – before we were absorbed by the Cavalry.

Once again 'Leakey's Luck' held out. I was driving, and stopped the second the 'jumping jack' exploded. The mine lifting course I had attended in Tobruk now paid off. Just 6 inches in front of the wheel of our vehicle was an anti-tank mine which would have blown us to bits. That was not the only one I removed before we extracted ourselves from the minefield.

It was at this time that the adverse confidential report caught up with me. By then I had been in command of a squadron for some two months, and Ian Spence kindly agreed to my holding that appointment. A week later he returned to his Regiment because his predecessor, Lt Col David Silvertop, who had been wounded, returned. He was a 14/20th Hussar and continued to command the 3rd until shortly before VE Day, when he was killed. He, too, accepted me, despite the report; he had been Brigade Major to Brig Richards in HQ 4th Armoured Brigade, so was aware of my past record.

After three weeks' stay in the Tunis area, we moved to Homs near Tripoli. We were under canvas on the shores of the Mediterranean, and life was not unpleasant. There was much speculation as to where next we should find ourselves. The invasion of Sicily was on, and we had been left out of the order of battle. Then came Italy, and again we were left behind. Finally, orders came through that we were to go to Cairo. Well, at least that meant the bright lights, and everybody was happy.

Being the most newly joined Major, I was denied the pleasure of driving back across the desert with the Regiment. Instead, I was given charge of our few remaining tanks, which were to go by ship to Alexandria. On the whole, mine turned out to be the more amusing journey. The tanks were loaded into a very old merchant ship which was too slow to accompany any normal convoy. The Captain was told to make his way to Alexandria unescorted and chance to luck. Off we set, and never once during the whole long journey we were more than a few miles off the shore. 'If they sink us, I am damned if I want a long swim,' commented the Captain.

When we arrived in Alexandria, he and I went ashore to enquire when the tanks were to be unloaded. The officials were far from cooperative. 'We don't want any old tanks here – take the blasted things away.' 'Where?' 'Anywhere you bloody well like, but get your old ship out of this port.' The Captain was not in the least perturbed. 'Why argue? They might well order me back to Tripoli, and those waters are still too dangerous for my liking.' So we steamed out of Alexandria, and made our way to Port Said. Here we again tried for permission to unload the tanks, but this time the official merely pointed to the door, and we went.

By the time we arrived at Suez, we had been on board for almost a month, and my twenty soldiers and I were getting a little tired of life at sea. So this time, when the officials told us to get to hell out of the place, I dug my toes in, despite the opposition from the Captain, who felt sure I would enjoy a voyage to South Africa. The Egyptian State Railways took the tanks to Cairo, and we rejoined the 3rd there. Then the good news came through. We were to return to England. I had been overseas for five years, so for me and many others this was indeed good news. This time, however, 'Leakey's Luck' failed me.

On 3 November 1943, the Regiment boarded a luxury troopship in Alexandria harbour. I was in charge of the 'rear party', and so was the last person to embark. I arrived on deck, and the gangway was already being hoisted when I heard my name being called. I looked down, and there was Maj Gen McCreery looking up with his usual delightful smile. The gangway was lowered, and down I went. The General signalled for it to be hoisted, and the ship sailed for England. I looked him in the eyes, gave him a sickly smile, and asked, 'Baghdad?'

'No, not this time. You are to join that troopship' – pointing to one nearby – 'which is waiting for you, and it will sail to Taranto in Italy. You will join 44 RTR as Second in Command, and at least you will know the CO – Gerry Hopkinson.' So it was that once again I set off with nothing but the clothes I wore – no documents, no money, no toothbrush, and clearly not liked by the General. And that was not the last I saw of him.

The 44th RTR were under command of 4th Armoured Brigade, one of the original 'Desert Rats' formations, but no longer part of 7th Armoured Division. They were supporting a Canadian Division fighting north along the Adriatic coast. This Regiment was a Bristol-based Territorial Infantry Division which had been 'mechanized'. Their wartime record was outstanding, and to this day their annual Reunions continue to be very well attended. One of their COs was Bill Yeo; his son was Adjutant of 1 RTR, and in 1941 when the British forces in Tobruk 'broke out', he was killed minutes before his father, commanding 4 RTR, met up with them. Such are the fortunes of war.

Unlike the desert, this was not a terrain where armour flourished. Yet one learns to be versatile, and although the tanks found their way across rivers, up the valleys and on to the next ridge, wheeled vehicles could not follow. So it was that a Tank Regiment was issued with mules. When darkness fell, a column of these 'spirited' animals in charge of 'squaddies', set off across country carrying supplies. It was bitterly cold, but at least finding one's way was not difficult. At this stage in the contest the Italians were willing to co-operate with the 'Allies', and that made life for us a little easier.

Fighting under these conditions favoured the defender, and the Germans continued to give us a hard time. It was a very cold winter with a good deal of snow which was unusual for that part of Italy. So what a thrill it was when we were given orders to 'pull out' of the line, and return south to Taranto. On 28 March 1944 we disembarked at Gourock in Scotland, and then on to comfortable billets in Worthing.

While we were at sea, I went down with malaria; it was the first attack I had had since leaving hospital in Persia. It was many years later that I discovered how careful a check was kept on my health by the doctors. Certainly at this time they felt that I might well go mad, and thus I was put in a padded cell in the bowels of the ship. Fortunately, I recovered by the time we disembarked, but, even so, I had to report to a medical officer every day for the next two months.

In early May I attended an investiture at Buckingham Palace, and had the honour of receiving a medal from HM King George VI. It was a day I shall not forget. Shortly before having the medal pinned on my chest, 'nature called', and an attendant ushered me into a Royal loo. Each sheet of paper carried the Royal Crest, and I pocketed some of them.

Walking along Piccadilly after the ceremony with several friends, I spotted two Nursing Sisters coming towards us, and I recognized them. 'Watch this,' I said, and when they were a few yards from me I bent down, put my fingers in my ears, and let out an ugly screech. The last time we had met was in the Ahwaz hospital, and they had not forgotten me. My friends caught up with them as they fled for their lives, and assured them that I was more or less sane. So we had a splendid reunion in a Mayfair bar, and for once I was able to pay for the drinks, because I sold the Palace loo sheets for £1 each to an American.

We had two months to prepare for D-Day – not that we were told when that was to be, but we knew there was little time to spare. Soon our equipment came pouring in – new Sherman tanks, new guns, wireless sets still in their factory packing cases, and other items of equipment which we had not seen before.

The most time-consuming task was that of waterproofing the vehicles so they could disembark from the landing ships while still in deep water. This was particularly important for the tanks; not only did the hatches and turret rings have to be sealed with Bostik but they were lined with strings of cordite. Once out of the water these were exploded and the tank was then capable of fighting. In the summer evenings, when the shops closed, hundreds of girls would take over from the soldiers, and their hands were more adept at fixing the cordite and the electrical fittings. Without their help 44 RTR would not have been ready to embark on 4 June 1944 to take part in the Battle of Normandy.

Notes

1.   44 RTR had been formed – as 44th RTC – from the 6th Bn, The Gloucestershire Regiment (TA), at Bristol, when the Royal Tank Corps expanded in 1938. At the end of the year, the regular RTC staff arrived and conversion training started in earnest. Recruiting and training continued, then in May 1939 the 50th RTR was formed as a second line unit to the 44th. 44 RTR sailed to the Middle East, via Durban, in July 1940.

CHAPTER TWELVE

On To Normandy

Editor The 44 RTR, was still part of 4th Armd Bde, together with the Greys and the 4th County of London Yeomanry. The brigade was not part of the initial 'D-Day' landing force, but rather in the first 'follow-up' wave. It had been intended that the Regiment would arrive in France on 'D + 1' (i.e. 7 June 1944). However, due to the 'usual delays' they did not start to land until late evening of 7 June and continued on 8 June (D + 2), so Rea Leakey's personal recollection of dates for this period are slightly wrong. Life was fairly peaceful for the first few days, but on 26 June they took part in some savage 'dogfights' around Cheux, where they proved to their immense satisfaction that the new 17-pdr Fireflies could knock out the German Panther tank.[1] Then followed their first major battle, when they took part in the operation to cross the River Odon and exploit. For this operation, codenamed 'Epsom', they were under command of 11th Armoured Division – another 'Hobo' trained division, then in the capable hands of Maj Gen 'Pip' Roberts (late RTR) – the youngest divisional commander in the British Army at that time. On the first day the brigade commander, Brig J C Currie, was killed by a shell and his place taken by Brig (later FM) Mike Carver. The 44th crossed the Odon on the 28th and the following day took part in 11th Armd Div's attack on Point 112 – a very commanding position, that would change hands on a number of occasions. The history of 11th Armd Div describes the feature as: 'the notorious Hill 112'. Despite being: ' . . . neither impressive nor well defined', it did form a part of a ridge which dominated the Odon Valley and the country to its north. It was also untenable and: '. . . death stalked the rider who attempted to mount its broad saddle', an apt description of the vicious fighting which took place in the area. At that time the bulk of the German panzer divisions which had arrived in Normandy were engaged on the British flank – this was a deliberate ploy on Montgomery's part so as to distract the enemy from the intended breakout by the US Third Army, on the American flank in Brittany. So 44 RTR spent the last few days of June and most of July in close support and counter-attack roles in the Cheux and Point 112 area, very unpleasant jobs which were costly in casualties, especially from enemy shelling.

During this period of confused and bitter fighting, 7 RTR, which was also involved in the fighting around Hill 112, suffered heavy casualties, having four officers killed and losing eight tanks (but knocking out nine of the enemy's). Among the wounded was their Commanding Officer, Lt Col George Gaisford, who had been blinded in one eye, but had refused to be evacuated until later that day, his courage and leadership being described in the regimental history as being: 'superb and an inspiration to us all'. Rea was chosen to replace him and, as he explains, had little time to prepare himself for his new command. 7 RTR, together with 4 RTR, had fought itself to a standstill in the desert, where both regiments had virtually ceased to exist at the end of the second siege of Tobruk. It had been reformed in April 1943 from 10 RTR which had been formed in UK in November 1940, but never seen any action. The 'new' 7 RTR was equipped with the British A22 Churchill infantry tank, one of the most successful British tanks of the war and had landed on 22 June, having been delayed by the terrible gale which had spread havoc along the entire invasion coast and severely damaged the two prefabricated Mulberry harbours. They had also lost six tanks when one of the LCTs struck a mine, but fortunately all the crews were saved. Together with 9 RTR and 141 RAC, 7 RTR formed 31st Tank Brigade. Rea arrived on 20 July, while the Regiment was 'marrying-up' with the infantry in a little hamlet called Rocrenil, for an attack on Matlot. The subsequent loss of eight Churchills – and the reason why – is vividly told in his narrative.

Once the breakout had been achieved the Churchills of 7 RTR were clearly the wrong type of tank to take part in the 'race' to liberate the Low Countries, being too slow and heavy. Instead, they were switched to help in the reduction of the various German garrisons that had held out in the Channel ports. The first was to be Le Havre, which was assaulted by 1 Br Corps (1st Canadian Army) on 10 September at 1745 hrs, after the defences had been softened up by the heavy guns of the Royal Navy and a series of attacks by Bomber Command (nearly 5,000 tons of bombs were dropped). By dark, both 49 & 51 Divisions had penetrated the enemy defences. The assault continued all the next day with both divisions working their way into the town itself. By 1145 hrs on 12 September, the garrison commander had surrendered and 12,000 prisoners were taken. The success of this operation, which was against one of the strongest fortresses of the German Atlantic Wall, was described in a small diary produced in BAOR by A Sqn, 7 RTR, as follows: 'It was really a triumph for the RAF as they bombed the enemy stupid. But it was also a model "all-arms" battle with 79th Armd Div in the limelight, with their Flails, Bridging tanks, AVREs and Flame-throwers helping us over a sea of mines and obstacles. The General Commanding 49th Division, offered Five Pounds to the man who captured the Garrison Commander, Colonel Wildermuth. It was won by Lt Bland of B Squadron, who found him in his pyjamas. But our most vivid memories must surely always remain – the LOOT. Note: Kit Bland never got his "Fiver". The Field Cashier (a subaltern) said: "The general must draw the money himself, and not send in a *please pay bearer*."'

Rea Leakey When the tanks rumbled through the streets of Worthing, everybody knew that the eve of the great battle was at hand. The streets were lined with cheering people and we, who travelled in these tanks, felt proud that we had been chosen for this great task; yet we were sorry to say farewell to the kind people of this town who had done so much for us. As we drove past the quiet fields of the beautiful countryside I could not help wondering how many of us would survive to enjoy this beauty again. There must have been many who had a sinking feeling in the pit of their stomachs; I know I did.

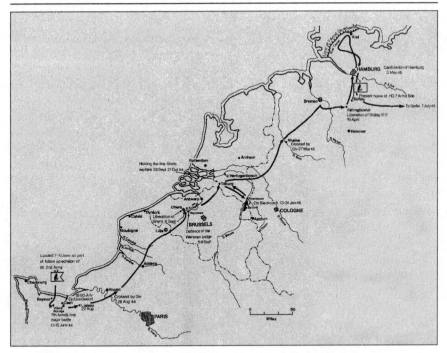

North West Europe. Route taken by 7th Armoured Division, June 1944–July 1945.

It was only when we reached the outskirts of Portsmouth that we really appreciated the magnitude of this undertaking. Every street, every square, in fact, every corner of the town was packed tight with lorries, tanks and guns, hundreds of thousands of them. We were guided to our parking places, and here each vehicle had its particular place – the number being chalked on the street, I was deeply impressed at the superb organization.

The inhabitants of Portsmouth must have given away tons of chocolate and hundreds of gallons of tea, and where they got it in the days of rationing, goodness knows. As we climbed into our tanks for the last short journey down to the hards, many old soldiers were moved to tears by the sincere farewell given by these brave people who had themselves suffered so much from German bombs. Old ladies tottered out of their cottages and kissed any soldier they could seize, and hundreds of little comforts were handed out.

The journey across the English Channel to the Normandy beaches was uneventful – certainly no sign of the enemy. We travelled in Landing Ships Tanks. They were flat-bottomed and each one carried some forty vehicles and their crews. Our ship 'beached' on the afternoon of D-Day, so our landing was unopposed.

As the large door of the ship dropped down into the sea, the driver of the tank at the exit climbed into his seat and pressed the starter. There was a loud bang and the inside of the tank was ablaze. The driver came back out of the turret like a cork out of a bottle with his clothes on fire. He was our first casualty in Normandy, and lucky to survive. The Navy doused the fire, but then we had a problem. Until this tank was offloaded and cleared out of the way, the rest of the vehicles were trapped inside, and there was an emergency. The beach controllers shouted at us to get going, because enemy tanks were closing in on this beach.

A second driver climbed through the turret into the driver's seat, pressed the starter, and we were away. The Worthing girls had done us proud. As each tank emerged from the water, the cordite rings were fired and the guns were ready for action. We were engaging the enemy within minutes. Certainly not as exacting a battle as that fought by those who came ashore at dawn that day, but for all those who took part in this campaign, it was only the beginning of what was to prove a very tough fight before the final breakout from the Normandy beachhead.

Before dark the Regiment was all ashore, and we had another fight which lasted until the light failed. But more than half the night was over before we had completed the replenishment of the tanks. At dawn we were once again on the move, but only a short distance, and the battle was on. So it went on day after day. Often there was hardly time for a meal, and at night we were too tired to eat. We suffered many casualties, the larger German Tigers tanks out-gunned us, and it cost between four and five Sherman tanks to destroy one Tiger. Fortunately, we had plenty of tanks, yet it was never fun to be 'brewed up', and trained crews were difficult to replace.

It was towards the middle of July that we had our worst spell. It started with an attack against a hill called Point 112 in which we were supporting an infantry Brigade. Although the attack was successful, the Germans counter-attacked, and retook the vital hill. By this time the infantry and ourselves were so reduced in numbers and so tired that it was all we could do to hold the lower slopes. The infantry dug in, and we tried to hide our tanks in what remained of the hedges.

But the enemy could see every single move we made. If a man got out of his tank to relieve nature, that tank would be accurately shelled. After a few hours and after many casualties, orders were given that under no circumstances would crews get out of their tanks. The days were very long, but even then darkness did not bring much relief. On the first night we moved from our deployed positions to squadron leaguers so as to make replenishment easier. The enemy seemed to know exactly where we were, and we were shelled incessantly. The second night was the same and we got no sleep. From then on, only the tanks that needed replenishment moved back – the rest stayed where they were. On about the fourth day of this hell I felt sure that I could see one of the German observation posts, but Regimental Headquarters was about 500 yards from the forward infantry and tank positions: argument ensued as to whether the slight movement on the forward slopes was enemy or our own troops.

Eventually I got Gerry Hopkinson to agree to my going forward on foot to find out exactly where our own infantry were. I jumped out of my tank, and ran like hell to where I knew there was a slit trench. I got to it about a second before the shells started falling on the area. When all was quiet I moved on to the next place of safety. I reached a farmyard where there was a Company Headquarters, and under cover of the walls I was able to stand up, which was a relief after crawling along hedges. The company commander was busy explaining to me which hedges to crawl along to reach the forward platoons, when suddenly the whole area was alive with bursting shells. I dropped where I was, and huddled up against the wall. The company commander and two other men tried to reach their dugouts, but they never got as far. The shelling stopped as suddenly as it started: my three companions lay dead a few paces from me.

Moving even more carefully, I slowly crawled forward and eventually reached the forward platoon position. From here I could clearly identify the general location of where the German observation post was. I asked the Platoon Commander if there were any of our troops forward of him, and he admitted that there were none, but he was sure the Germans had no positions within at least 300 yards of him. Yet, according to my calculations, this German position was in the middle of a wheatfield about 200 yards from where we were. Stupidly I decided to confirm my suspicions.

The corn was almost waist-high, and I had no trouble in remaining concealed as I crawled forward up the gentle slope towards the position where I suspected the observation post was. But, of course, my field of view was very limited, so after crawling about 100 yards, I slowly stood up, looking ahead very carefully. I was standing with my legs apart looking through my binoculars when the Germans fired at me. They had a very cleverly concealed anti-tank gun not more than 100 yards from me, and it was a shell from this gun that they fired at me.

I would like to have met that German gunner and congratulated him on his marksmanship. He had evidently been taught to shoot at the bottom of the 'bull', and as a result the shot passed between my legs, and all it did was to burn two holes in my trousers and singe my crutch. An inch higher and he would have claimed the family jewels! When I got back to my tank, I had much pleasure in hitting the anti-tank gun with my first shot. Yet even though we managed to subdue this particular observation post, the Germans evidently had another that was able to watch our every movement because their accurate shelling continued to make our life more than miserable.

For eight days and eight nights we were almost continually in our tanks: the driver was the best off, because he could sleep in his seat, but the three in the turret had a most uncomfortable existence. It is not humanly possible to lie down or even sit back in comfort, and so for most of that terrible time we were standing. After about the sixth day our ankles and feet began to swell, and by the end of this hell there was hardly a man who could wear even a pair of loosely fitting plimsolls.

Eventually we were relieved, and we drove back in the darkness to a field some 3 miles behind the front line. As each tank halted, the crew tumbled out and dropped into a deep sleep within seconds. We shared the field with a battery of medium guns that were in action most of the night; at least that is what they told us next morning, and they were not a little surprised to find that their dreadful bangings had not disturbed us.

I suppose it was about 10 o'clock in the morning when the messenger eventually managed to shake me out of my deep slumber, and I read his message and groaned with misery. 'You have been selected to command 7th Royal Tank Regiment. You are required to take over immediately. This is urgent.' I had not the heart to wake Gerry Hopkinson to ask for the loan of two 'stars' to convert myself into a Lieutenant Colonel, so I merely stole them off his jacket.

I must have presented a sorry sight to my new Regiment when I joined them two hours later. My eyes were still heavy with sleep, and my feet were clad in plimsolls which had been cut in several places to make room for my swollen feet. However, neither they nor I had time to worry about such matters, because we were to take part in a large attack which was due to start that afternoon. My predecessor had been seriously wounded, and his Second in Command killed the day before, hence the reason my presence was demanded so urgently. My task was not easy: I did not know one single officer or man in the Regiment, and to make matters worse for me they were equipped with Churchill tanks with which I had no previous experience or training.

The 7 RTR was a Regiment raised like many in the early days of the war and was, in fact, 10 RTR. When Tobruk fell 4 and 7 RTR were 'put in the bag' so Whitehall renamed 10 RTR, 7 RTR, and 144 RAC Rgt became 4 RTR. I suppose this confused the enemy and the public! The Regiment was under command of 31st Tank Brigade whose two 'Churchill Regiments' would be 'farmed out' to infantry divisions for close support operations. They arrived in Normandy towards the end of June, and this was the first time any of them had been in battle. My Second in Command was Maj Howard-Jones, the only prewar officer in the Regiment. I mention this because RTR officers were in short supply, unlike the Cavalry.

At 3 p.m on the day I took over command, my Regiment was involved in an attack to capture the village of Maltot. This village lies beneath the slopes of Hill 112, not far from where 44 RTR had spent the last eight days and nights under fire. We were supporting an Infantry Brigade, part of 43 Infantry Division commanded by Maj Gen G.I. Thomas. I remember well the two battalions we supported were men from Wiltshire. The attack worked like clockwork. By dusk the village was in our hands, and the infantry took up defensive positions with the tanks of 'A' Squadron commanded by Maj Dick Jocelyne and 'B' Squadron commanded by Maj Allan Taylor. 'C' Squadron was in reserve – it had suffered heavily in previous engagements, and the Commander was young and inexperienced. When I joined them, the 7th had lost half their officers in action.

For me, this could not have been a better start, as the CO of this 'new' Regiment, and a few hours before dawn I fell asleep a happy man. At dawn, my Adjutant, Jackie Fitt, woke me and said the Divisional Commander wanted me to report to his Headquarters immediately. So it was some 30 minutes later I appeared before this Senior Officer in a beautiful Normandy orchard some 5 miles from the famous Hill 112.

Maj Gen Thomas, whose nickname was 'Von Thoma', was a ruthless tough soldier, a Gunner by 'trade' commanding an Infantry Division. Like many of the Infantry Division, his had suffered heavy losses in the Normandy 'bocage' country, and indeed his Division had captured Maltot, but had been counter-attacked and driven out. On that occasion 9 RTR had supported the attack, and Thomas considered that they had pulled back and left the infantry to look after themselves. This was understandable, because the armoured regiments had been trained only to operate by day, and at the end of a battle withdrew to replenish and carry out repairs.

This fiery little General looked me up and down, probably noted my footwear – plimsolls cut to accommodate swollen feet, and understandably took a dislike to me. I don't blame him. 'Where are your Squadrons? – Back replenishing, no doubt, and leaving the infantry with no support, as usual, I suppose.' I explained to him that this was not the case. A and B Squadrons were forward in the village with two Wiltshire Battalions. C Squadron with the third Battalion – the Somersets – were in reserve some 2 miles back from Maltot. General Thomas 'blew up'. 'That Squadron should be well forward, there,' he said, pointing to the slopes of Hill 112 and some 400 yards forward of the village. I tried to explain to him that not only was there no cover for them, but also they would be sitting targets for Tiger tanks on Hill 112. 'Do as you are bloody well told. Order them to move there immediately, and don't argue,' he shouted. 'I refuse,' I replied.

He went pink in the face, strode over to my scout car, picked up the radio microphone, and started to shout out orders for C Squadron. As he had little idea of our codes, the orders were meaningless. I gave in, and told the poor young Squadron Commander to proceed into the 'valley of death'. As I put the microphone down, the General picked it up and shouted his final order. 'This is the General speaking. Bloody well get a move on, or you will be sacked!' He knew only too well that the minute his back was turned I would cancel the order, and thus he propelled me deeper into the orchard and proceeded to tell me what he thought of me and my ancestors. When eventually I was allowed to leave the Divisional Headquarters, many minutes had passed, and worse was to follow – I could not get through to my Regiment on the wireless.

I arrived in Maltot village in time to see the twelfth tank 'brew up' and the Squadron virtually ceased to exist. It was my turn to lose my temper, and I did. I transferred to another scout car, and sent the following message to my Adjutant. 'Tell General Thomas that I am on my way to General Montgomery's headquarters to get him sacked.' When I arrived, the two Generals were outside the famous caravan obviously discussing my future. I think I would have strangled him had I been allowed to get near him.

It was only after he had gone that the C in C sent for me. I was about to tell him that it was now impossible for me to go back to that Regiment after this disaster, but he stopped me. 'I know all about it – most unfortunate – but I order you to return to your Regiment immediately and resume command. By the time you rejoin them, you will find they have moved from Thomas's Division, and I assure you that never again will you serve under him – never.' 'Monty' kept his word.

In fact, I did see Gen Thomas on several occasions after the end of the war,[2] and the last occasion was when, as Quartermaster General, he paid an official visit to HQ East Africa Command in 1950. I was serving on the staff of this Headquarters in Nairobi and, being Kenya born, I escorted him. His final week in the country was spent with my father at his beautiful farm beneath the slopes of Mount Kenya. But that is another story.

Two days after the battle of Maltot we were involved in another attack – this time supporting 53 Division. Again a success, and then on to support another Division in its attack. Rarely did we get a day's rest and we must have fought in every sector of the British Normandy beachhead. In six weeks we suffered thirty-five officer casualties. But this was nothing in comparison to the casualties suffered by the infantry. It was they who were constantly thrown into battle by Monty in his effort to stop the Germans putting in a major attack against the Americans, and they succeeded.

Slowly but surely the Allied Forces pushed forward, away from the beaches where we had landed towards the great trunk roads that led to the River Seine and Paris. Finally came the great battle of the Falaise Gap where so many Germans were killed or captured, and the battle of Normandy was over. The race forward to Belgium and Holland took place, and the slow heavy Churchill tanks were almost non-starters. Not because these tanks were unreliable mechanically, far from it, but because their task in the hard slogging match was over. The Armoured Divisions now came into their own, and they were not equipped with Churchill tanks.

For a week we were left at peace camped in a beautiful Normandy orchard, a land literally flowing in milk and honey. Yet we were busy all day repairing our tanks and training new crews. Then came the order to move, and we were glad that we had not been forgotten. Two days later we were across the Seine, and moving towards the great port of Le Havre. The Germans had left behind strong garrison forces guarding the Channel ports, many of which had been turned into vast fortresses which were capable of holding out, unsupported, for many months. Le Havre was one of these, and we were now to take part in its reduction. My Regiment played a notable part in the attack; we were the first to cross the start line, and the first to reach the final objective – the Town Hall!

I was with my leading troop of tanks when they arrived at the Town Hall, and it was a memorable occasion. The Mayor and all his minions were there to welcome us, dressed in their best robes and ready to ladle out as much champagne as we cared to drink. Pretty girls surrounded us, and never before had I been kissed so often by old and young. I enjoyed it. Unfortunately we were ordered out of the town within an hour, but not before we had a collected a large quantity of loot. The German Officers' mess wine cellar was perhaps our best find.

A few days later we were once again on the move, and this time we were told our destination was north of Brussels in Belgium. It was now September and beginning to get a little cold, but the countryside was beautiful and one had plenty of time to admire it in a slow-moving Churchill tank. There was no fighting, there was no great hurry, and I had very few worries. But it was not to last. When we were less than a day's march from the Belgian frontier, I got orders to halt my Regiment and report to the Brigade Commander. I always thought that Brig 'Wahoo' Clarke had a habit of picking on my Regiment for nasty jobs, and this now confirmed my suspicions.

In 1940 when Czechoslovakia was overrun by the German forces, many Czech officers and men escaped to Britain. Here they were formed into an independent Infantry Brigade. Later, in fact not long before D-Day, they were converted to an Armoured Brigade. Now there was a shortage of infantry, and this armoured brigade, which had yet to fight in battle, was ordered to take over an infantry task. To soften the blow, it was decided that a regular British tank unit should suffer the same fate, and Brig 'Wahoo' told me that my Regiment was the one chosen.

Thus it came about that towards the end of September 1944, the 7th Royal Tank Regiment came under command of the Czech Independent Armoured Brigade commanded by Gen Lishka. Now to explain our task. Dunkirk was another of the fortified ports and contained a garrison of some 30,000 men. As it was so strongly fortified, it was not to be attacked; instead, a force was to be left behind investing it and ensuring that the Germans did not break out. The Czech Brigade was to take over this task, and thus relieve a brigade of 51st Highland Division who were at that time holding the ring. 'Wahoo' Clarke bade me a fond farewell and wished my Regiment luck in their new role as infantrymen. He promised to visit us!

Notes

1.   The Panther was one of the best, if not the best, medium-heavy tanks of the Second World War. Its design was a direct result of the shock the Germans had received from

encountering such Soviet tanks as the T 34 and KV 1. Weighing some 43–5 tons, it was armed with a 7.5cm KwK 42 L/70 gun. Its graceful lines, good protection and mechanical reliability (after a few initial problems), made it well-liked by its crews and feared by its opponents.

2.   Rea Leakey was commanding 5 RTR after the war as part of the British Army of the Rhine and, in early 1946, was stationed in terrible barracks in the Hamm area (Rea described them as being little better than the conditions experienced living rough in the North African desert!). He had complained about their appalling living conditions and, as a result, was told to expect a visit from the Corps Commander. This turned out to be 'Von Thoma', namely, Lt Gen Sir Ivo Thomas. After his visit, he asked if he could speak to all the officers alone in the mess. As Rea later recalled: 'His talk to us went something like this – "I have seen your barracks and you will get priority for building repairs, sports facilities and so on . . . But my main purpose in visiting you today is a very personal one, and this is why I have come here with none of my Staff Officers. In June 1944, I was commanding 43 Infantry Division in Normandy. In one of our more successful battles we captured the village of Matlot, resting beneath the slopes of the notorious Hill 112. The next morning I summoned the Commanding Officer of 7 RTR to my Headquarters. I had never met him because he took over command of that Regiment two hours before the battle started. To cut a long story short, I ordered him to move his third squadron to take over a position on Hill 112. He refused, but I bullied him into giving the order and made sure that he would not cancel it when I let him return to his scout car, because I knew he would cancel it. The Squadron was destroyed and the fault was mine. I have come today to apologize." For the two of us it was a moving occasion; the tears were streaming down his face. Some three years later I met him again. I was Military Secretary (Major) at HQ East Africa Command in Nairobi, and said farewell to him at the airport. He was a lonely man, a ruthless soldier, not liked by many, but that is not uncommon if you rise to the higher rank and have to win battles or be sacked.'

CHAPTER THIRTEEN

Dunkirk:
September–December 1944

Editor It was the Canadian 2nd Corps that was operating in the coastal belt, on the far left flank of 21st Army Group, Montgomery's intention being for them to clear the area west of Antwerp up to the southern shores of the Scheldt estuary and, at the same time, reduce the garrisons of Boulogne and Calais, while investing the even tougher nut of Dunkirk. The port had become a major German naval base and bastion of the 'Westwall'.[1] Some 30,000 German troops were holding Boulogne, Calais and Dunkirk. Whilst operations for the clearing of the Scheldt were developing, Boulogne and Calais were both stormed. The assault on the former began on 17 September, the latter on 25 September. Boulogne surrendered on 22 September and Calais on 30 September, after heavy fighting in both fortresses. It was then decided that the Canadians should concentrate on clearing the Scheldt, so Dunkirk, which continued to be invested, became an Army Group responsibility and Montgomery put the Czechslovak Independent Armoured Brigade in charge of the investing forces.

Dunkirk would in fact hold out until 10 May 1945 when, with the unconditional surrender of Germany, it was the last French town to be liberated. Rea Leakey would, however, not remain throughout these long months of siege. Indeed, he would be on his way to command yet another Regiment – 5 RTR – soon after his twenty-ninth birthday (30 December 1944). Nevertheless, the action around Dunkirk was a tough one and 7 RTR, dismounted in the infantry role, would suffer a fair number of casualties until Rea decided on a novel approach to make up for his lack of numbers. His employment of tanks to hold positions at night was similar to the tactics employed by the Commonwealth Division during the latter part of the Korean War, when Centurion tanks, equipped with searchlights, fought by night in frontline positions, in support of the dug-in infantry, along the 38th Parallel. 7 RTR's highly successful operations in support of the Czechs, would also result in the well-deserved award of the Czechoslovak Military Cross to their CO.

Rea Leakey What a grand crowd those Czechs were; the more we saw of them the more we liked them, particularly Maj Gen Alois Lishka. When I met him he told me, most apologetically, that my Regiment was to take over the most difficult sector because, after all, we were a regular Regiment. I learned later that, in their eyes, this was a great honour! I then visited the 1st Battalion the Black Watch from whom I was to take over. They were holding some 6,000 yards of front to the south of Dunkirk, and guarded the direct route to Calais. The Commanding Officer, Lt Col John Hopwood, greeted me with joy. 'Thank goodness for a few tanks in this area; we need them as things are a bit hot round here. Last night the Germans were throwing hand grenades at me here at my headquarters. Not so funny, as we are at least 2 miles behind the frontline. Who are your infantry?' I then explained that my Regiment was to relieve them, and that we were the infantry who were to relieve him. He just roared with laughter and explained that his Battalion, up to full strength and augmented by two dismounted anti-aircraft batteries, was finding very great difficulty in holding the line.

'How many men can you raise?' I would have to leave some men guarding the tanks, so at the most 400 officers and men would be available to man the defensive positions. And I explained that few would be armed with rifles, and we had a few Bren guns, but, of course, no support weapons, such as mortars or anti-tank weapons. He told me he had well over double that figure. 'If you are still holding the line in a fortnight's time, send me a signal, and you will receive a crate of whisky – and I would remind you that I am a Scotsman.'

So we dumped our tanks in a small town called Gravelines, and on a dark September night took over from the Black Watch. We knew we were going to be employed as infantry for some time, so it would be necessary to have one of the Squadrons out of the line in reserve. As a result, where the Black Watch had a platoon defensive post manned by thirty men, we put in no more than ten.

Our sector was flat, mostly waterlogged, and the only cover was one small village and a few farmhouses. Two roads led in towards the town of Dunkirk, and there was also a short road leading from the small village directly to the seashore. Vehicles could not move across country. By day we saw few Germans. They had plenty of artillery, but not a lot of ammunition. By night, however, they were very active.

I well remember the night we took over; the Black Watch put on a firework display, the like of which I had not seen before. They certainly had a great variety of weapons and plenty of ammunition. As a result the Germans left us alone, and the handover was completed by midnight. From then on there was silence, and no doubt the enemy was anxious to know what was going on. It did not take them long to find out.

Our first night was peaceful, although various positions were shelled and German patrols were active. On the second night one of our posts held by a dozen men was attacked and overrun. Two men escaped, but the rest were killed or captured. The next night the same thing happened to another post, and this was to be the pattern of operations for the following two nights. On the sixth night the strongest and most important of our positions astride the road leading to Calais, manned by 23 men, was attacked by a force of 500 men (so we discovered later), and this time none of our men escaped. At dawn we found the Germans had occupied this position and were holding it in strength.

The situation was serious, because now there was little to stop the Germans pushing on to Gravelines and even to Calais – now one of the most important posts in our hands. By midday I had assembled a company of about 100 men armed with a variety of weapons, and ten Churchill tanks moved forward, fully crewed. We had little difficulty in recapturing the post, killed a number of the enemy, and took over 50 prisoners. That certainly kept things quiet for a while, and in due course the whisky arrived, but it was a near thing.

Before long the Germans were at us again, and night after night our isolated posts were attacked. It was now becoming bitterly cold and most nights the temperature fell below freezing point. The morale of my men in their waterlogged weapon pits was beginning to drop, and I realized that this state of affairs could not go on. Studying the map, I found there was a lateral road running across our front some 2,000 yards plus of our positions. There were two 'feeder' tracks leading up to this road from our area. This gave me an idea. If we could attack and capture this lateral road not only would we narrow our front, but it would also be invaluable for our tanks, because they could then use it to move across the front. I arranged for as many tanks as possible to be fitted with a spotlight.

Once again I called in all the men from the forward posts and this time formed two teams; each team consisted of ten tanks and about fifty men. With this small force I launched an attack against the German positions. Each team was based on one of the two feeder roads leading up to the lateral road; the tanks were, of course, roadbound, but, as the country was flat and open, they could give supporting fire to either flank for a considerable distance. We caught the Germans 'napping', and within 2 hours we had reached the lateral road, and we continued to push forward. By this time we had captured quite a number of prisoners, and they were becoming a bit of an embarrassment; when we asked Brigade to come and collect them, they quite naturally asked how we had collected them. I had forgotten to tell Gen Lishka about the attack! He was just a little annoyed. However, later on he awarded me the Czechoslovakian Military Cross, so he must have forgiven me.[2]

As darkness closed in on us we fell back to the lateral road, more tanks were brought forward, and we took up our future defensive positions that were to last until Germany surrendered. No longer did the men occupy damp holes in the ground; the tanks, fully manned, were spaced across the front on the lateral road and acted as pill-boxes, each equipped with a spotlight. At dawn the tanks moved back down the feeder roads and spent the day hidden around farmyards. The crews slept; at dusk they moved forward again and took up station on the lateral road. It was certainly a novel way of holding a front line, and many Senior Officers were most sceptical. Brig 'Wahoo' paid us a visit shortly after we had adopted these tactics, and, to give him his due, he refrained from criticism. He evidently decided to wait and see!

The Germans soon realized our game and tried every means possible to make us abandon it. Almost every night aircraft from Germany used to drop supplies for the beleaguered garrison. We used to send up recognition flares, and thus received a number of these supply drops. Mostly they consisted of short-range anti-tank weapons, although we did collect a proportion of their mail.

Armed with these anti-tank weapons, German patrols were out every night trying to destroy our tanks. Only once did they achieve any degree of success, and this was early in December in a blinding snowstorm. By this time they knew the position of almost every tank so it was not surprising that even at night in a snowstorm one patrol located a tank. From a range of a few yards they fired a hollow-charge armour piercing shell at the tank, and hit it. Fortunately, the shell hit the outer edge of one of the tracks, and expended its force on the track plates. It did very little damage to the tank, and not one member of the crew was even scratched. The crew could, of course, see nothing, but opened fire in the direction of where they thought the enemy patrol might be. Next morning they discovered two dead bodies.

As a result of this novel system of holding the line, our casualty rate dropped from a high figure to nil. Also, we found that we needed fewer men actually in the line, and so we could ring the changes and get people away on short leave. Before long we had trained patrol teams who would go out on almost every night giving the enemy a little of their own medicine. They also made sure that no mines were laid on the roads which the tanks used, and just as well! One night twelve anti-tank mines were laid on one of the roads which was used. Fortunately a patrol found them.

During the day there was very little activity, and we tended to think that the Germans would never venture out of their defences in daylight. How wrong we were. One Sunday afternoon in November my Second in Command, Bob Romsey, and I decided to walk down to the seashore. I now had some French soldiers under my command, and they were manning a position in the sand dunes. We decided to visit them.

As we arrived, all hell was let loose, and I realized that the Germans were about to assault this small strongpoint. This was the first time these men had been in action, and it was just as well we turned up, despite the fact that we were only armed with walking sticks, because they panicked and there was little chance of their escaping. Bob was slightly lame, so I told him to take command while I set off at the double across the open ground to get help. Fortunately, I was some 300 yards away before the enemy opened fire on me, and once again my luck held. I was able to wake up the crews of these tanks and get them into action, but it was a close thing, and taught us a lesson.

On Christmas Day all was peace and quiet on our front, and we celebrated in the usual Army manner. Our rations were excellent, and there was no lack of champagne. I felt that life for me in command of the 7th Royal Tank Regiment was good. But it was not to last. The day of 30 December is my birthday, and I gave a party for those officers who could leave the front. At about 8 p.m., when the party was in full swing, I received a telephone call from Army Group HQ. It was Maj Gen Rickie Richards, who was now FM Montgomery's tank adviser. He was short and sharp. 'You will move at once and take over 5 RTR. They are in action near a village called Sittard in Holland. And don't argue.' My birthday party then developed into a farewell party, and many officers and men, including Czechs, called in, even if only for a few minutes. I was very sorry to leave the 7th. I think they had accepted me despite my disastrous second day in command, and they were certainly a very good Regiment. It had been an honour to have commanded them.

Notes

1.   During the invasion Hitler had declared the following places to be 'fortresses': Ijmuiden, Walcheren Island, Dunkirk, Calais, Cap Gris Nez, Boulogne, Dieppe, Le Havre, Cherbourg, St Malo, Brest, Lorient, St Nazaire, Lapallise, Royan and the mouth of the Gironde. This tied up some 200,000 troops and much valuable material and did not really hinder the Allies drive eastwards.

2.   Maj Gen Lishka, wrote to Rea Leakey on 1 May 1945, telling him that the President of the Czechoslovak Republic had awarded him the Czechoslovak Military Cross 1939, in appreciation of all services rendered to his Brigade. he went on: 'I want to take this opportunity to congratulate you on behalf of myself and all officers and men of the Brigade. Your assistance to the Brigade has been most valuable and the fact that I am in the position to express the recognition of your work in this way gives me great satisfaction.' The Investiture Parade was held on 6 May.

CHAPTER FOURTEEN

Holland and Germany

Editor Rea Leakey was now about to join his fifth wartime Regiment, appropriately enough, the 5th Royal Tank Regiment. 5 RTR had also fought both in North Africa and Italy, returning home with the rest of the 7th Armoured Division to prepare for the invasion. Together with 1 RTR, they had landed on 7 June as part of 22nd Armd Bde and had fought throughout the difficult battles in France and the Low Countries. Their Commanding Officer since landing, Lt Col C.A. 'Gus' Holliman, was killed when a shell hit his scout car just outside RHQ 1 RTR, where he had gone for a conference. Rea would replace him in January 1945, and take the Fifth on into Germany and victory. When Rea arrived 5 RTR was taking part in Operation Blackcock, which was designed to clear the area between the Meuse and the Roer in preparation for the northward drive to the Rhine of the US Ninth Army, which was aimed to coincide with the 21st Army Group's assault through the formidable Siegfried Line positions in the Reichswald forest area. The weather was appalling – first snow and ice, then the mud and slush of a quick thaw.

This chapter, despite its brevity, covers the last five months of the war, when the Allies were moving steadily forward, following the failure of the German Ardennes offensive. Hitler had ordered his troops to stand fast west of the Rhine and not allow the Allies to cross. However, this proved too much for the now weakened German forces, who were assailed in the west by three Allied Army Groups: Devers's 6th in the south, Bradley's 12th in the centre and Montgomery's 21st in the north. The Supreme Commander, Gen Eisenhower, had planned to cross the Rhine on a broad front, but first his armies had to tackle the Siegfried Line, plus the flood-swollen river barriers of the Moselle, Sauer and Our. To this had to be added the bitter winter weather. However, despite all these problems, by March all three Army Groups had reached the Rhine. Although US First Army were the first to secure a crossing on 7 March – at Remagen – followed by the US Third Army on 22 March, the 21st Army Group's major crossing on a 25-mile front between Emmerich and Rheinberg (codenamed Operation Plunder) on 23 March was a resounding success, which Montgomery reckoned was one of his best organized operations. Three days later, Gen Miles Dempsey, C in C British 2nd Army, in which 7th Armd Div was serving in XII Corps, told his troops as they crossed the great river: 'This is collapse! The German line is broken. The enemy no longer has a coherent system of defence between the Rhine and the Elbe. It is difficult to see what there is to stop us now.' And 45 days later it was all over. However, there was still plenty of fighting to be done in those last seven and a half weeks of the war.

Towards the end of the chapter, Rea Leakey delineates the route which the Fifth took towards the great city of Hamburg, together with the rest of 7th Armoured Division, 1 RTR being the first to capture the vital bridges over the Elbe, leading into the city on 3 May. The first troops to officially enter the centre of Hamburg were the Division's armoured car regiment, the 11th Hussars, followed by 1/5th Queens and 5 RTR, who passed through the much bombed city to the Adolf Hitler Platz, establishing their HQ at the Streits Hotel. The surrender of the city was received by a party led by Brig John Spurling, commander 131 Bde, on the afternoon of 3 May 1945. Gen Alwin Wolf was accompanied by the Mayor and a Nazi Intelligence Officer, sporting a Christchurch scarf with his uniform – to show that he had been educated at Oxford University! Thereafter, 7th Armoured were ordered to press on towards Denmark, but were then halted around the Kiel Canal area, where as well as enemy soldiers, 10,000 German sailors surrendered to the divisional commander, Maj Gen Lou Lyne. The final capitulation of the Third Reich was now only a matter of time and on 7 May 1945, Germany surrendered unconditionally; the following day was Victory in Europe Day (VE Day). The Fifth, according to their War Diary, celebrated VE Day: 'in the usual way with bonfires and the shooting of Verey lights.' The war was over!

Rea Leakey At about 9 a.m. on 1 January 1945, I found HQ 22 Armoured Brigade – under command of 7th Armoured Division – and reported to Brig Tony Wingfield. He had been Second in Command of 34 Tank Brigade under Brig 'Wahoo' Clarke, so he knew me well. I have a suspicion that he had asked for me. 'Glad you have arrived. Your Regiment is having a pretty tough battle a few miles from here, and the sooner you join them the better.'

It was snowing quite hard, and visibility was poor as I drove forward to where I could hear the tank guns in action. Before long I was up among the forward troops, and I asked the driver of a passing vehicle if he could tell me where I could find RHQ 5 RTR. He guided me forward for another 500 yards, and then pointed to four tanks which were moving across a snow-covered field. I thanked him and set off in pursuit of them in my Humber staff car. When they halted, I climbed on to one of the tanks and was about to introduce myself to the occupants when, in a second, the area around was alive with bursting shells. 'Get off this bloody tank – I am moving for cover.' And with that the tank rolled forward. I jumped off and ran back to my staff car. It had been hit by shell splinters, but fortunately neither the driver nor it had suffered serious damage. We followed the tanks to the cover of a small wood.

'Blimey, sir, what a reception to your new Regiment; don't you wish you was back with the 7th?' How right, what a reception, and indeed I longed to be back with the 7th. I was cold, hungry, miserable and lonely; I knew only one officer in the 5th, and I was not sure that he was still with them. I had no map, I did not know this country, and I had no idea what was going on. But at least this Regiment was part of 7th Armoured Division, the Desert

Rats, and I had known them well in the Western Desert. When I came up to the tanks a second time, an officer dismounted and came forward to meet me. He happened to be the only officer I knew in the 5th, Maj Macdonald. 'We have just heard from Brigade that you are coming to command us.' He then explained what had happened. The previous CO, an old friend of mine called 'Gus' Holliman, had been killed at the start of this particular battle. The Second in Command and the Adjutant were away in England, and he, Macdonald, was called in from his squadron to take over temporary command. Once again I found myself in a new type of tank; this time it was a Cromwell, a very fast but lightly armoured tank, certainly a change from the slow heavy Churchill.

For about another week this battle continued, and then we reached the Siegfried Line, which was the final objective. It had been hard fighting, but the weather was almost as bad as the enemy; it was bitterly cold and, more often than not, it snowed. Our tanks were painted white to match the landscape, and we wore white smocks. For another fortnight we remained in the front line and carried out many minor raids against the enemy positions. The area in which we operated was heavily mined, but we did not discover this until the ground began to thaw and we had several tanks and other vehicles badly damaged by these mines.

Then we were relieved, and we moved back to a Belgian village called Bree, where we remained for the next fortnight. Up to this time I had not had the chance or the time to meet many of the officers and men, and I had been in command of the Regiment for a month. I discovered that a large number of them had been with the Regiment for many years and the Regiment had seldom been long out of action throughout the war. Many were beginning to get war weary, and they had certainly had their 'bellyfull'. I soon noticed the difference between this Regiment and the 7th. The 5th fought as hard as any and with a good deal of cunning; where the 7th would lose two tanks, they would lose one. Even so, I missed that 'urge to go' which the 7th never lacked.

I was glad of our stay in Bree, because it gave me the chance to get to know the Regiment; I met the QM and his staff for the first time, and others who had been on leave. Gus Holliman was a hard man to follow – the Regiment rightly thought the world of him. I was the 'new broom', and I had to make changes, and they are never popular.[1] One of the squadron commanders, Pat Wood, was an Army boxer, senior to me – and suffered from deafness. The Adjutant, Jackie Garnett, I had first met before the war in 4 RTR when I was a very junior officer and he was a corporal with several years service. We had one thing in common – neither of us was good at reading and writing, and, thank goodness, I was his senior; one of us had to go. In his place, I chose a young officer called Roy Dixon, and this caused a little friction because of his age, but he had won an MC and he was educated. I think that at that time my only friend in the Regiment was L Cpl King. He was my scout-car driver/operator, and he was some eight years older than me. He was a married man who had been called up in 1944, and so, like me, he was a newcomer to this well-tried Regiment.

Too soon for our liking came the orders to get moving, and we all prayed that this would be our final run to victory. The next ten days were spent in moving forward and preparing for the assault across the Rhine. On the great day of the crossing we were not involved, but we had a grandstand view of the airborne drop across the river, and it was certainly an impressive spectacle. By the time we reached the banks of the river a floating bridge had been erected, and we drove our tanks across in perfect safety. In fact, we moved forward for another 4 miles before the enemy made his presence felt. I had gone ahead of the Regiment in a scout car, and got heavily shelled as I entered a small village. I saw a number of German soldiers moving back through the village and decided to wait until the leading squadron came up before tackling them.

Our orders were merely to push on as fast as possible into the heart of Germany, and those orders held good until the very end. By last light we had not got very far; we had yet to learn that the fields were still very soft after heavy rain, and it was almost impossible to move off the roads without getting bogged. So roads and tracks became, as always in war in Europe, all-important. We were confined to one country track, and thus the Regiment advanced on a one-tank front. The speed of the advance was almost entirely governed by the speed and daring of the leading vehicle. At this stage the Germans held no organized line; they mainly operated in small groups who were ordered to block the routes and die at their posts. They had large quantities of short-range anti-tank weapons, and these were ideal for use in wooded country and villages. The leading vehicle got knocked out sooner or later, and nobody enjoyed the honour of leading the Regiment.

On 1 April we captured the town of Rheine on the River Ems, but all the bridges were blown, and we received orders to pull back and try to find a crossing further to the south. Two days later we were lucky to find a bridge intact, and early next morning we entered the town of Diepholtz. As this town was full of hospitals, the Germans did not fight for it. We were now on a good main road, and by last light we had covered over 40 miles. As usual each village or town was defended, and we had to fight our way through. Often we found it necessary to set fire to the odd house or shop to discourage snipers who used to lie up in the attics and shoot at us as we passed beneath.

In one town I asked the Mayor why he did not tell the soldiers to get out of his town, and thus avoid houses being burnt or damaged by shellfire. He replied that he had not thought of it. I asked him if he was in telephonic communication with the next town on our route, and he confirmed that the line was still working. 'Well, phone the Mayor and tell him he had better surrender his town and so avoid houses being burnt down.' Sure enough, when we reached this town, white flags were waved, and we passed through without a shot being fired. After this we made a point of phoning through to the Mayors and telling them not to fight. In most cases it worked.

It was in the wooded areas that we had most of our troubles, and, of course, in towns where there was a natural obstacle such as a river or canal. But all the same, our casualties were very light, and we continued to advance rapidly. Then we were ordered to make for Bremen. It was the same drill – keep going on the one road until the leading vehicle was 'brewed up'. I remember that on this occasion it was a scout car from the reconnaissance troop. As it approached a wood, it was hit and the crew of two killed – one, a young officer who had joined the Regiment three months earlier.

The road was mined, and the enemy were in strength in the wood either side of the road. We had a company of the 1st Rifle Brigade working with us and, supported by the tanks on the road they entered the wood. The battle was short and sharp. The infantry got a bloody nose, lost a number of men and had to withdraw. The leading tank hit a mine and was promptly 'brewed up'. The crew were killed, and the tank commander was a man named Sgt Jake Wardrop. Like Jackie Garnett, he and his family were Yorkshire miners, and they knew each other well. When the 5th went into action for the first time in France in 1940, Wardrop was a tank driver. He kept a diary throughout the war, and regularly sent instalments home to his mother. In 1963, when I was commanding 7th Armoured Brigade (Desert Rats) stationed at Soltau in Germany, Garnett was commanding a squadron in 5 RTR under my command. He had edited the Wardrop diaries given to him by Jake's mother, and he asked me to vet them before publication. I had to 'blue pencil' some of his comments about officers he named, because they were far from complimentary. The diaries have been published and are well worth reading.[2]

We managed to find a way round the wood and just as we started to move into Bremen, the Brigadier ordered me to withdraw because enemy tanks were attacking his Headquarters which was following behind the 5th. So we failed to be the first British troops to enter Bremen. The next day we were ordered to move south-east and join 53 Infantry Division. Their task was to cross the River Aller. For the next few days all three Squadrons were supporting Infantry Battalions fighting through woods and villages. It was tough going, and we suffered our fair share of casualties.

I recall two incidents that occurred during this phase. A troop (4 tanks) commanded by Lt Keith Crocker (a nephew of Gen Sir John Crocker) was leading a column of infantry on a road – as usual – and as they entered a wood, all four tanks were hit by anti-tank rockets and 'brewed up'. Most of the crews escaped uninjured, and Crocker then led them in an attack against the enemy post and won the day. It was a gallant action and maybe he should have been recommended for a medal, but the 5th were not generous in this respect – so I discovered.

Another troop commanded by Lt Lou Jones found themselves well ahead of the infantry they were supporting, when darkness fell. They had captured a small enemy position occupying farm buildings in a wood. They decided to stay the night in comfort with their prisoners. At about midnight a strong enemy patrol rushed the buildings, and within a few minutes the fighting was over. Lou and the soldiers not on sentry duty were caught with their 'boots off'. The first Lou knew about the incident was when he was kicked in the ribs and told to get dressed. Whilst they were preparing themselves for inevitable captivity, the German officer in charge of the patrol stood guard over them brandishing his pistol. Stupidly he turned his back on Lou and that was his end. Lou was a tough rugby forward and that officer died quickly. Jones knew how to use his boots. Minutes later the tables were turned. Jones removed his boots and resumed his 'Egyptian physical training.'

The 53rd Division closed in on the town of Rethem on the River Aller, and it was heavily defended. One of the Brigades was given the task of capturing it and hopefully the bridge across the river. They were to have the support of the Corps and Divisional Artillery and 5 RTR. Like all the British Infantry Divisions, the 53rd had suffered heavy casualties, and at this stage of the war, nobody was very keen to earn medals. So the policy was, correctly, to use fire-power, shells and tanks, of which there were plenty.

The attack started at 3 p.m. with a heavy artillery bombardment, including smoke. The Infantry Battalions, supported by my tanks, moved forward across open ground and met heavy opposition. They failed to penetrate the defences, and when darkness fell, the order was given to withdraw. Our casualties were light, as were those of the infantry. Several tanks were knocked out, and I remember one in particular had its track broken, so it was immobile and the crew abandoned it, hoping the Germans would not set fire to it during the night.

The capture of this small town and bridge was considered vital, and 'Monty' decided to call in the RAF. 500 bombers were to obliterate it and the defending troops, but we had not been informed of this decision. At dawn L Cpl King and I set off in the scout car to visit the squadrons. As we approached 'C' Squadron we saw Maj Arthur Crickmay, the Squadron Commander, walking towards the enemy positions to see if his disabled tank had been 'brewed up'. 'Hop on,' I said, 'I will give you a lift.'

We sat on the top of the scout car, chatting about this and that and taking little notice of what was going on around us. Our minds must have been far removed from battle on that beautiful morning, and we got a rude shock when King remarked, 'Blimey, sir, I have not seen so many dead Germans lying around for many a day.' We had driven through the main defensive position on the outskirts of the town – the Germans had gone. Knowing only too well that in the town itself we should meet opposition – certainly snipers in the houses – we waited until Arthur's squadron should take over the lead.

As the leading tank approached the T-junction in the centre of the town, the troop commander went forward on his feet to peer round the corner to see if there was an anti-tank gun waiting for a 'kill'. As he poked his large nose round the corner, a bullet whistled past his head. He instantly disappeared down the road towards the sniper. I happened to be just behind him and witnessed this large Welshman, John Gwilliam by name, return carrying a small German soldier by the scruff of his neck, not unlike a cat with a mouse. 'Gwilliam,' I asked, 'was this the soldier who just missed your big nose?' Indeed it was, and I asked him why he did not kill him 'Oh, no,' he replied in his splendid Welsh voice, 'much too small.'

When last we met in 1976 he bullied me into being the Guest of Honour at his annual School Speech Day. These can be, I was told, dull occasions for the pupils and their parents. Fortunately I was in a position at least to tell the boys a little of their Headmaster's past history and so raise some interest in the closing speech. I told them of the incident involving the sniper. The story certainly caused a laugh. I thought of telling the schoolboys of another incident I witnessed concerning their Headmaster, but I lost my nerve before this formidable man. Watching one of our rugby matches, there was a bundle of fighting forwards on the ground, and from the depth of this mêlée came the cry of a large Welshman, 'Let go of my testicles, you silly little man.'

Divisional Headquarters would not believe that we had captured Rethem, and told us that 500 bombers were on their way to flatten the place. We were told to keep clear. An argument over the wireless is never really satisfactory, so while I continued to send messages I drove like mad for Divisional Headquarters. The next direct route was via three villages which had not yet been cleared of the enemy. But as this road saved me about 4 miles I decided to take it and trusted to luck that the Germans had withdrawn. As we approached the first village I could see German soldiers moving about, but it was too late to turn back. I told King to keep moving at a steady pace and, as we passed each group of soldiers, I grinned at them and gave them a wave. Not a shot was fired. The second village was also occupied and, to make matters worse, a convoy of German military vehicles was crossing my road. A policeman was directing the traffic. I had a German hunting horn with me, and I blew this hard as we approached him. He held up the traffic and let me through. Fortunately the Germans had moved out of the third village!

Divisional Headquarters were still not convinced that I had a squadron in Rethem, but when I told them exactly what had happened, they agreed to cancel the bombers. Had I arrived 15 minutes later, the bombing would have taken place. The RAF must have been just a little annoyed at having to turn back still carrying their bombs, but possibly not quite so annoyed as Crickmay would have been had they unloaded their bombs on him, or the Germans living in the town. The capture of Rethem was important, as it provided a site for a bridge across the River Aller. On 15 April we resumed the advance, once again under command of 7th Armoured Division. For the next five days we fought our way north heading direct for Hamburg. There was still a good deal of opposition and we had a particularly tough battle for the town of Soltau. As we approached the town of Hamburg we hit a series of strongly defended positions, and it was obvious that a major attack would have to be launched to break through and so to the large bridge spanning the Elbe, with Hamburg on the north bank of the river.

On 28 April I was wounded for the second time and almost in the same place. Accompanied by Maj Dennis Cockbaine, I was reconnoitring ahead of our forward tanks on foot, and the Germans shelled us. By this stage of the war, we were fairly adept at judging when a shell was going to land too close for comfort. We dropped to the ground at the same moment, but even so a shell splinter lodged itself in the right cheek of my bottom, and, as on the previous occasion, the Medical Officer removed it in the Officers' Mess with the aid of a knife and fork off the dining-table.

That must have been one of the last shells to have been fired at us, because next morning two German officers walked down the main road from Hamburg towards our forward positions carrying a white flag. This was the beginning of the end. For the next few days German officers passed through our lines, and finally on 3 May 1945 it was agreed that Hamburg would surrender. At 3 p.m., leading my Regiment from the front, we passed through the Hamburg defences and so on to the bridge crossing the Elbe. Well I remember looking down at that bridge and noticing that the explosive charges were still in position ready to drop it into the mighty river.[3]

The RAF had certainly made one hell of a mess of that great city. At the city centre the Burgomeister and his minions in their full regalia, were awaiting us. With due pomp and ceremony he handed over the keys of the city. After the ceremony I asked for a guide to take me to the best hotel still standing in this mess of rubble. So it was that I slept in the bridal suite of the Atlantic Hotel, having dined and wined better then at any time since the war had started almost six years previously.

At dawn I received orders to move north and head for Denmark as fast as the tanks would travel. As we were about to cross the Kiel Canal we were told to halt and go no further. It came in clear as a personal message to 7th Armoured Division direct from Churchill. Evidently if we had gone on, we would have captured Admiral Doenitz, and then there would have been nobody with whom to negotiate the surrender of Germany. Hitler was dead. That night the news came through that hostilities would cease at eight o'clock next morning. We were too tired mentally and physically to celebrate, but never have I slept so well.

The war in the Far East against Japan was still in progress, and I volunteered to go there. Yes, I could go, and with my Regiment. Soon I was busy going round other Regiments collecting volunteers – not that many were needed to fill our ranks because the 5th was a family that sticks together. However, the atom bomb was exploded, and the 5th Royal Tank Regiment remained in Germany. For the next eighteen months I continued to command, and my cup was full when my great friend, Dennis Coulson, joined the Regiment as my Second in Command.

But at the end of 1946 peacetime Army conditions were the vogue, and I was relieved of my command. I was much too young to be a Lieutenant Colonel! Eight years later I rejoined the 5th as Second in Command, and sailed with them to fight in Korea. I was still too young to command.

Notes

1.   Peter Vine, then a trooper serving in 5 RTR, told me that his abiding memory of Rea Leakey's arrival concerned personal hygiene: 'The first thing he said was "you men will shave". So we used to save half-an-inch of tea and use that for shaving. Since that day, except when in hospital, I have never missed a day shaving, it made an indelible print on me. He was right of course.'

2.   The edited version which Jackie Garnett produced was purely for Regimental consumption within the RTR. With permission from the late Jackie Garnett's widow and that of Jake's family, I re-edited Jake Wardrop's war diary some years ago and it was published under the title, *Tanks Across the Desert*, William Kimber & Co Ltd, 1981.

3.   Although various members of various regiments of 7th Armd Division are convinced that they were 'first into Hamburg', I discovered quite by chance that it was a staff car driver from HQ 7th Armoured Division who, when the German Garrison Commander, Gen Alwin Wolf's own Mercedes broke down, was lent with his car to the Hamburg commander to return him to the Town Hall in time to prepare for the official entry ceremony!

Postwar

In October 1945, Rea Leakey, still commanding 5 RTR in Germany, was awarded the Distinguished Service Order (DSO), for the brilliant way in which he had led the Fifth in the last year of the war. At twenty-nine, he was still far too young to be a substantive lieutenant colonel in the peacetime army – his true substantive rank was actually that of captain! He also soon found that there were lots of officers at least six years older than he lining up to take over command of the eight regular RTR Regiments that remained postwar. It was inevitable, therefore, that he would be posted to a job at a level at least one rank below the one he was presently occupying and this happened in early 1947, when he was selected to join the teaching staff at the newly opening Royal Military Academy, Sandhurst.[1] He was chosen to be the company commander (Major) of Dettingen Company, Old College, where, for two happy and rewarding years, he passed on his hard-earned wartime knowledge and battlefield expertise to future regular officers. His success can be judged by the fact that during his tenure, Dettingen won the Champion Company Competiton. His task was described by the then Chief of the Imperial General Staff, FM Montgomery, as being: 'to produce officers who will be fit, morally, mentally and physically, to lead the British soldier.' Rea was an ideal choice for such a task and took a full part in all Academy activities, running both the squash and tennis.

His next posting was most appropriately to Kenya in 1949, where he was initially selected to take command of an East African armoured car squadron. However, just as he arrived, he was 'grabbed' by the C in C (Gen Dowler) to be his Military Secretary at HQ East Africa Command.[2] This meant that he was stationed in Nairobi, only some 120 miles from his father's farm in Kignajo, rather than being several hundreds of miles further away in what had been Italian Somaliland, where the armoured cars were then operating. His tour in Kenya lasted for just over a year and during that time he married Muriel, a Kenyan-born girl, whose parents ran a hotel near Mombasa. Then it was back to teaching again, this time at the Staff College, Camberley, where for the first time since leaving 5 RTR, he was once again wearing the badges of rank of a lieutenant colonel – although he was still only being paid as a major!

In October 1953, after three staff jobs in a row, it was back to Regimental duty, this time as Second in Command of 5 RTR (only six years earlier he had been commanding!), who had been warned for operational service with the United Nations forces in their war against the North Koreans and their Chinese allies. The war had started when the North Koreans invaded South

Korea on 25 June 1950 and the British Army had provided a major part of the Commonwealth Division, including an armoured regiment of Centurion tanks. While Rea was on his way to the Far East in a 'trooper', Muriel and their two sons boarded an old passsenger liner, bound for Mombasa, where they would stay with her parents until Rea returned. 5 RTR's arrival in Korea was something of an anti-climax, as an Armistice had been signed before their ship docked at Pusan and they were moved, in unheated cattle-trucks, up to the war zone on the 38th Parallel. The Regiment was camped in Gloucester Valley, close to the hill on which the 'Glorious Glosters' had won imperishable fame in April 1951. They lived in difficult conditions, especially because of the bitter winter weather – far colder than any of them had ever experienced before in their lives. Nevertheless, despite their spartan existence and lack of amenities, they were a happy and united Regiment. In February 1954, Rea left Korea and the Fifth, sailing back to the Middle East, disembarking at Port Said, then flying on to Jordan, where he took command on the 1st Armoured Car Regiment of the Arab Legion.[3]

Rea Leakey received his commission from HM King ibn Talal Hussein, who had ruled Jordan since 1952 and had earlier been a cadet at RMA Sandhurst. As Rea himself put it: 'What a challenge!' He had last studied Arabic back in 1939 just before the war and then only for a few weeks, so it took a great deal of hard work and determination to become fluent in the Bedouin dialect, but he managed it in just six weeks. His Regiment was almost immediately moved to the Jordan valley, north of Jericho, where he and his 800 men had the task of stopping the Israelis from crossing the Jordan River. Fortunately, that particular crisis blew over and the Regiment returned to their barracks in Zerka near Amman, where Rea was reunited with his family. However, the Middle East was constantly in turmoil and it was not long before they found themselves embroiled in another border engagement with the Israeli Army, as their task was to defend the frontier on the 'West Bank' between Jordan and Israel. During his year with the Arab Legion, Rea found himself involved in no less than twenty such operations, with the United Nations peacekeepers, as he put it: 'acting as umpires'. He got to know a number of senior Jewish officers quite well, including Moshe Dayan, who later became the Israeli Defence Minister. While serving with the Arab Legion, he received the heartbreaking news that his father had been murdered by the Mau-Mau[4] and he immediately flew to Nairobi. He found out from Dr Louis Leakey at the Nairobi Museum, who was his father's first cousin, that his father had been savagely beaten, then buried alive, after the house had been surrounded by some sixty Mau-Mau. His wife, Mary, had managed to hide their daughter, Diana Hartley,[5] before she was caught, taken outside and strangled, then hacked to pieces while their cook, who had bravely tried to defend them, had himself been disembowelled. The house and farm were in chaos, but Rea did manage to find his brother Nigel's Victoria Cross before leaving to return to Jordan.

Rea Leakey's service with the Arab Legion came to an abrupt end in March 1956, when Glubb Pasha and all the other British officers serving with the Legion were ousted. He returned to England where, after nearly a year's leave on full pay, he was posted to Colchester as GSO 1 of the 3rd Infantry Division. Then, in 1958, he returned to Camberley for a second tour as a member of the Directing Staff (Colonel) at the Staff College. Two years later, he was on the move again, this time to take command of the 7th Armoured Brigade, which had its headquarters in Soltau, Germany, so he had at long last returned to the 'Desert Rats' with whom he had fought for so much of the war. Rea's three inspirational years as Commander, 7th Armoured Brigade, were legendary as all those who had the privilege to serve under him will recall.

His next job was probably his most influential, namely as Director General Fighting Vehicles (DGFV),[6] in the rank of Major General, part of the Master General of the Ordnance's department at the War Office. One of the major bones of contention during his tour was the ill-advised acceptance into service of the Chieftain main battle tank, with its ailing L60 multi-fuel engine. Against Rea's advice the issue was forced through, a decision which the Army as a whole, and the Royal Armoured Corps in particular, lived to regret. This contentious issue led directly to him putting in his request to leave the Army and to join Jaguar, who had offered him a very good job. However, it was not to be allowed, the powers that be ruling that he would not be permitted to accept such an appointment for at least two years after retirement, so Rea had to 'soldier on'. He was made a Companion of the Bath (CB) in 1967.[7]

His final Army posting was to Malta in January 1967, as General Officer Commanding British Troops Malta and Libya, a post which he held for the next eighteen months, his tenure coinciding with the rundown of British forces in Malta, some 150 years after Admiral Lord Nelson had taken possession of the island; the Arab-Israeli Six Day War which began on 5 June 1967; and the declaration of UDI in Rhodesia, to name but three of the major happenings of the period. After thirty-two years of soldiering, Rea then left the Army in 1968.

Still only fifty-three, he went on to become the Director and Secretary of the influential Wolfson Foundation,[8] a post which he held from 1968 to 1980. Finally, from 1980 until 1982, he was Fund Raiser for St Swithun's Girls' School in Winchester. Rea and Muriel divorced in 1984, but have remained close friends. In 1994, he was remarried to Joan Morant, widow of Maj George Morant. Rea's younger son, David, followed in his father's footsteps, entering the RTR and making a highly successful career in the Army. He commanded 2 RTR some years ago and is currently serving as Director, Military Operations at the MOD, in the rank of Brigadier, and was recently awarded a CBE for his sterling work in Bosnia.

There are very few men or women who deserve the accolade of 'Bravest of the Brave', but undoubtedly Rea Leakey is one. His sustained courage throughout six long years of war and his many individual acts of heroism put him into that class. Utterly fearless and determined, he was also an enormously popular commander, never asking his men to undertake anything he would not cheerfully do himself, while constantly inspiring others by his example. He is a born soldier who clearly loved fighting and excelled in battle, just like his brother Nigel, who won a posthumous VC in Abyssinia in 1941. Rea is not only a brave man, but also an extremely intelligent one, as he proved time and time again during his staff tours – although he had an abiding hatred for the 'gilded staff' and tried valiantly to avoid being chained to a desk! I have barely mentioned his sporting prowess, but it is worth recording that he represented the Army at athletics and squash, and his Regiment at athletics, squash, tennis, rugby, hockey and boxing. He was also a good shot and is still a keen fisherman – in short, the perfect soldier!

Notes

1.   The RMA Sandhurst was formed on 7 November 1946 and took the place of both the prewar RMC which Rea had attended and the RMA Woolwich (known to all as 'The Shop'), which, prewar, had trained Officers for the technical arms such as the Royal Artillery and Royal Engineers.

2.   The Military Secretary's post was the channel for all business relating to the appointment and promotion of Officers, which included the selection of Officers as suitable for all staff and command appointments, Officers' annual confidential reports and Honours and Awards.

3.   The Arab Legion had been formed in Transjordan in 1920 and was a highly efficient well-disciplined force. Its commander was Gen Sir John Bagot Glubb (known as 'Glubb Pasha') and it recruited Arabs, Circassians, Palestinians, Armenians and, most importantly, Bedouins, all of whom were British-trained, equipped and officered. The British Government also paid an annual subsidy towards its upkeep. Its strength was some 6,000 all ranks, organized into a mechanized Brigade, plus numerous independent companies.

4.   The Mau-Mau was a secret society of the Kikuyu tribe who were both 'warriors and witch doctors' and who exercised great power over the native population. They began a terror campaign against the government and white settlers in 1952, causing a state of emergency to be declared on 20 October, which lasted for three years and cost many lives.

5.   Mrs Diana Hartley, having escaped from the Mau-Mau, was killed by a lion just six years later.

6.   The post of DGFV at the War Office (which became the Ministry of Defence (Army Department) on 1 April 1964), added an 'E' for 'Engineer Equipment' to become 'DGFVE' during Rea's tenure, when he took control of the Royal Engineer Research Establishment at Christchurch, Dorset. Rea always worked closely with his opposite number in the Civil Service, the Director of the Fighting Vehicle & Research Establishment (FVRDE), Alec Dunbar. DGVFE came under the Master General of the Ordnance (MGO) in the War Office hierarchy.

7.   The Most Honourable Order of the Bath was founded in 1725 when there was just one class and one division, the recipients being known as 'Knights of the Bath' or simply as 'KBs'. Following the Napoleonic wars a military division was added, with three classes: 'GCB' (Knight Grand Cross); 'KCB' (Knight Commander) and 'CB' (Companion of the Bath). Then, in 1847, the civil division was also divided into three classes. Admission is granted only sparingly, so it is probably the most highly regarded of the 'lesser' orders.

8.   Sir Isaac Wolfson, a Scottish businessman and philanthropist, set up the Wolfson Foundation in 1955, for the advancement of health, education and youth activities in the UK and Commonwealth. He also founded Wolfson College, Oxford.

Appendix

Details of Tanks used by A.R.L. and fought against by A.R.L.

Srl	Type of tank	Unit where used	Weight (tons)	Crew	Armament (main & secondary)	Armour thickness (mm)	Engine type & rating	Top speed (mph)
1	Vickers Medium Mk II	4 RTC	12.5	5	3pdr QF 2 × Vickers (mted sides) 4 × Hotchkiss (dismted)	8	Armstrong Siddeley V8 air cooled 90bhp	15–16
2	Vickers Light Mk VI	1 RTC/1 RTR	5	3	1 × .5 Vickers 1 × .303 VMG	4–14	Meadows 89bhp	30-35
3	Cruiser Mk 1 (A9)	1 RTR	12	6	1 × 2pdr 3 × .303 VMG	6–14	AEC 6 cylinder 150 bhp	25
4	Infantry Tank Mk II Matilda	7 RTR	26.25	4	1 × 2pdr 1 × .303 VMG or 7.92 Besa MG	40–78	Two AEC 6 cylinder 174 bhp	15
5	Medium M3 Grant	1 RTR	27.68	6	1 × 75mm 1 × 37mm 3 × .30 MG (one flexible AA) 1 × 2in bomb thrower (smoke)	12–37	Wright Continental R975 EC2 9 cylinder radial	21
6	Medium M4 Sherman (mid-production M4)	3 RTR & 44 RTR	29.87	5	1 × 75mm 2 × .30 MG 1 × .50 MG (AA) 1 × 2in bomb thrower (smoke)	12–75	as for M3	24–29
7	Sherman Firefly	44 RTR & 5 RTR	There were three models of Sherman upgunned to mount the British 17pdr high velocity gun, viz: Sherman IIC, IVC & VC which were the British designation for the Firefly using the American Sherman M4A1, M4A3 and M4A4 respectively						
8	Infantry Tank Mk IV A22 Churchill III	7 RTR	39	5	1 × 6pdr QF 2 × Besa 7.92mm MG 1 × 2in bomb thrower (smoke)	16–102	Bedford twin six 350bhp	15.5
9	Cruiser Tank Mk VIII A27M Cromwell IV	5 RTR	27.5	5	1 × 75mm QF 2 × Besa 7.92mm MG 1 × 2in bomb thrower (smoke)	8–76	Rolls-Royce Meteor V12 600bhp	40
10	Cruiser Tank A34 Comet	5 RTR	32.7	5	1 × 77mm QF 2 × Besa 7.92mm MG 1 × 2in bomb thrower (smoke)	14–76	as for Cromwell	32

Enemy Tanks*

Srl	Country of origin	Type	Weight (tons)	Crew	Armament Main & secondary	Armour (mm)	Engine	Top speed (mph)
1	Italy	CV 33	3.2	2	1 or 2 × 6.5mm MG or 1 × 13mm HMG	5–15	SPA CV3 4 cylinder 43bhp	26

(also the L35/11 armed with a flame-thrower (lanciaflamme))

2	Italy	M 13/40	14	4	1 × 47mm 3 × 8mm MG	14–4	SPA 8 TM40 V8 145 bhp	20

3	Germany	PzKpfw III Ausf F/G	20.3	5	1 × 50mm 2 × 7.92mm MG	18–30	Maybach HL 120 300 bhp	25

Many other Marks of PzKpfw III were in service – up to Ausf M on all fronts up to the end of the war.

4	Germany	PzKpfw IV Ausf F1	22.3	5	1 × 75mm 2 × 7.92mm MG	10–50	Maybach HL 108 300 bhp	27

The F2 'Special' had the long-barrelled more powerful KwK 40 L 43 gun and thicker armour, plus wider tracks. It was far superior to any British armour of the same period, viz: summer of 1942.

As with the PzKpfw III, the PzKpfw IV was built in many Marks – up to Ausf J and remained the backbone of the Panzer Divisions throughout the war.

5	Germany	PzKpfw V Panther Ausf G	45.5	5	1 × 75mm KwK L42 L /70 2 × 7.92 mm MG 34	16–110	Maybach HL 230 700 bhp	28.5

Panther Ausf D, Ausf A and Ausf F also produced. Towards the end of the war, Panther comprised half the tank strength of most Panzer divisions.

* These are just examples of the types of AFVs employed in all theatres and on all fronts, but have been deliberately chosen for the purpose of comparison with opposing British armour (including those originating from the USA).

Bibliography

Baynes, John: *The Forgotten Victor*, Brassey's, 1989

Farran, Roy: *Winged Dagger*, Collins, 1948

Forty, George: *Tanks across the Desert*, William Kimber & Co Ltd, 1981

—— *Tank Action*, Sutton Publishing, 1993

—— *The Armies of Rommel*, Arms & Armour Press, 1997

Harrison, Frank: *Tobruk, the Great Siege Reassessed*, Arms & Armour Press, 1996

Playfair, Maj Gen I.S.O.: *The Mediterranean and Middle East Vol 1 (part of the official history of WWII)*, HMSO, 1954

Smith, Denis Mack: *Mussolini*, Weidenfeld & Nicolson, 1981

Thesiger, Wilfred: *Arabian Sands*, Longman, Green & Co, 1959

Thomas, Hugh: *The Story of Sandhurst*, Hutchinson, 1961

Index